Praise for

The Socrates Express

"Eric Weiner's *The Socrates Express* rekindled my love for philosophy. A smart, funny, engaging book full of valuable lessons, *The Socrates Express* is not an explanation—it's an invitation to think and experience philosophy filtered through Weiner's words. . . . The structure of this book is brilliant. . . . An engaging read . . . With plenty of humor and straightforward prose [Weiner] engages with deep thought and encourages us to focus on questions instead of answers. . . . A fun, sharp book that draws readers in with its apparent simplicity and bubble-gum philosophy approach and gradually pulls them in deeper and deeper until they're contemplating desire, loneliness, aging, and death."

—NPR

"With signature clarity and humor, [Eric Weiner] picks up where *The Good Place* left off. In a rare philosophy book that's a delight to read, he illuminates what deep thinkers through history have known about a life well lived."

—Adam Grant, bestselling author of *Originals*

"[Weiner's] writing is fresh and even revelatory as he pulls together seemingly disparate notions and asks meaningful (and often unanswered) questions. His tone alternates between informative and insightful to cheeky and challenging. . . . Readers will enjoy Weiner's unique approach and ultimately satisfying conclusions."

—*Booklist* (starred review)

"Such a globe-trotting tour of philosophy can only be as good as its guide, and Weiner proves to be a curious, sincere, and generous companion. His good cheer alone serves as a model for how to live, and many readers will appreciate his method of taking what's useful for him and leaving what's not. . . . 'The world needs more philosophical enthusiasts,' Weiner writes. This book is sure to generate its share."

—*Kirkus Reviews*

"A pleasant surprise. Part high-level survey of the central ideas of a diverse group of philosophers, part memoir, part 'how to' book and part travelogue, [*The Socrates Express*] is an invigorating introduction to some of philosophy's eminently practical uses. . . . A serious man of ideas . . . refreshingly free of prescriptiveness."

—*Bookreporter*

"Weiner makes a convincing and winningly presented case for the practical applications of philosophy to everyday existence in the twenty-first century. With humor and thoughtfulness, he distills the wisdom of thinkers from throughout history . . . into ways to slow down, ask questions, and pay attention. . . . His book offers an appealing way to cope with the din of modern life and look at the world with attentive eyes and ears."

—*Publishers Weekly*

"Equal parts vivifying travelogue and Philosophy 101 crash course . . . Weiner's gift is his lively ability to unearth fresh insights about their ideas that relate to the chaos of the present day."

—*Boca*

"Weiner offers bubble-gum philosophy that provides a quick, sweet taste. . . . Those looking for lite insights will be drawn in gradually from the shallow (getting out of bed and walking) to the deep end (aging and death)."

—*Library Journal*

ALSO BY ERIC WEINER

The Geography of Bliss

Man Seeks God

The Geography of Genius

The SOCRATES EXPRESS

IN SEARCH OF LIFE LESSONS FROM DEAD PHILOSOPHERS

ERIC WEINER

AVID READER PRESS

NEW YORK LONDON TORONTO SYDNEY NEW DELHI

Avid Reader Press
An Imprint of Simon & Schuster, Inc.
1230 Avenue of the Americas
New York, NY 10020

First Avid Reader Press trade paperback edition August 2021

Interior design by Carly Loman

Manufactured in the United States of America

10 9 8 7 6 5 4 3 2

Library of Congress Cataloging-in-Publication Data

ISBN 978-1-5011-2901-8
ISBN 978-1-5011-2902-5 (pbk)
ISBN 978-1-5011-2903-2 (ebook)

For Sharon

“Sooner or later, life makes philosophers of us all.”

—MAURICE RISELING

Contents

INTRODUCTION

Departure

We are hungry. We eat and eat some more, yet still we are hungry.

Sometimes we experience the hunger as a faint presence; other times, when the world is upended and fear roams unchecked, the hunger swells, and threatens to consume us.

We reach for our smartphones. With a swipe of a finger, we can access all human knowledge: from ancient Egypt to quantum physics. We gobble it up, but still we are hungry.

What is this hunger that cannot be sated? We don't want what we think we want. We think we want information and knowledge. We do not. We want wisdom. There's a difference. Information is a jumble of facts, knowledge a more organized jumble. Wisdom untangles the facts, makes sense of them, and, crucially, suggests how best to use them. As the British musician Miles Kington said: "Knowledge is knowing that a tomato is a fruit. Wisdom is not putting it in a fruit salad." Knowledge knows. Wisdom sees.

The difference between knowledge and wisdom is one of kind, not degree. Greater knowledge does not necessarily translate into greater wisdom, and in fact can make us less wise. We can know too much, and we can mis-know.

Knowledge is something you possess. Wisdom is something you do. It is a skill and, like all skills, one you can learn. But it requires effort. Expecting to acquire wisdom by luck is like expecting to learn to play the violin by luck.

Yet that is essentially what we do. We stumble through life, hoping to pick up scraps of wisdom here and there. In the meantime, we're confused. We mistake the urgent for the important, the verbose for the thoughtful, the popular for the good. We are, as one contemporary philosopher puts it, "misliving."

I am hungry, too—more than most, I suspect, owing to a persistent melancholy that has shadowed me for as long as I can remember. Over the years, I've tried various means of satisfying the hunger: religion, psychotherapy, self-help books, travel, and a brief, and ill-fated, experiment with psychedelic mushrooms. Each method slaked the hunger, but never fully nor for long.

Then, one Saturday morning, I ventured to the underworld: my basement. That's where I quarantine books deemed unfit for the living room. There, amid titles such as *The Gas We Pass* and *Personal Finance for Dummies*, I unearthed Will Durant's 1926 book, *The Story of Philosophy*. It had real heft and, when I opened the cover, emitted an actual cloud of dust. I wiped it clean and began to read.

Durant's words elicited no thunderclap of revelation, no road-to-Damascus moment. Something kept me reading, though. It was not so much the ideas embedded in the book as the passion with which they were presented. Durant was clearly a man in love, but with whom? With what?

"Philosopher," from the Greek *philosophos*, means "lover of wisdom." The definition says nothing about possessing wisdom any more than the Declaration of Independence says anything about obtaining happiness. You can love something you don't possess, and never will. It is the pursuit that matters.

As I write these words, I am on a train. I am somewhere in North Carolina, or maybe South Carolina, I'm not sure. On a train, it's easy to lose track of place, and of time, too.

INTRODUCTION

I love trains. More precisely, I love riding trains. I am no "foamer"—a rail enthusiast who froths at the sight of, say, an SD45 diesel-electric locomotive. I could not care less about tonnage ratings or track gauges. I love the experience: that rare combination of expansiveness and coziness only travel by train provides.

There is something amniotic about the inside of a train. The toasty temperature, the warm light. Trains transport me to a happier, preconscious state. A time before 1040 forms and college tuition savings and dental plans and traffic. A time before the Kardashians.

My mother-in-law is suffering from late-stage Parkinson's. It is a cruel disease, robbing her of abilities and memories. She has forgotten much. Yet she retains vivid recollections of childhood train rides in upstate New York. Albany to Corning to Rochester, then back to Albany. The sights and sounds and smells flood back as if they happened yesterday. There's something about a train that stays with us.

Philosophy and trains pair well. I can think on a train. I cannot think on a bus. Not even a little. I suspect it has something to do with the different sensations, or perhaps it's associative: buses remind me of childhood trips to school and camp, places I didn't want to go. Trains take me where I want to go, and do so at the speed of thought.

Yet both philosophy and trains possess a certain mustiness: once-vital parts of our lives reduced to quaint anachronisms. Today few people take the train if they can help it, and no one studies philosophy if their parents can help it. Philosophy, like riding trains, is something people did before they knew better.

I subscribe to a magazine called *Philosophy Now*. It arrives every other month in a brown manila envelope, like pornography. One recent headline read "Is the World an Illusion?" Another asked: "Is the True the Same as the Truth?" When I read these to my wife, she rolled her eyes. For her, like many people, articles like these epitomize all that is wrong with philosophy. It asks absurd, unknowable questions. Only in a dictionary do the words "philosophy" and "practical" appear in proximity.

Technology seduces us into believing philosophy no longer matters. Who needs Aristotle when we have algorithms? Digital technology so excels at answering life's smaller questions—Where can I find the best burrito in Boise? What is the fastest route to the office?—we assume it's good at the big ones, too. It is not. Siri may shine at finding that burrito joint, but ask her how best to enjoy it and she will draw a blank.

Or consider a train journey. Technology, and its overlord, science, can tell you the velocity of the train, its weight and mass, and why the onboard Wi-Fi keeps cutting out. Science cannot tell you whether you should take the train to your high school reunion, or to visit Uncle Carl, who always annoyed you but is now gravely ill. Science cannot tell you whether it's ethically acceptable to cause bodily harm to the screaming child kicking your seat. Science cannot tell you whether the view outside your window is beautiful or clichéd. Philosophy cannot either, not definitively, but it can help you see the world through a different lens, and there is great value in that.

At my local bookstore, I notice two sections: "Philosophy" and, adjacent to it, "Self Transformation." In the Barnes & Noble of ancient Athens, these two sections would be one. Philosophy *was* self-transformation. Philosophy was practical. Philosophy was therapy. Medicine for the soul.

Philosophy is therapeutic but not the way a hot-stone massage is therapeutic. Philosophy is not easy. It is not nice. It is not palliative. Less spa than gym.

The French philosopher Maurice Merleau-Ponty called philosophy "radical reflection." I like how he imbues philosophy with the edginess and whiff of danger it deserves. Philosophers once captured the world's imagination. They were heroic. They were willing to die for their philosophy, and some, like Socrates, did. Now all that is heroic about philosophy is the epic struggle for academic tenure.

Most schools today don't teach philosophy. They teach *about* philosophies. They don't teach students how to philosophize. Philosophy is different from other subjects. It is not a body of knowledge but a way of thinking—a way of being in the world. Not a "what" or a "why" but a "how."

How. The word doesn't get much respect these days. In the literary world, how-to books are an embarrassment, the successful but uncouth cousin. Serious writers don't write how-to books, and serious readers don't read them. (At least they don't admit reading them.) Yet most of us don't stay up at night wondering "what is the nature of reality?" or "why is there something rather than nothing?" It is a how question—how to live?—that grabs hold of us and won't let go.

Philosophy, unlike science, is proscriptive. It not only describes the world as it is but as it *could be*, opening our eyes to possibility. The author Daniel Klein said of the ancient Greek philosopher Epicurus what could be said of all the good ones: read them not so much as philosophy but as "life-enhancing poetry."

I've spent the past few years imbibing that poetry, slowly, at the speed of thought, cocooned in a window seat on a train. I have taken trains wherever and whenever possible. I traveled to where some of history's greatest thinkers thought. I braved Stoic Camp in Wyoming and the Indian Railways bureaucracy in Delhi. I rode New York City's F train for longer than anyone should. These journeys were my intermission, a chance to stretch my legs, and mind, between philosophical acts. They gave me pause, in the best sense of the word.

Google "philosophers" and you will find hundreds, perhaps thousands. I've chosen fourteen. How? Carefully. They are all wise, though in different ways. Different flavors of wisdom. They cover a vast span of time—Socrates lived in the fifth century BC, Simone de Beauvoir in the twentieth century—and of space, too: from Greece to China, Germany to India. All fourteen are dead, but good philosophers never really die; they live on in the minds of others. Wisdom is portable. It transcends space and time, and is never obsolete.

My list includes many Europeans but not exclusively. The West has no monopoly on wisdom. Some of my philosophers, such as Nietzsche, were remarkably prolific. Others, such as Socrates and Epictetus, didn't pen a single word. (Fortunately, their students did.) Some achieved great fame in their lifetimes. Others died unknown. Some you will recognize as philosophers; others, such as Gandhi, you probably don't think of as a philosopher. (He was.) A few names, like that of the Japanese courtier and author Sei Shōnagon, may be new to you. That's okay. In the end, my criteria boiled down to this: Did these thinkers love wisdom and is that love contagious?

We usually think of philosophers as disembodied minds. Not this bunch. They were corporeal, active beings. They trekked and rode horses. They fought wars and drank wine and made love. And they were, to a man and woman, practical philosophers. It was not the meaning of life that interested them but leading meaningful lives.

They were not perfect. They had their peccadilloes. Socrates lapsed into trances that sometimes lasted hours. Rousseau exposed his buttocks in public on more than one occasion. Schopenhauer talked to his poodle. (Don't even get me started on Nietzsche.) So be it. Wisdom rarely wears a Brooks Brothers suit, though you never know.

We always need wisdom, but we need different kinds of wisdom at different stages of our lives. The "how to" questions that matter to a fifteen-year-old are not the ones that matter to a thirty-five-year-old—or a seventy-five-year-old. Philosophy has something vital to say about each stage.

The stages, I'm learning, fly by. Too many of us hum along, cluttering our minds with the trivial and the silly, as if we have all the time in the world. We don't. *I* don't. I like to think of myself as middle-aged. My teenage daughter, a math whiz, recently pointed out that unless I live to the age of 110, I am technically not *middle* age.

So, despite the slowpoke train I'm riding as I write these words, a sense of urgency propels my pen. It is the urgency of someone who does not want to die having not lived. Life is not a problem for me, not yet, but I feel the hot breath of time on my neck, and a little stronger every day. I want—no, need—to know what matters and what doesn't, and before it's too late.

"Sooner or later, life makes philosophers of us all," said the French thinker Maurice Riseling.

When I first encountered those words, several years ago, the world was a happier place. Pandemics were the stuff of history books and Hollywood screenplays. Yet Riseling's words moved me because, even then, I had a nagging suspicion I was misliving.

Impulsively, and with uncharacteristic prescience, I thought, "Why wait?" Why wait until life becomes a problem for me? Why not let life make a philosopher of me today, right now, while there is still time?

PART ONE

DAWN

1.

How to Get Out of Bed like Marcus Aurelius

7:07 a.m. Somewhere in North Dakota. Aboard Amtrak's Empire Builder, en route from Chicago to Portland, Oregon.

Morning light slants across my cabin window. I'd like to say it wakes me gently, but the truth is I was not asleep. My head feels as if it's been tumble-dried. A dull pain radiates from my temples to the rest of my body. A fog, thick and toxic, clouds my brain. Mine is a body at rest but not a rested body.

When it comes to sleep, there are two types of people. The first type views slumber as a bothersome interruption of life, an inconvenience. The second considers sleep one of life's unalloyed pleasures. I fall into the latter category. I have few ironclad rules, but one is this: do not mess with my sleep. Amtrak has, and I am not happy.

The relationship between train travel and sleep is, like most relationships, complicated. Yes, the rocking motion lulled me to sleep, but soon other kinetic sensations—including, but not limited to, the Lateral Lurch, the Sudden Jolt, and the Undulating Roll (aka the Wave)—jarred me awake repeatedly throughout the night.

The sun summons me from bed with all the sweetness of a drill sergeant. Our demons do not haunt us at nighttime. They strike in the morning. We are at our most vulnerable when we wake, for that is when the memory of who we are, and how we got here, returns.

I roll over, pulling the baby-blue Amtrak blanket against my body. Sure, I could get out of bed—really I could—but why bother?

"Good morning, everyone!"

I had dozed off but am awakened, not by a Lateral Lurch or an Undulating Roll, but by a voice. It is crisp and perky.

Who *is* that?

"My name is Miss Oliver, your café car attendant. Your café car is open and serving. But if you want service from Miss Oliver you must always wear shoes, shirts—and kindness!"

Good Lord. There's no going back to sleep now. I reach into my backpack and fumble for a book, careful not to disrupt my blanket. There it is. *Meditations*. A thin volume. Not more than 150 pages, and with wide margins. The jacket cover features a relief of a man, bearded and muscular, astride a horse. His eyes possess the quiet power of someone with nothing to prove.

Marcus Aurelius, Roman emperor, commanded an army of nearly half a million men, and ruled over an empire that comprised one-fifth of the world's population and stretched from England to Egypt, from the shores of the Atlantic to the banks of the Tigris. But Marcus (we're on a first-name basis) was not a morning person. He lingered in bed, doing most of his work in the afternoon, after a siesta. This routine put him at odds with his fellow Romans, most of whom rose before dawn. On the streets of Rome, bleary-eyed children walked to school in the predawn darkness. Marcus, thanks to his elite background, had been homeschooled. He could sleep in. And he did, throughout his life.

Marcus and I don't seem to have much in common. Centuries separate us, not to mention a not-insignificant power differential. Marcus controlled an empire that covered an area equal to roughly half the continental United States. I control an area roughly half the size of my desk and, truth be told, even that is a struggle. I'm forever deflecting revolts by rebellious business cards, magazine subscription notices, cat hair, three-day-old tuna sandwiches, the cat, Buddhist trinkets, coffee mugs, back issues of *Philosophy Now*, the dog, 1099 forms, the cat again, and for reasons not entirely clear, given that I live 150 miles from the nearest ocean, sand.

Yet I read Marcus and these differences dissolve. We are brothers, Marcus and I. He, running an empire and wrestling with his demons; and me, feeding the cat and wrestling with my demons. We have a common enemy: mornings.

Mornings set the tone for the day. Bad days follow bad mornings. Not always, but more often than not. Under the covers on a cold and gray Monday morning, rank and privilege count for nothing. Wealth, so helpful in other aspects of life, is useless. If anything, affluence conspires with the duvet to detain you in the horizontal position.

Mornings provoke powerful, conflicting emotions. On the one hand, morning smells of hope. Every dawn is a rebirth. Ronald Reagan didn't campaign on a slogan of "Late Afternoon in America." It was his promise of "Morning in America" that catapulted him to the White House. Likewise, great ideas don't dusk on us. They dawn on us.

For some of us, though, mornings smell of simmering despair. If you don't like your life, chances are you don't like your mornings. Mornings are to an unhappy life what the opening scene is to *The Hangover Part III*. A taste of the awfulness to come.

Mornings are a time of transition, and transitions are never easy. We're leaving one state of consciousness, sleep, and entering another, wakefulness. To put it in geographic terms, mornings are the border town of consciousness. A Tijuana of the mind. Disorienting, with vague hints of danger.

Philosophers are as divided about mornings as they are everything else. Nietzsche woke at dawn, splashed cold water on his face, drank a glass of warm milk, then worked until 11:00 a.m. Immanuel Kant made Nietzsche look like a slacker. He woke at 5:00 a.m., the Königsberg sky still ink-black, drank a cup of weak tea, smoked a pipe—only one, never more—then got to work. Simone de Beauvoir, bless her, didn't wake until 10:00 a.m., and lingered over her espresso. Marcus, alas, had no such luxury: he was born some 1,200 years before the invention of coffee.

Suicide, said the French existentialist Albert Camus, is the "one truly serious philosophical problem." Is life worth living or not? The rest was just so much metaphysical claptrap. Simply put, if there is no philosopher, there is no philosophy.

Camus's proposition is logically sound but, in my mind, incomplete. Once you've wrestled with his suicide question, and concluded that, yes, life is worth living (*for now*; existential conclusions are always contingent), you confront another, even more vexing question: Should I get out of bed? This question, I believe, is the one truly serious philosophical problem. If a philosophy can't extract us from under the covers, what good is it?

The Great Bed Question, like all great questions, is actually many questions disguised as one. Let's pull back the comforter and examine it. On one level, we're asking *can* I get out of bed. Unless you are disabled, the answer is yes, you can. We are also asking whether it is beneficial to get out of bed, and crucially, *should* you get out of bed. This is where it gets tricky.

The Scottish philosopher David Hume thought a lot about these sorts of questions, though rarely from bed. He divided any inquiry into two parts: an "is" and an "ought." The "is" part is observational. We observe, without judgment, the empirical benefits of getting out of bed: increased blood flow, for instance, and earning potential.

The "ought" part contains a moral judgment. Not what are the benefits of getting out of bed but why we *ought* to do so. Hume thought we jumped too quickly from "is" to "ought." A moral "ought" never follows directly from a factual "is." (That's why the "is-ought problem" is also known as "Hume's Guillotine," since he cleaves "is" from "ought" and insists on a gap between the two.) Embezzling money from your employer *is* likely to lead to negative outcomes; therefore you *ought* not to embezzle.

Not necessarily, says Hume. You can't move from a statement of fact to a statement of ethics. Getting out of bed may be healthy and lucrative, but that doesn't mean we "ought" to do so. Maybe we don't want better blood flow and increased earning potential. Maybe we like it just fine here, under the covers. It is this pesky "ought" that, I think, explains our predicament. We feel we ought to get out of bed, and if we don't there must be something wrong with us.

To rise or not to rise? Under the covers, warm and coddled, competing impulses duke it out with the vigor of a Socratic dialogue, or a cable news show. The stay-in-bed camp makes a strong case. It is warm and safe in bed, not womblike but close. Life is good, and no less a philosopher than Aristotle said the good life was all that mattered. Conversely, it is cold *out there*. Bad things happen out there. Wars. Pandemics. Easy-listening music.

It seems like a slam dunk for the stay-in-bed camp. Yet nothing in philosophy is ever clear-cut. There is always a "yet." Entire philosophical systems, cognitive superstructures, towering edifices of thought, have been built upon that one monosyllabic word: yet.

Yet life out there beckons. We have precious little time on this planet. Do we really want to spend it horizontally? No, we don't. Surely the life force, pulsing through our weary veins, is powerful enough to wrest a middle-aged man, slightly overweight but not obese, from bed. Isn't it?

This conversation, in some form, has been taking place under the covers for as long as there have been covers and people to hide under them. We've made significant advances since Roman times, but the Great Bed Question remains essentially unchanged. No one is immune. President or peasant, celebrity chef or Starbucks barista, Roman emperor or neurotic writer, we're all subject to the same laws of inertia. We're all bodies at rest, waiting for an outside force to act upon us.

I close my eyes and Marcus materializes, as real as the day-old Styrofoam coffee cup perched on the edge of my tiny bed. I can picture him cocooned in his private tent in the Roman encampment along the River Gran, a tributary of the Danube. I imagine the day is cold and damp, his spirits low. The war is not going well. The Germanic tribes have ambushed Roman supply lines. Morale among Marcus's troops is low, and who can blame them? More than fifty thousand Roman soldiers have been killed.

Marcus no doubt missed Rome. Especially his wife, Faustina, loving, if not always faithful. The past decade had not been easy, marred not only by those nettlesome Germanic tribes but also an abortive revolt by the scheming Cassius. Then there were his children. Faustina bore at least thirteen. Fewer than half survived childhood.

Marcus was a rarity: a philosopher-king. What was it that drove the most powerful man in the world to study philosophy? As emperor, he could do, or not do, as he pleased. Why take time from his busy schedule to read the classics and ponder life's imponderables?

Marcus's early years offer a few clues. He had that rarest of childhoods: a happy one. Bookish, he'd rather read than go to the circus. This tendency put him in a distinct minority of Roman schoolchildren.

Later, enamored of the Greek way of life, he'd sleep on the hard ground covered only in a *pallium*, a philosopher's threadbare cloak, until his mother scolded him and insisted he give up "this nonsense" and sleep in a proper bed.

The Romans viewed Greek philosophy the way most of us view opera: something worthy and beautiful, and we really should go more often, but it's so darned difficult to follow and, besides, who has time? Romans liked the idea of philosophy more than actual philosophy. This made Marcus, an actual philosopher, highly suspect. Even as emperor, people snickered behind his back.

Marcus was an accidental emperor. He never wanted the job. It was his predecessor, Hadrian, who set events in motion that led to Marcus being crowned emperor in AD 161. He was forty years old.

Marcus enjoyed a honeymoon period. For six months. Then came a deadly flood, the plague, and the invasions. Aside from these wars, Marcus had relatively little blood on his hands. It's living proof that absolute power does not always corrupt absolutely. Marcus routinely handed down lenient sentences for deserters and other lawbreakers. When the empire faced a financial crisis he auctioned off imperial goodies—robes, goblets, statues, and paintings—rather than raise taxes. And in an act I find particularly touching, he decreed that all tightrope walkers, often young boys, should henceforth perform over thick, spongy mattresses.

Marcus displayed great courage in battle but, as biographer Frank McLynn says, his most courageous feat was "his constant strivings to curb his natural pessimism." I can relate. I, too, wrestle with the forces of negativity, always scheming to recruit me to their side. For we wannabe optimists, a half-empty glass is better than no glass at all, or one that has shattered into a hundred slivers and pierced a major artery. It's all a matter of perspective.

Marcus had trouble sleeping. He suffered from indeterminate chest and stomach pains. His physician, an arrogant but accomplished man named Galen, had prescribed theriac (possibly laced with opium) to help him sleep.

Marcus, like me, aspired to be a morning person. A wide gap, though, separates actual morning people from aspiring morning people. Lying here now, feeling the train's gentle rocking, the Amtrak blanket warm against my body, it is a gap that feels insurmountable.

You'd think nothing could be easier. Place one foot on the floor, then the other. Pull yourself to a vertical position. Yet I fail to achieve vertical status. Not even diagonal. What's wrong with me? Help me, Marcus.

Meditations is unlike any book I've read. It is not really a book at all. It is an exhortation. A compilation of reminders and pep talks. Roman refrigerator notes. What Marcus Aurelius fears most is not death but forgetting. He constantly reminds himself to live fully. Marcus had no intention of publishing his refrigerator notes. They were intended for himself. You don't so much read Marcus as eavesdrop on him.

I like what I hear. I like Marcus's honesty. I like how he lays himself bare on the page, exposing his fears and vulnerabilities. Here the most powerful man in the world confesses to insomnia and panic attacks and to his, at best, perfunctory performance as a lover. ("He deposits his sperm and leaves," is how he describes the act of copulation.) Marcus never lost sight of the Stoic precept that all philosophy begins with an awareness of our weakness.

Marcus constructs no grand philosophical system, to be picked apart by generations of earnest graduate students. This is philosophy as therapy, with Marcus playing the role of both therapist and patient. *Meditations* is, as translator Gregory Hays observes, "a self-help book in the most literal sense."

Time and again, Marcus exhorts himself to stop thinking and act. Stop describing a good man. Be one. The difference between philosophy and talking about philosophy is the difference between drinking wine and talking about wine. A single sip of a good pinot noir tells you more about a vintage than years of rigorous oenology.

Marcus's ideas didn't simply materialize. No philosopher's does. He was a Stoic, but not exclusively. He imbibed other sources: Heraclitus, Socrates, Plato, the Cynics, and Epicureans. Marcus, like all great philosophers, was a wisdom scavenger. What mattered was an idea's value, not its source.

To read *Meditations* is to witness an act of philosophy in real time. Marcus is live-streaming his thoughts, uncensored. I am watching "someone in the process of training himself to be a human being," as the classicist Pierre Hadot puts it.

Several entries in *Meditations* begin with the phrase "When you have trouble getting out of bed . . ." As I read further, it occurs to me that much of the book is a covert treatise on the Great Bed Question. Not only how to get out of bed but *why bother?* Camus's suicide question swaddled in a fluffy down comforter. Marcus seesaws between opposing views, debating himself.

"What do I have to complain of, if I'm going to do what I was born for—the things I was brought into the world to do?"

"Or is *this* what I was created for? To huddle under the blankets and stay warm?"

"But it's nice here. . . ."

"So you were born to feel 'nice'? Instead of doing things and experiencing them?"

Back and forth he goes. Hamlet under the covers. He knows there are great deeds to do, great thoughts to think.

If only he could get out of bed.

"Good mooooorning, passengers. Peek-a-boo, I see you. The café is still open and serving!"

Miss Oliver is back, more cloyingly cheerful than ever.

That's it. I am now seriously considering getting out of bed. Any minute now. I examine my Styrofoam coffee cup and notice fragments of Amtrak wisdom. "Change How You See the World" and, on the other side, "Experience the Taste of a Better World." Not exactly erudite, I concede, but I find the childlike simplicity endearing.

Sonya, my thirteen-year-old daughter, likes her sleep as much as I do. "I self-identify as a lazy human being," she announced one day. Trying to pry her out of bed on weekday mornings requires a marshaling of resources not seen since Normandy. Yet on weekends and snow days, she springs to life, unaided. When I asked about this discrepancy, she explained, philosophically, "It's the activity that gets you out of bed, not the alarm clock."

She's right. When I struggle to get out of bed, it is not the bed that is my enemy, or even the world out there. It is my projections. Lying under the covers, I imagine a hostile world determined to upend me. Just like Marcus. True, his world featured belligerent barbarians, the plague, and palace revolts. Obstacles are relative, though. One person's messy desk is another's ruffian invasion.

Perhaps the greatest obstacle is other people. Marcus doesn't go as far as the French philosopher Jean-Paul Sartre, who famously declared "hell is other people," but he comes close. "When you wake in the morning, tell yourself: the people you deal with today will be meddling, ungrateful, arrogant, jealous, and surly." Little has changed since Marcus's day.

Marcus suggested dealing with difficult people by disempowering them. Revoke their license over your life. Other people can't hurt you, for "nothing that goes on in anyone else's mind can hurt you." Of course. Why do I care what others think when thinking, by definition, occurs entirely inside *their* minds, not mine?

I've always suspected that at the heart of my inability to get out of bed lies an insidious self-loathing, one I can't fully acknowledge. Marcus, braver than I, does. "You don't love yourself enough," he says, and seems on the verge of self-compassion when, a page or two later, he's on the attack again. "Enough of this wretched whining, monkey life. . . . You could be good today. But instead you chose tomorrow." He saves his sharpest barbs for his perceived selfishness. "When I laze in bed, as I am now, I am thinking of only myself." Remaining under the covers is, in the final analysis, a selfish act.

This realization gets Marcus moving. He has a duty to get out of bed. "Duty" not "obligation." There is a difference. Duty comes from inside, obligation from outside. When we act out of a sense of duty, we do so voluntarily to lift ourselves, and others, higher. When we act out of obligation, we do so to shield ourselves, and only ourselves, from repercussions.

Marcus was aware of this distinction, but, as usual, needed to remind himself of it. "At dawn, when you have trouble getting out of bed, tell yourself: 'I have to go to work—as a human being.' " Not as a Stoic or an emperor, or even as a Roman, but as a human being.

"Dee-dah, Dee-dah. Miss Oliver here. Did I mention the café car is open? I look forward to meeting each and every one of you! Dee-dah."

That's it. I'm getting out of bed.

I peel off the Amtrak blanket. It offers little resistance. I pull myself upright. What, I wonder, was all that whining and ruthless self-scrutiny about? This was nothing.

I'm about to celebrate my small but decisive victory over gravity when a Lateral Lurch—or maybe a Sudden Jolt, I'm not sure—knocks me off my feet and back into bed.

This is what's so nettlesome about the Great Bed Question. It's not enough to answer it once. It's like going to the gym, or parenting. It requires repeated and regular exertions.

"Dee-dah, Dee-dah. Miss Oliver here again, ladies and gentlemen!"

I pull the covers tight. Five more minutes, I tell myself. Just five more minutes.

2.

How to Wonder like Socrates

10:47 a.m. On board train No. 1311, en route from Kiato to Athens.

Train of thought. A throwaway expression, a cliché, but a good one. Each one of our thoughts is connected to the next like boxcars on a freight train. They depend on one another for their forward momentum. Every thought, be it about ice cream sundaes or nuclear fusion, is pushed by the previous thought and pulled by the next.

Feelings travel in trains, too. My periodic bouts of melancholia seem as if they come from nowhere, but when I stop and investigate their origin, I discover a hidden causality. My sadness was triggered by a prior thought or feeling, which was triggered by a prior one, which was triggered by something my mother said in 1982. Feelings, like thoughts, never come out of the blue. There's always a locomotive pulling them along.

I order a pastry and coffee, and my train of thought slows. I think and feel nothing. I am not numb, not exactly. I experience neither happiness nor sadness nor the vast spectrum in between. I am vacant, in a good way. Lulled by the gentle sway of the train, so unlike rough-and-tumble Amtrak, savoring my coffee, not only the taste but the way the mug, warm and with a satisfying heft, nestles in my hand, my anxieties take a holiday. I watch the red roofs and blue lonian sea glide by as if they, not I, were moving. I gaze out the window at nothing in particular, and I wonder.

I wonder. Two simple words, yet they contain the seeds of all philosophy, and more. All great discoveries and personal breakthroughs began with those two words: I wonder.

Rarely, once or twice in a lifetime if you're lucky, you stumble across a sentence so unexpected, so plump with meaning, it stops you cold. I found such a sentence buried inside an odd little book called *The Heart of Philosophy*, by Jacob Needleman. I say odd because at the time I didn't know philosophy had a heart. I thought it was all head.

Here is the sentence: "Our culture has generally tended to solve its problems without experiencing its questions."

I put the book down and turned the words over in my mind. I knew they contained an important truth but I didn't know what. I was confused. How does one experience questions? And what is wrong with solving problems?

A few weeks later, I found myself sitting across from the man who wrote that profound and perplexing sentence. Jacob Needleman is a professor of philosophy at San Francisco State University. Age has slowed his gait. His voice has grown reedy, his skin thin like crepe paper, but his mind remains nimble. Jacob thinks before speaking and, unlike most professors of philosophy, uses words normal people use. Words like "question" and "experience." The way he combines them, though, is anything but normal.

As we sit on his deck overlooking the Oakland Hills, sipping Earl Grey tea and water infused with lemon, I ask Needleman, in so many words: Are you nuts? We ask questions. Sometimes we pose questions. We might grapple with questions. We do not *experience* questions. Not even in California.

Needleman is silent. For a long time. So long that I fear he has dozed off. Finally, he stirs, and speaks in a voice so low I have to inch closer to hear.

"It's rare but it's possible. Socrates experienced questions."

Of course. The inscrutable, inevitable Socrates. Philosophy's patron saint. The King of the Question. Socrates didn't invent the question, but he altered the way we ask them and, in turn, the answers they yield. You think and act differently because of Socrates, even if you know nothing about him.

Socrates isn't an easy man to know. Perched so high on the pedestal we've erected for him, he's barely visible. Just a speck. An idea, and a fuzzy one at that.

This is a shame. Socrates was not a speck. He was not an idea. He was a man. A breathing, walking, defecating, lovemaking, nose-picking, wine-drinking, joke-telling man.

An ugly man, too. The ugliest man in Athens, it was said. His nose was broad and flat, his lips full and fleshy, his belly large. He was bald. He had crablike eyes, widely spaced, that endowed him with great peripheral vision. Socrates may or may not have known more than other Athenians (he insisted he knew nothing), but he definitely saw more.

Socrates ate little, bathed rarely, and always wore the same shabby clothes. He walked barefoot everywhere, even in the dead of winter, and with a strange gait, somewhere between a waddle and a swagger. He could go days without sleep, drink without getting drunk. He heard voices—well, *a* voice. He called it his *daemon*. "This began when I was a child," he explained during his trial on charges of impiety and corrupting the youth of Athens. "It is a voice, and whenever it speaks it turns me away from something I am about to do, but it never encourages me to do anything."

Taken together, Socrates's peculiar appearance and idiosyncrasies made him otherworldly. "He seems to have entered mankind's 'great conversation' from outside, as if from another planet," says the contemporary philosopher Peter Kreeft.

This is true, I think, of all philosophers. They possess an otherness that borders on the alien. Even Marcus, a Roman emperor, felt like a misfit. Diogenes, a founder of Cynicism, was the ultimate oddball philosopher. He lived in a barrel, masturbated in public, and in general traumatized the good people of ancient Athens.

This otherness, if not the public masturbation, makes sense. Philosophy is all about questioning assumptions, rocking the boat. Captains rarely rock their own boats. They have too much at stake. Not philosophers. They're outliers. Aliens.

Socrates was a practitioner of "Crazy Wisdom." Found in traditions as disparate as Tibetan Buddhism and Christianity, Crazy Wisdom operates on the premise that the path to wisdom is crooked. We must zig before we can zag.

Crazy Wisdom means casting aside social norms and risking ostracism, or worse, to jolt others into understanding. The original shock therapy. No one likes to be shocked, and we often dismiss practitioners of Crazy Wisdom as more crazy than wise. Here is how Socrates's student Alcibiades describes him: "He will talk of pack-asses and blacksmiths, cobblers and tanners, and he always seems to be repeating the same things so that someone who wasn't used to his style and wasn't very quick on the uptake would naturally take it for the most utter nonsense." Yet, Alcibiades concludes, spend some time truly listening to Socrates and you realize it's anything but nonsense. "This talk," he says, "is almost the talk of a god."

As he pours another cup of Earl Gray, Jacob Needleman tells me about the first question he experienced. He recalls it clearly. Jacob was eleven years old. He and his friend Elias Barkhordian were sitting on a low stone wall in their Philadelphia neighborhood, just as they did several times a week, even on days when the wall was covered in ice and snow.

A year older than Jacob, Elias was tall for his age, "with a big, round face and brilliant, dark eyes." The two enjoyed chewing over weighty scientific questions, about everything from the movement of electrons to the nature of dreams. These questions intrigued young Jacob, but on this particular day, Elias asked a question that floored him: "Who created God?"

Jacob recalls staring at Elias's "great, smooth forehead as though I was trying to look into his brain" and realizing that "when he asked that question he was not merely challenging me, but challenging the whole universe. It sent an extraordinary feeling of freedom through me. And I remember saying to myself the words, *This is my best friend.*"

Jacob Needleman was smitten with the unexpected joy of asking, and experiencing, big questions.

Socrates's story parallels Jacob's. The setting, of course, is different—the mean streets of Athens, not Philadelphia—but the trajectory is similar. There was a pivot to a new and unexpected direction and, again, a friend was responsible, in Socrates's case a young man named Chaerephon. One day, Chaerephon visited the oracle at Delphi and asked the soothsayer a question: Is there any man in Athens wiser than Socrates?

"No," came the reply. "There is none."

When Chaerephon relayed the oracle's words to Socrates, he was flummoxed. No one wiser than he? How could this be? He was a mere stonecutter's son who knew nothing. Oracles, though, are never wrong, so Socrates decided to investigate. He buttonholed revered Athenians, everyone from poets to generals. Socrates soon discovered these men were not as wise as they thought they were. The general couldn't tell him what courage is, the poet couldn't define poetry. Everywhere he turned he encountered people who "do not know the things that they do not know."

Perhaps the oracle was right, Socrates concluded. Maybe he did possess a kind of wisdom, the wisdom of knowing what he didn't know. For Socrates, the worst kind of ignorance was the kind that masquerades as knowledge. Better a wide and honest ignorance than a narrow and suspect knowledge.

It is the introduction of this innocent ignorance, this "marvelous new naiveté," as the philosopher Karl Jaspers puts it, that is Socrates's greatest contribution to human inquiry, one that still drives the philosophical impulse today.

Socrates was not the first philosopher. Many came before him: Pythagoras, Parmenides, Democritus, and Thales, to name a few. These men turned their gaze heavenward. They strived to explain the cosmos, to penetrate the mysteries of the natural world. Results were mixed.

Thales, brilliant in many ways, was convinced all matter in the universe consisted of water. Like Socrates, these philosophers asked questions, but theirs were mainly "what" and "why" questions. What is everything made of? Why do the stars disappear during the day?

These sort of questions didn't interest Socrates. They were unanswerable, he thought, and, in the end, unimportant. The universe may be fascinating, but it's not much of a conversationalist, and conversation was what Socrates craved the most.

"Every question is a cry to understand the world," said the cosmologist Carl Sagan. Socrates would agree, up to a point. Every question is a cry to understand *ourselves*. Socrates was interested in "how" questions. How can I lead a happier, more meaningful life? How can I practice justice? How can I know myself?

Socrates couldn't fathom why his fellow Athenians weren't more interested in these kinds of questions, given their zest for improvement, be it a better way of making statues or practicing democracy. Athenians, it seemed to Socrates, worked tirelessly to improve everything—except themselves. That needed to change, he thought, and he made it his life's mission to do so.

This marked a major shift in philosophy. No longer is it fuzzy-headed speculation about the cosmos. It is about life, *your life*, and how to make the most of it. It is practical. Indispensable. As the Roman politician and philosopher Cicero said, "Socrates was the first to call Philosophy down from the heavens, and establish it in the towns, and introduce her into people's homes."

Socrates didn't behave the way we think philosophers must. He displayed no interest in amassing followers. (When students inquired about other philosophers, Socrates happily directed them.) He bequeathed no body of knowledge, no theories or doctrines. He published no dense tomes. In fact, he never wrote a single word. We know Socrates today thanks to a handful of ancient sources, most notably his student Plato.

There is no such thing as "Socratic thought," only Socratic thinking. Socrates was all means, no ends. We remember the gadfly of Athens today not for what he knew but how he went about knowing it. He cared more about method than knowledge. Knowledge doesn't age well. Methods do.

Scholars deploy many fancy terms to describe Socrates's method: the dialectic, the *elenchus*, inductive reasoning. I prefer a simpler term: talking. I realize that doesn't sound sophisticated, and probably won't snag me the Nobel Prize, but it's true. Socrates talked to people. "Enlightened kibitzing," the contemporary philosopher Robert Solomon calls it. I love that. It brings philosophy down to earth and elevates it at the same time.

The examined life demands distance. We must step back from ourselves to see ourselves more clearly. The best way to achieve this perspective is through conversation. For Socrates, philosophy and conversation were virtually synonymous.

Socrates talked to all sorts of people: politicians, generals, craftsmen, as well as women, slaves, and children. He talked about all sorts of subjects, too, but only important ones. Socrates wasn't much for chitchat. He knew life was short and he wasn't about to waste one second of his allotted time on trivialities. "We are considering how to live the best possible life," he said, exasperated, to a sophist named Gorgias. "What question can be more serious than this to a person who has any sense at all?"

As much as he loved conversation, Socrates, I think, saw it as simply another tool in his kit. All this enlightened kibitzing had a goal: to know himself. By talking to others he learned how to converse with himself.

Philosophy may be the art of asking questions, but what is a question? Ah, now there's a question Socrates would love! Take a word everyone knows, everyone *thinks* they know, and examine it, probe it, poke it from many angles. Shine a bright and unforgiving light on it.

Some twenty-four centuries have elapsed since the barefoot philosopher of Athens roamed the city's winding, dirty streets and asked questions. We've made much progress since then: indoor plumbing, almond milk, broadband. We've had more than two thousand years to hone our definitions. We're pretty good at it, too, judging by the nearly half a million entries in *Webster's Third New International Dictionary*. We needn't dirty our fingers with pages, print or even digital. We can always turn to our faithful aide-de-camp: Siri.

"Hello, Siri."

"Hey, Eric."

"I have a question."

"Ask and you shall receive."

"What is a question?"

"Interesting question, Eric."

Then silence. Nothing. I shake my phone. Still nothing. Siri clearly thinks I'm yanking her algorithm, and she's having none of it. I try a more literal approach.

"Siri: What is the definition of a question?"

"A sentence worded or expressed to elicit information."

That is accurate, I suppose, but woefully incomplete. Socrates wouldn't be satisfied. He was a stickler for definitions. He'd find Siri's answer at once too broad and too narrow. According to Siri's definition, both the question *Have you seen my keys?* and *What is the meaning of life?* exist on an equal plane. Both aim to elicit information, of a sort—and both are difficult to answer, at least in my house—but the information they seek differs so widely as to be of a different kind. The bigger the question, the less interested we are in a reply that provides merely information. *What is love? Why does evil exist?* When we ask these questions, it is not information we desire but something larger: meaning.

Questions aren't one-way; they move in (at least) two directions. They seek meaning, and convey it, too. Asking a friend the right question at the right time is an act of compassion, of love. Too often, though, we deploy questions as weapons, firing them at others—*Who do you think you are*? and at ourselves, *Why can't I do anything right?* We use questions as excuses—*What difference will it make*? and, later, as justification, *What more could I have done?* Questions, not the eyes, are the true windows to the soul. As Voltaire said, the best judge of a person is not the answers they give but the questions they ask.

Siri's response captured none of the magic embedded in every good question, the kind Socrates had in mind when he said, "All philosophy begins with wonder." Wonder, Socrates thought, isn't something you're either born with or not, like blond hair or freckles. Wonder is a skill, one we're all capable of learning. He was determined to show us how.

"Wonder" is a wonderful word. It's impossible to say it aloud without smiling. It comes from the Old English *wundor*, meaning "marvelous thing, miracle, object of astonishment." On one level, to wonder is to seek information, in Siri fashion. *I wonder where I can find some dark chocolate?* On another level, to wonder is to suspend inquiry, at least momentarily, and simply behold. *I wonder what it is about good Belgian chocolate, spiked with sea salt and almonds, that makes my brain dance and my heart sing?*

When we question, we are constrained by the topic at hand. Any queries that extend beyond that topic are deemed superfluous and therefore discouraged. Think of a lawyer chided by the judge for veering into "immaterial" lines of questioning, or a high school student reprimanded by her teacher for straying "off topic."

Wondering is open-ended, expansive. Wondering is what makes us human. That's been true ever since the first caveman wondered what would happen if he rubbed two sticks together, or dropped a large rock on his head. You never know until you try and you never try until you wonder.

We often conflate wonder with curiosity. Yes, both provide helpful antidotes to apathy, but in different ways. Wonder is personal in a way curiosity is not. You can be curious dispassionately. You can question dispassionately. You cannot wonder dispassionately. Curiosity is restive, always threatening to chase the next shiny object that pops into view. Not wonder. Wonder lingers. Wonder is curiosity reclined, feet up, drink in hand. Wonder never chased a shiny object. Wonder never killed a cat.

Wonder takes time. Like a good meal or good sex, it can't be rushed. That's why Socrates never hurried his conversations. He persevered even when his conversers grew weary and exasperated.

Socrates was the original therapist. He tended to answer a question with another question. Unlike a therapist, Socrates did not bill by the hour (he never charged a single drachma for his sessions) and never uttered the words "I'm afraid that's all the time we have." He always had more time.

Even when alone, Socrates liked to linger, a friend reports in the *Symposium*. "He sometimes stops and stands wherever he happens to be." Another friend recounts an even more unusual episode that occurred when both men served together during the battle of Potidaea.

> One time at dawn he [Socrates] began to think something over and stood in the same spot considering it, and when he found no solution, he didn't leave but stood there inquiring. It got to be midday, and people became aware of it, wondering at it among themselves, saying Socrates had stood there since dawn thinking about something. Finally some of the Ionians, when evening came, carried their bedding out to sleep in the cool air and to watch to see if he'd also stand there all night. He stood until dawn came and the sun rose; then he offered a prayer to the sun, and left.

Good philosophy is slow philosophy. Ludwig Wittgenstein called his profession the "slow cure" and suggested all philosophers greet one another with "Take your time!" I think that's a fine idea, not only for philosophers but all of us. Rather than "Have a good day" or similarly empty expressions, let's greet each other with "Take your time" or "Slow down." Utter these imperatives often enough, and we might actually decelerate.

On some level, I think, we already recognize the cognitive benefits of slowing down. When something makes us stop and think, we say it "gives us pause." A pause is not a mistake or a glitch. A pause is not a stutter or an interruption. It is not emptiness but a kind of latent matter. The seed of thought. Every pause is ripe with the possibility of cognition, and of wonder.

We rarely question the obvious. Socrates thought this oversight was a mistake. The more obvious something seems, the more urgent the need to question it.

I take it as a given that I want to be a good father. It is so self-evident it hardly requires stating.

Not so fast, Socrates would say. *What do you mean by "father"? Are you speaking in strictly biological terms?*

"Well, no. Actually, my daughter is adopted."

Ah, so a "father" is something more than biological?

"Yes, absolutely."

What defines a father, then?

"Someone, a male, who cares for a young child."

So if I take your daughter to, say, Delphi for a few hours am I her father?

"No, of course not, Socrates. Being a father entails a lot more than that."

What is it then, that separates a male adult who cares for a child from a male adult worthy of the title "father"?

"Love. That is what makes a father a father."

Very good. I like that answer. Of course, we need to define "love," but we'll save that for another time. Now, you say you want to be a "good" father?

"Yes, I do, very much so."

What do you mean by good?

Here I confess I haven't a clue. Only the vaguest notions—inchoate, cartoonish images—spring to mind: ice cream sundaes, band recitals, soccer practice, homework coaching, college tours, jokes when she's feeling down, and even if she's not, sleepover pickups, yin to my wife's yang. Good cop, mostly.

These are fine images, Socrates would say, but what do they add up to? You don't really know what you mean when you say "good father," do you? And, with a final twist of the philosophical knife, Socrates would suggest that until I knew, really knew, what I mean by "good father," I couldn't possibly become one. I was chasing a ghost.

For Socrates, all misdeeds, such as bad parenting, are committed not out of malice but ignorance. If we understood the ramification of our missteps—not only for our children but for ourselves, too—we wouldn't commit them. A genuine understanding of a particular virtue leads to virtuous behavior. Automatically. To know—truly know—what it means to be a good father is to be one.

It was Take Your Child to Work Day. I always dread this day. Other parents take their children to shiny, serious offices with conference rooms and phone banks and gravitas. My office (one of them anyway) is a local diner called Tastee. The food does not live up to its name, but the booths are large, the waitresses friendly, and the coffee infinite. This year, for the first time, my daughter agreed to tag along.

How to break through to a thirteen-year-old is a mystery the world's great philosophers have yet to solve. If a tree falls in the woods and her friends don't share it on Snapchat, it didn't fall. Sonya showed no interest in my work, in philosophy, in anything, it seems, beyond her teenage world. I suspected the only reason she agreed to go to work with me that morning was so she could skip a day of school.

As we picked at our breakfast—heart-healthy omelet for me, chocolate chip pancakes for her—I stared down the great void that is parenthood. I felt inadequate and, worse, invisible. What would Socrates do?

He would ask questions, of course. I'd been wrestling with one question in particular, a sort of meta question. Is that old saw true—is there really no such thing as a stupid question? I put this question to my daughter, who, with a barely perceptible twitch of her left eyebrow, indicated: *I have registered your question, Father, and deemed it unworthy of a response, so I shall now return to my pancakes and Snapchat.*

I persisted, like Socrates. "Is there such a thing as a stupid question?" I repeated, louder.

She lifted her head from the screen and thought for a while. At least I surmised she was thinking. Then, to my amazement, she spoke.

"Yes," she said. "A stupid question is one you already know the answer to." And with that she returned to her pancakes and her phone and her adolescent pique.

Not for the first, or last, time had she surprised me. She was right. Unless you happen to be a prosecutor, asking a question you already know the answer to is indeed stupid. We do this more often than you might think, and in various ways. We might ask a question to show off our knowledge, or to elicit information that buttresses an unswerving, unexamined conviction we already hold.

For Socrates, none of these qualified as serious questions. A serious question steps into uncharted waters. A serious question carries risk, like striking a match in a dark room. You don't know what you'll find when the room illuminates—monsters or miracles—but you strike the match anyway. That's why serious questions are uttered not confidently but clumsily, hesitantly, with all the gangly awkwardness of a teenager.

For Socrates, nothing was more important, or courageous.

Professor Jacob Needleman pours me another glass of lemon-infused water, his hands slow but steady. The ice cubes clink as they strike the glass. The California light has grown softer, the colors richer, as the sun dips low.

I ask Needleman more about himself. He takes a deep, wheezy breath and transports me back to the 1940s Philadelphia of his youth. Elias and he continued their philosophical gabfests on the stone wall, though with decreasing frequency. One day when Jacob phoned Elias's home, his mother answered and, in a peculiar voice, said he was resting. Jacob knew something was wrong well before he heard the word "leukemia."

He recalls one of the last questions he experienced with Elias. "I wonder what happens to a person when we fall asleep," Jacob asked his friend. "Where does he go?"

For the first time, Elias had no answer. He died shortly before his fourteenth birthday.

Death, especially an unnaturally early one, has a way of focusing the mind. Questions flooded Jacob's. Why Elias and not him? What should we do with this short time allotted? He received no satisfying answers from his parents or his teachers or his rabbi. So he turned to Socrates and philosophy.

"Why philosophy?" I ask.

"Why do you love something? You feel called. Called to the ultimate questions. Who are we? What are we? Why are we here? Human beings need meaning. So, yes, it was a calling."

Jacob's parents weren't thrilled with his calling. "As the older son, I was obliged by God to become a doctor," he deadpans. Jacob did become a doctor, only not the medical kind. He earned a PhD in philosophy. He still recalls the first time he was introduced socially as "Dr. Needleman" in his mother's presence. She interrupted to point out, "He's not the kind of doctor that does anybody any good, you know."

Needleman spent the rest of his life proving her wrong. He amassed academic accolades and promotions, always eager to reach a wider audience. He couldn't fathom why these "ultimate questions" received so little attention. "Our culture has no place where the ultimate questions are honored as questions. Every institution and social form we have is devoted either to solving problems or providing pleasure," Needleman says.

He pauses, letting his words loiter in the soft California air. He's right, I realize. Solving a problem before you experience it is like trying to cook a meal before buying groceries. Yet so often we reach for the quickest solution, or the most expedient pleasure. Anything to avoid sitting with our ignorance.

My eyes wander across the Oakland Hills, a dusty brown this time of year. My ears register the pleasant jingle of a nearby wind chime, mingling with a wordless presence that fills the space between me and Jacob Needleman, and connects us.

Socrates was suspicious of the written word. It lies lifeless on the page, and travels in only one direction, from author to reader. You cannot talk to a book, not even a good book.

That's why I decide not to read Plato's dialogues but to listen to them. I download the lot. I'm not sure what the ancient Greek word for "megabyte" is, but it's an awful lot of them.

The dialogues become the soundtrack of my life. I listen as I ride the train and as I drive my daughter to soccer practice. I listen as I pump my legs on the elliptical. I cook to Socrates and I drink to Socrates. I wake to Socrates and I go to sleep to Socrates.

The dialogues feature Socrates and one or more interlocutor wrestling with the meaning of, say, justice or courage or love. These are no dry treatises. They are full-throated conversations, at turns contentious and, to my surprise, funny, too. "A wisdom full of pranks," as Nietzsche put it.

A conversation with Socrates was often infuriating and disorienting, as one character from the *Dialogues*, Nicias, attests. "Anyone who is close to Socrates and enters into conversation with him is liable to be drawn into an argument, and whatever subject he may start, he will be continually carried round and round by him, until at last he finds that he has to give an account both of his present and past life, and when he is once entangled Socrates will not let him go until he has completely and thoroughly sifted him."

Another interlocutor complained that Socrates reduced him to a "mass of helplessness" and compares the philosopher to a "torpedo fish" (also known as an electric ray) that numbs people's minds.

Conversing with Socrates was frustrating the way conversing with an inquisitive five-year-old is frustrating.

Can we have ice cream for dinner?

No.

Why?

Because ice cream isn't good for you.

Why?

Because it contains sugar.

Why is sugar bad for you?

Because it is stored in the fat cells of your body.

Why?

Because it just is! Now go to your room.

The child's questions irk us not because they are silly but because we are incapable of answering them adequately. The child, like Socrates, unmasks our ignorance, and while that may be beneficial in the long run, in the short run it's annoying. "If you do not annoy anyone, you are not a philosopher," says Peter Kreeft.

I read that and perk up, hopeful. I have it on good word, and from multiple sources, that I am indeed annoying. World-class. I see other similarities with Socrates. The outlier status. The paunch. The wandering, wondering mind. The love of talk.

Where we part ways, though, is persistence. I tend to walk away from a fight, real or imagined. Not Socrates. He displayed great courage. Fighting in the siege of Potidaea, in 432 BC, he demonstrated remarkable strength and stamina, saving the life of his friend Alcibiades.

In the philosophical arena, too, Socrates was unrelenting. He was an unsparing auditor, demanding people account not only for their beliefs but for their lives. You couldn't wiggle out of a debate with Socrates. He saw through the smoke screen of obfuscation favored by intellectual posers, then and now. *Look at you, a general, who doesn't know what courage is. A priest who can't tell me what piety is. A parent who doesn't know what love is.*

The goal was not to humiliate but to illuminate, to facilitate a kind of intellectual photosynthesis. Socrates as gardener. He loved nothing more than "planting a puzzle in a mind and watching it grow."

This puzzle planting was tricky business. Nobody likes having their ignorance exposed, especially so publicly, and many of the dialogues grew heated. "I don't understand you, Socrates, so I wish you'd ask someone who did," said one of his annoyed companions in a dialogue called *Gorgias*. "You are a tyrant, Socrates. I wish you'd either bring an end to this argument or get someone else to argue with you." Sometimes more than strong words were exchanged. "Men pummeled [Socrates] with their fists and tore his hair out," reports the third-century-AD biographer Diogenes Laertius.

Socrates annoyed others for a good cause: better vision. Socrates as optometrist. People walk around with faulty eyeglass prescriptions.

Naturally, this lapse affects how they see, and what they see. They have mistaken their distorted view of reality as the only view. Worse, they don't even know they're wearing glasses. They stumble through the day, bumping into furniture, tripping over people, all the while blaming the furniture and the people. Socrates thought this was silly, and unnecessary.

The sun has turned a glowing crimson, and a slight chill has crept into the air. Jacob Needleman and I have been talking for hours but neither of us has tired of this enlightened kibitzing. We turn to the subject of false beliefs.

The philosopher, Needleman suggests, is like a burly bouncer at the Nightclub of Ideas.

"A philosopher says to his opinions, 'You are my opinions. How did you get in here? You didn't ask me. I didn't examine you. Yet I believe you. You're taking over my life.'"

I think of my opinions and how they colonize my mind. Like all wily colonizers, they trick me into believing I invited them. Did I? Or did they show up unannounced, these ideas of others, and dress themselves in my clothing?

I circle back to that intriguing, beguiling notion of "experiencing questions." What does he mean?

Jacob explains that he distinguishes ordinary questioning from "deep questioning." Ordinary questioning skates along the surface, like Siri. Deep questioning is slow and immersive.

"If I really live a question, let it haunt me, then this state of deep questioning is transformative in itself."

"Live the question?"

"Yes, live the question. Have it in the back of your mind a lot of the time. Living a question. Not just trying to fix it. Too often we jump to the solution."

This sounds good, makes me want to spend the rest of my days living questions, but what about answers? Where do they fit in? This is the rap on philosophy: that it's all talk, endless questions and no answers. The train that is always departing, never arriving.

Not true, says Needleman. Philosophy is definitely interested in the destination, but the journey can't be rushed. That is the only way to ensure you arrive not merely at clever answers but "answers of the heart." The other kind, answers of the head, are not only less satisfying but, in the deepest sense, less true.

Arriving at answers of the heart demands not only patience but a willingness to sit with your ignorance. Staying with the doubt, the mystery, rather than rushing to solve the problem, to check off another item on your endless to-do list. This takes time, and courage. Others will mock you. Let them, says Jacob Needleman, and Socrates, too. Ridicule is the price of wisdom.

A while ago, I was speaking with my friend Jennifer. To clarify: I was speaking; she was listening, as I relayed my usual catalog of worries.

I suffer from a distribution problem, I told her. I have enough of any given attribute, but it's distributed unevenly. Hair, for instance. I've got plenty on my chest, and in my nostrils, but not nearly enough on my head.

Success, though, is more problematic. That is not a distribution problem, I explained, but a genuine shortage. "I am not," I told her, "successful enough."

Jennifer paused the way people do when they are either about to say something profound or are plotting an escape strategy. Fortunately, Jennifer's pause was the former.

"What does success look like?" she said.

"What does success look like?" I said.

"Yes, what does success look like?"

Normally, when you parrot a question back to someone they feel obliged to elaborate, to connect the dots for you. Not Jennifer. My question boomeranged and hit me upside the head. What does success *look* like? This had never occurred to me. I had always thought of success in terms of quantity, not aesthetics.

How we frame a question matters. Jennifer could have asked, "Why do you want to be successful?" or "How much success is enough?" I would have dismissed those queries, swatted them like the mosquitoes circling as we sat on her deck in New Jersey. *Why do I want to be successful?* I just do—doesn't everybody? *How much success is enough?* More than I currently have.

Jennifer didn't ask me those questions, though. She asked me what success looked like. Implied in her question was the personal. What does it look like *to me*? Would I recognize it if I saw it?

I just sat there, stunned, as if a torpedo fish had stung my brain. A good question does that. It grabs hold of you and won't let go. A good question reframes the problem so that you see it in an entirely new light. A good question prompts not only a search for answers but a reevaluation of the search itself. A good question elicits not a clever reply but no reply at all. From ancient times, long before Socrates, Indian sages have practiced *brahmodya,* a competition where contestants aim to articulate absolute truth. The contest always ends in silence. As author Karen Armstrong explains, "The moment of insight came when they realized the inadequacy of their words, and thus intuited the ineffable."

Silence is not my usual state. Words are like oxygen for me. Yet I silently turned Jennifer's question over in my mind, looked at it from different angles. A good question triggers more questions, and sure enough Jennifer's single query sparked dozens of my own. I was no longer conversing with her but with myself.

This is exactly what Socrates aimed to induce: a state of ruthless self-interrogation, questioning not only what we know but who we are, in hopes of eliciting a radical shift in perspective.

Tolstoy's novella *The Death of Ivan Ilyich* contains one of my favorite passages in literature, perhaps because it is so unexpectedly redemptive, and also involves a train. The protagonist is a successful government official. He is terminally ill, gripped by fear and regret. Toward the end of the story, the dread lifts, replaced by a new perspective "like the sensation one sometimes experiences in a railway carriage when one thinks one is going backwards while one is really going forwards and suddenly becomes aware of the real direction."

Looking back at my conversation with Jennifer, I realize how I, like Ivan, suddenly intuited my real direction. It was the most Socratic experience I've ever had. It took place not in the dusty streets of ancient Athens but on my friend's deck in Montclair, New Jersey. No matter. Genuine wisdom isn't bound by place and time. It's portable.

Now, whenever I'm striving to achieve something, anything, I stop and ask: What does success look like? To be honest, I haven't answered that question, and may never do so. That's okay. I've changed the prescription on my glasses, and can see more clearly.

The doors glide open. I step into a sleek subway car, shiny and metallic. In modern Greek parlance, I am embarking on a *metaforá*. Derived from the ancient root *metamorphoo*, to transform completely from the inside out, it is where we get the English word "metaphor." Today, Greeks use *metaforá* to denote travel on public transport. Whenever someone takes a bus to work or the subway to meet friends or a streetcar to pick up dry cleaning, she is, in a way, taking a metaphor, and engaging in a transformative act. I love Greece. Everything exists on two levels, often more. Even a subway ride offers the promise of self-renewal.

Not only does the Athens subway run smoothly, but a history lesson comes with each ride. When it was under construction, workers unearthed ancient artifacts from the city's golden age. Archaeologists removed some of the artifacts ("rescue archaeology," it's called) but others were incorporated into the stations, so that today locals call their subway "a museum with a train running through it."

I have come to Greece, the land of metaphors, to walk where Socrates walked, to breathe the air he breathed. I have come to remind myself that Socrates was not an idea but a man, flesh and bone. Socrates wondered, but he didn't wonder just anywhere. He wondered *here,* in Athens, a city he loved like no other.

I disembark at the Agora Station and walk. The agora, or marketplace, was Socrates's favorite haunt. It was a crowded and smelly place, rife with hawkers and thieves and everyone else. Socrates loved it. The agora was his classroom, and his theater.

Archaeologists began excavating the site relatively late, in 1931, decades after other big digs, including those at Pompeii and Olympia. They've made up for lost time, though, as the thousands of artifacts recovered attest: pottery shards, inscriptions, sculptures, coins, and other ancient treasures.

Today the site, spread over two dozen acres, is mostly rubble, but enough remains of the old marketplace that, with a bit of imagination, I can picture the scene. I can see hawkers selling their wares, everything from spices to water clocks; defendants awaiting trial; young men loitering, as young men do. Taking it all in is Socrates, barefoot, those crablike eyes swiveling wildly, on the prowl for philosophical companions. Socrates practiced retail philosophy. He didn't wait for people to come to him. He went to them.

"The unexamined life is not worth living," Socrates famously said. When I first heard that, as a mopey teenager, I sighed. Life is difficult enough. You want me to examine it, too? The examined life. I don't care for the term. For starters, it contains the root "exam," which stirs dormant memories of number-two pencils and cold doctor hands. It sounds like too much work. We can do better. So, with all due respect, I offer two corollaries to Socrates's examined life.

Corollary Number One: The examined life that doesn't produce practical results isn't worth living. Contemplating one's navel has its pleasures but it is far more satisfying to see results, a better navel. *Eudaimonia,* the Greeks called it. Often translated as "happiness," the word signifies something larger: a flourishing, meaningful life. Consider, as the contemporary philosopher Robert Solomon suggests, two people. One has an elaborate theory of generosity, while the other does not. "Generosity just flows from him, unthinkingly, as water flows from a fountain." The second person is clearly leading the exemplary, meaningful life.

Corollary Number Two: The unexamined life may not be worth living, but neither is the overexamined one. "Ask yourself if you are happy and you cease to be so," said the British philosopher John Stuart Mill, articulating the Pleasure Paradox (also known as Paradox of Hedonism). The more we try to seize happiness the more it slips from our grasp. Happiness is a by-product, never an objective. It's an unexpected windfall from a life lived well.

So was Socrates wrong about this whole unexamined life nonsense? Or am I missing something?

My instinct is to answer those questions quickly so I can scratch them off my to-do list and move on. I restrain this impulse. Instead, I let the question loiter in the soft Greek air, unanswered but not unexamined. Then I take a metaphor back to my hotel.

Socrates was a failure. I know that sounds harsh, but it's true. Many of the dialogues end not with a thunder-of-Zeus breakthrough but an impasse. Philosophy produces more problems than it solves. That is its nature.

Socrates didn't publish, and he perished, executed by his fellow Athenians. Again, his alleged crimes were impiety and corrupting the youth but, really, he was executed for asking too many impertinent questions. He was philosophy's first martyr.

After his trial, his fate sealed, he gathered with a few of his followers. They were heartbroken, but not Socrates; he remained sanguine, and coyly opaque, until the end. "And now it is time to go, I to die, and you to live, but which of us goes to a better thing is unknown to all but God," he said.

Those are excellent last words, and indeed that is how many a biography of Socrates ends. There's only one problem. They were not the philosopher's last words. Plato, in a dialogue called *Phaedo*, tells us what transpired during Socrates's final minutes.

"Crito," says Socrates, speaking to his friend. "We owe a rooster to Asclepius; make this offering to him and do not forget."

"It shall be done," replied Crito. "But have you anything else to say?"

There was no reply. Socrates was dead.

What to make of this seemingly pedestrian exit? For centuries, scholars have pondered that question. Some interpret Socrates's last words darkly. At the time, roosters were offered to the god of healing, Asclepius, so perhaps Socrates was saying life is like a disease we must cure. Or maybe it was Socrates's way of calling us back down to earth, even as he ascended to heaven. Maybe he was reminding us, as we grapple with life's big questions, not to forget the small stuff. Don't overlook your obligations as a citizen and a friend. Be a person of honor. If you owe someone a rooster, give him a rooster.

There's a simpler and less profound possibility: the hemlock had begun to take effect, and an addled Socrates was mumbling gibberish. No one knows for certain, and probably no one ever will.

I do know this: it is deliciously fitting that the King of Questions departed in a cloud of them, leaving us scratching our heads, wondering. Socrates couldn't resist planting one more puzzle in our minds. One more question to experience.

3.

How to Walk like Rousseau

2:42 p.m. On board Swiss Federal Railways, Train No. 59, en route from Basel to Neuchâtel.

I glance out my window and watch the Swiss countryside unfurl in slow motion. At least I think it's slow. Speed is relative. Train travel, viewed through the rosy haze of nostalgia, represents a throwback to a simpler, analog time. I take the train to change the rhythm of my life, to remind myself what dawdling feels like.

It wasn't always this way. When people first rode trains, in the nineteenth century, they reacted with an unease bordering on terror. "I felt like a projectile," said one early passenger. "Like a human parcel," said another. The speed—faster than humans had ever traveled on land—transformed the hallowed countryside into an ungodly blur. In a letter dated August 22, 1837, Victor Hugo described the view from his train's window: "The flowers by the side of the road are no longer flowers but flecks, or rather streaks, of red or white . . . everything becomes a streak; the grainfields are great shocks of yellow hair; fields of alfalfa, long green tresses. . . . [F]rom time to time, a shadow, a shape, a specter appears and disappears with lightning speed behind the window." Hugo's train was traveling at about 15 miles per hour. Speed is relative.

The art critic John Ruskin, one of the loudest voices decrying this newfangled form of transport, devised a maxim that still holds true: "All traveling becomes dull in exact proportion to its rapidity."

As my Swiss train glides (Swiss trains really do glide) through the landscape, whisper-quiet, I wonder what Ruskin would make of air travel. Nothing good, I'm sure.

Transportation traces its own evolutionary arc, a survival of the fastest that erases its antecedents as it speeds ahead. We're moving too fast to pause and ask how exactly we got here, strapped into an aluminum tube and hurtling through space at a speed so fast it doesn't blur the scenery but obliterates it. This acceleration didn't just happen, of course, any more than our outsize brains and opposable thumbs just happened. Before the airplane was the train and before the train the coach and before the coach the saddle. We need to reach further back, though, to the beginning.

In the beginning was the foot.

Jean-Jacques Rousseau was a man of multitudes: philosopher, novelist, composer, essayist, botanist, autodidact, fugitive, political theorist, masochist. Most of all, he was a walker. He walked often and he walked alone. Yes, a stroll with a close friend has its pleasures, as do walking clubs, but at its heart walking is a private act. We walk by ourselves and for ourselves. Freedom is walking's essence. The freedom to depart and return when we wish, to meander, to, as Robert Louis Stevenson put it, "follow this way or that, as the freak takes you."

Rousseau followed his freak. It took him across Europe, from Venice to Paris, Turin to Lyons, and beyond. Rousseau was among the first truly rootless souls, what today we'd call an urban nomad. At home everywhere, and nowhere.

For most of human history, walking was not optional. If you wanted to get anywhere, you had to walk. Today walking is a choice. Rousseau didn't have as many choices as we do—train travel was not yet invented—but he had some. An extensive network of carriage service crisscrossed Europe. He detested carriage travel and walked whenever he could. "I have never thought so much, existed so much, lived so much, been so much myself . . . as in the journeys which I have made alone and on foot," he said. Walking saved Rousseau's life. It also killed him.

Rousseau grew up in Geneva, the son of an irascible watchmaker named Isaac. His mother died shortly after his birth, a trauma that haunted him. Young Rousseau regularly teamed up with friends to explore the countryside. "I always went farther than any of them without thinking about my return, unless others thought of it for me," he recalls in his memoir, *The Confessions.*

One pleasant spring afternoon, in 1728, Rousseau took a walk that changed the vector of his life. He was sixteen years old, apprenticed to an engraver, a job he despised, and feeling "restless, disconnected with everything and with myself." A typical sixteen-year-old. He had ventured outside the city. It was getting late. He knew he had to return before the city's gates closed for the night. Rousseau had missed two curfews in the past, and been beaten by his employer. He dreaded what might happen this time.

He ran frantically, but it was no use. He was too late. Sleeping outside the city walls that night, Rousseau vowed never to return to Geneva. From that day, he led a nomadic life, traveling ceaselessly, and almost always by foot.

Rousseau lived in many cities but was not a city person. He describes his first encounter with Paris, a city most of us associate with beauty and romance, this way: "I saw nothing but dirty stinking little streets, ugly black houses, a general air of squalor and poverty, beggars, carters, menders of clothes, sellers of herb-drinks and old hats." Then there were the people of Paris, "tiresome" and forever mouthing "stupid witticisms." No, not a city person.

Not a people person, either. Rousseau was what today we'd call high maintenance. "A difficult friend, a disappointing lover, and an impossible employee," says author Leo Damrosch in his excellent biography of Rousseau.

Walking enabled Rousseau to escape the eyes of others. He was shy. Severely nearsighted, an insomniac like Marcus, and with a lifelong urinary problem (eventually diagnosed as an enlarged prostate) that required frequent visits to the toilet, he avoided social contact whenever possible. Throughout his life, he imagined people were staring at him. It probably didn't help that he had an odd compulsion to expose his rear end to strangers. Rousseau was an avowed masochist who enjoyed a good spanking, like the one he received as a delinquent schoolboy. "I found in the pain, in the shame even, a mixture of sensuality that left me desiring more," he writes in his memoir, among the first to contain such personal, and salacious, details.

Walking was an obvious fit with Rousseau's philosophy. He advocated a return to nature, and what is more natural than walking? Natural, that is, for most of us.

I am no Rousseau. I am not a child of nature—or even a distant cousin. I do not go camping, nor do I go glamping. My car is not adorned with a bumper sticker that says "I'd rather be fishing." Ditto hunting, camping (see above), spelunking, kayaking, snorkeling, rock climbing, and bird-watching. I do not own hiking boots. I do not own a sleeping bag. I do not own a crampon. I do own several backpacks, but they are sleek models with names like "city edition" and "urban renegade."

Mother Nature is something of a nag. She's constantly reminding me of my core incompetence. I do not know how to pitch a tent or unpitch a tent or do anything involving a tent. I do not know how to navigate using the stars or the sun or any other celestial bodies. My incompetence extends beyond the natural world. I do not know how to change the air filter on my car or talk to my teenage daughter or ease the suffering of an aging parent or do downward dog or sit quietly with my thoughts for more than five seconds without my head exploding.

I thought I knew how to walk, but reading Rousseau, I now question even that basic skill. Yes, I can put one foot in front of the other, repeating as necessary, but that is merely bipedal locomotion. It is not walking.

You can tell a lot about a person by how they walk. The Pentagon recently developed advanced radar that can identify up to 95 percent of individual walks, as distinct as a person's fingerprints or signature. Everyone has a walking style.

I have several, and they, like my moods, vacillate. I either charge ahead full tilt, like a Black Friday shopper, or lumber like an out-of-shape elephant that's just downed the all-you-can-eat Indian buffet. Should you find yourself walking behind me, don't. I am not an easy man to follow.

I wake in Neuchâtel, a city Rousseau didn't care for, and take the train to a small town called Môtiers, which he cared for even less. "The vilest and most venomous place that one could inhabit," Rousseau recalled. Apparently, the feeling was mutual.

The house that Rousseau despised in the town he despised is now a small museum, proving that there's nothing a lot of time and a little curation can't remedy. A plaque marks the dates that Rousseau lived here: July 10, 1762, to September 8, 1765. Factually accurate, yes, but incomplete. It fails to capture the poisonous animosity between Rousseau and the residents of Môtiers, furious over his writing.

Inside, I find early editions of the two books that ignited that anger: *Emile* and *The Social Contract*. I also spot a portrait of Rousseau wearing a caftan, a flowing tunic popular in the Middle East. It was comfortable, but odd-looking. It irked the townsfolk, as did Rousseau's daily walks, which became fodder for ridicule. One day, that simmering animosity boiled over. Residents, egged on by the town minister, hurled stones at Rousseau's house. Rousseau, a man who often misread social signals, got this one right. He fled Môtiers, never to return. I do the same.

That evening, back in Neuchâtel, I install myself at a *crêperie*, order a glass of chardonnay, which I hope pairs well with early Romanticism, and retrieve Rousseau's memoir from my backpack. I dive in. You don't dip into Rousseau. You plunge headfirst or not at all.

What grabs my attention and doesn't let go is the language. Clear, accessible, not your typical philosophical gobbledygook. Nice, I think, taking another sip of my chardonnay, which does in fact pair well.

Soon I realize that the clarity is accompanied by something else. Rousseau is—how do I put this politely?—a drama queen. So impassioned are the words that I swear the pages feel moist. Rousseau cries, regularly and voluminously. He is prone to fits of rapture. He has been known to swoon. He is forever abandoning himself to "the sweetest melancholy" or "the fatality of my lot" or, my favorite, "the indolent and solitary life." His preferred organ, the heart, is busy. It is either "opening" or "kindling" or "stirring." Mostly, it beats. It beats with "impatience" or with "joy" or, on more than one occasion, "violently."

I usually find this sort of cardiac writing off-putting, but not Rousseau's. The words, while overwrought, are free of artifice. Rousseau isn't faking it.

Rousseau's philosophy can be summed up in four words: nature good, society bad. He believed in the "natural goodness of man." In his *Discourse on Inequality*, he paints a picture of man in his natural state, "wandering in the forests, without industry, without speech, without domicile, without want and without liaisons, with no need of his fellow-men, likewise with no desire to harm them." Nobody is born mean-spirited, petty, vindictive, paranoid. Society makes them that way. Rousseau's "savage man" lives in each moment with no regrets about the past or worries about the future.

Much of what we take to be human nature is social habit, Rousseau believes. We're convinced our love of smoked Brie or Instagram is natural when it is cultural. After all, in the 1970s people thought shag carpeting and neckties as wide as a runway were "natural." Only now do we recognize them for the abominations they are. Even something as "natural" as scenery is prone to cultural influence. For most of European history, people considered mountains barbaric; no sane person would voluntarily travel to one. Only in the eighteenth century did they become objects of admiration. The good news, says Rousseau, is we can change these social habits, provided we recognize them for what they are: social artifices as easily jettisoned as an old pair of bell-bottom jeans.

Rousseau's Savage Man regularly experiences feelings of self-love, which Rousseau calls *amour-de-soi*. This healthy emotion differs from the more egoistical variety, which he calls *amour-propre*. The first stems from human nature, the second from society. *Amour-de-soi* is the joy you feel when singing in the shower. *Amour-propre* is the joy you feel while singing at Radio City Music Hall. You may sing poorly in the shower but the delight is yours alone, independent of others' opinions, and therefore, Rousseau argued, more authentic.

So you can see why Rousseau walked. Walking requires none of the trappings of civilization: no domesticated animals, no carriages, no roads. The walker is free, unencumbered. Pure *amour-de-soi.*

Sometimes a single walk changes everything. So it was with Rousseau one summer afternoon in 1749. He was on his usual six-mile jaunt from Paris to Vincennes to visit fellow philosopher and friend Denis Diderot, imprisoned for writings deemed blasphemous. It was an especially hot day, and the road was dusty. Rousseau stopped to rest. Sitting in the shade, idly leafing through an issue of *Mercure de France*, he spotted a prize offered by the Academy of Dijon for the best essay on the topic "Whether the restoration of the sciences and arts has contributed to purify morals."

Rousseau felt dizzy, disoriented, "like a drunkard." In that moment, he recalls, "I beheld a different universe and became a different man." His essay won first prize, launching his career into a high orbit.

Might Rousseau have had the same revelation while sitting in his study, or riding in a carriage? Perhaps, but the walk had primed his imagination. The mind thrives at three miles per hour, the speed of a moderately paced walk. Freed of the pettiness of the office, the tyranny of expectations, it roams, and when the mind roams, unexpected and wonderful things happen. Not always, but more often than you'd think. Walking supplies just the right balance of stimulation and repose, exertion and idleness.

When we walk, we are simultaneously doing and not-doing. On one level, our minds are engaged: focusing on the terrain ahead, cognizant of the periphery. Yet none of this thinking occupies much cerebral space. There's plenty left over for meandering, and freak following.

No wonder so many philosophers walked. Socrates, of course, liked nothing more than strolling in the agora. Nietzsche regularly embarked on spirited two-hour jaunts in the Swiss Alps, convinced "all truly great thoughts are conceived by walking." Thomas Hobbes had a walking stick custom made with a portable inkwell attached so he could record his thoughts as he ambled. Thoreau regularly took four-hour treks across the Concord countryside, his capacious pockets overflowing with nuts, seeds, flowers, Indian arrowheads, and other treasures. Immanuel Kant, naturally, maintained a highly regimented walking routine. Every day, he'd eat lunch at 12:45 p.m., then depart for a one-hour constitutional—never more, never less—on the same boulevard in Königsberg, Prussia (now Russia). So unwavering was Kant's routine that the people of Königsberg set their watches by his perambulations.

Good walkers, all of them. None, though, compares with Rousseau. He'd regularly walk twenty miles in a single day. He once walked three hundred miles from Geneva to Paris. It took him two weeks.

For Rousseau, walking was like breathing. "I can scarcely think when I remain still; my body must be in motion to make my mind active." As he walked, he'd jot down thoughts, large and small, on playing cards that he always carried with him. Rousseau was not the first philosopher to walk but he was the first to philosophize so extensively about walking.

The walking philosopher gives the lie to one of the discipline's greatest myths: that it is a mental pursuit wholly divorced from the body. From Archimedes's eureka moment in the bath to Descartes's masterful fencing to Sartre's sexual escapades, philosophy has a swift corporeal current running through it. There are no disembodied philosophers, or philosophies. "There is more wisdom in your body than in all of your philosophy," said Nietzsche.

Consider an emotion like anger. When you are outraged, where does "anger" reside? In your mind, yes, but also in your body, as the French philosopher Maurice Merleau-Ponty explains: "I could not imagine the malice and cruelty which I discern in my opponent's looks, separated from his gestures, speech and body. None of this takes place in some other-worldly realm, in some shrine located beyond the body of the angry man." Likewise, when we philosophize we do so not only with our minds, but with our bodies, too.

Back at the *crêperie*, I plunge again. Same wine, different Rousseau: his final and unfinished work, *Reveries of the Solitary Walker*. It is an odd yet endearing volume, "a book that is and is not about walking," as Rebecca Solnit points out in her history of walking. Then again, walking itself is and is not about walking.

Reveries is my favorite of Rousseau's writings. It pulses with the moral clarity and leavened wisdom of a man who, having been expelled, stoned, and ridiculed, no longer gives a fuck. This is not Rousseau the contrarian, or Rousseau the confessor or Rousseau the reformer. This is Rousseau at rest.

The book is arranged in a series of ten walks, or reveries. In each, Rousseau embarks on an outing, but that is merely the vehicle, so to speak, for the real subject of the book: memory. How do we retrieve life's sweet moments, and do they taste as sweet, or sweeter even, on the second bite?

In the fifth walk, Rousseau recalls his time living on a small island called Saint-Pierre, his refuge from the stone throwers of Môtiers. It was his paradise. "The happiest time of my life," he recalls.

I read those words and nearly spit up my chardonnay. Rousseau, connoisseur of his own pathologies, wasn't exactly prone to bouts of happiness. I want to see this island for myself.

I walk toward the train station. It is not a Rousseauvian walk. Too rushed, I say to myself. Too mindless. *Focus, damn it*, I say, out loud this time, startling the Swiss passersby.

At Neuchâtel's small but busy station, I board a regional express bound for Rousseau's happy isle. It departs on time, naturally. Swiss trains deserve their reputation for exceptional punctuality, but their cold efficiency seems at odds with the messy, emotive life of the country's greatest philosopher.

It's a short ride, just a few stops, but I decide to sample *Reveries*. "Everything is in constant flux on this Earth," Rousseau writes, echoing the Greek philosopher Heraclitus's dictum: "All is flux." The river we step in is never the same twice, nor are we.

The train glides along the tracks so smoothly that, were it not for the changing scenery, I'd swear we weren't moving at all. And movement, Rousseau tells me, is vital. It must be of a certain kind, though. "If the movement is irregular or too violent it arouses us from our dreams."

Rousseau's mention of violent movement reminds me of my Amtrak journey across the United States, in the company of that insomniac philosopher-emperor Marcus. Somewhere in North Dakota, bored by the monotonous scenery, I needed to do something, *anything*.

On the hard rails of Amtrak, routine activities are fraught with difficulty. Shaving, for instance. (My one attempt left me a bloody mess.) Walking, too. I teetered and tottered like a drunkard at sea. This made sense from an evolutionary perspective. We humans come from the sea, a fact reflected in the etymology of the word "walk." In the eleventh century, it meant "to roll about, toss" like the sea. It wasn't until the thirteenth century that "walking" came ashore, toweled off, and acquired its contemporary meaning. Words evolve.

Not me. As I attempted to walk, I was devolving, straight back to the eleventh century. I rolled and tossed down the aisles. I careened into luggage. I body-slammed strangers.

"You've got to dance with the train," said an older woman witnessing my incompetence.

She was right. I had been fighting the train. I needed to dance with it. Let the train lead. It took me a while, but I got the hang of it. The secret, I learned, is to stay loose. The train pitched left then right, and so did I. No resistance. Finally, I made it to my destination, the lounge car, as elated as if I had summited K2.

About six million years ago, early hominids got off their knuckles, stood up straight, and walked on two feet. This new, erect posture had many unexpected benefits. It freed up hands for toolmaking, as well as pointing, caressing, gesturing, hand-holding, bird-flipping, nose-picking, and nail-biting. Walking is about more than walking, and always has been.

Walking may be natural but that doesn't mean it comes easily. Here Joseph Amato, in his encyclopedic history of walking, *On Foot,* describes the physiology of a single stride. "It requires spending three-fourths of one's time on one foot or the other. As one strikes the ground with one stiff leg after another, all of one's weight is set against a descending heel, only to be transferred to the big toe as one rotates hips and redirects the plane of foot and leg." All of this happens automatically, of course. Think about the biomechanics too much and you might fall on your face, as I nearly did after reading the above passage.

We walk on two feet but we do so on a skeleton designed for four. This disconnect between ancient anatomy and modern usage keeps podiatrists in business. Flat feet, swollen feet, blisters, bunions, and hammertoes are just a few of the podiatric prices we pay for our bipedal existence. Rousseau suffered from painful corns most of his life. He walked on his heels, defiantly.

Rousseau was a devoted walker but not a heroic one. He walked slowly, owing to his corns, and could "never jump an ordinary ditch." He did not carry a loaded rucksack, or other accoutrements. He did not fend off thieves or wild dogs. He did not rescue those in distress, damsels or otherwise. He just walked, without judgment or expectation. When we walk like this, the experience approaches the sacred.

The train pulls into a small station a short bus ride from Saint-Pierre. It is an island full of surprises. For starters, it is no longer an island. Since Rousseau's time, a small land bridge has formed, connecting it to the mainland. All is flux.

I step onto the island that is no longer an island and see why Rousseau was so fond of it. It's idyllic in an unpretentious way, lush but not luscious, green but not *too* green. From nearly every vantage point, there's a view of Lake Bienne. This view is nature at her best, what the poet Philip Larkin called "serious earth."

I can picture Rousseau taking long and aimless walks here, accompanied by his beloved dog, Sultan, or perhaps collecting plant samples. I find the path that traverses Saint-Pierre, and I walk. One foot in front of the other, I say to myself, just as I've been doing all my life, only better. I translate "better" into "faster" and soon I'm moving at a ridiculous clip. I catch myself and compensate by slowing to elephant speed. Why can't I find my middle gear? What is wrong with me?

To my surprise, it is the philosopher-emperor Marcus who answers. *Respond to adversity, real or imagined, not with self-pity or hand-wringing, but simply by starting over.* Viewed this way, life no longer feels like a narrative gone awry, or a botched ending. None of that is real. There are no endings. Only an infinite chain of beginnings.

So I begin. One foot in front of the other. Good. Now again.

I follow the trail, stopping occasionally to gaze at the lake or the wispy clouds. Eventually I find the small room where Rousseau lived. It's a simple space, with a canopied bed, a Spartan sitting area, and, in one corner, a wooden trapdoor Rousseau used to make his getaway when fans, or enemies, tracked him down.

His herbarium is here, too: dried and pressed plants, long delicate stalks, frozen in time. A small plaque mentions Rousseau's "contradictory personality," an understatement if ever there were one.

Something is noticeably absent: books. So hurried was Rousseau's escape from Môtiers he didn't have time to pack his considerable library. In *Reveries*, he calls this dearth of reading material "one of my greatest joys." This observation seems awfully peculiar for a man who spent a lifetime reading and writing books. At another point, Rousseau describes walking to a secluded spot by the edge of the lake and listening to the ebb and flow of the water, "lapping against my ears and my eyes . . . and it was enough to make me pleasantly aware of my existence without troubling myself with thought." Okay, first he stopped reading; now he has stopped thinking. Was he devolving—or was he onto something?

Rousseau, like Socrates, was a kind of antiphilosopher. He had no patience for "empty logic-chopping" or "hair splitting metaphysical subtleties." He was a thinker but not an overthinker. Rousseau knew that his favorite organ, the heart, possessed its own intelligence, one we access not with furrowed brow and tight jaw but with loose legs and swinging arms.

People strut and swagger in front of others, but rarely alone. These are social gestures. Walking, the slowest form of travel, is the quickest route to our more authentic selves. We can't return to some long-lost paradise that probably never was. But we can walk. We can walk to work. We can walk our daughter to school. We can walk, alone, to nowhere in particular on a crisp and breezy autumn afternoon.

We walk to forget. We walk to forget the cranky boss, the spat with the spouse, the pile of unpaid bills, the flashing warning light in your Subaru, indicating either that the tire pressure is low or the car is on fire. We walk to forget, if only momentarily, a world that is "too much with us," as William Wordsworth, another fine walker, put it.

We walk to forget ourselves, too. I know I do. The surplus fifteen pounds resistant to every diet known to man, the recidivist nasal hair, the decade-old blemish that suddenly, for reasons known only to it, has decided to self-actualize on the crown of my bald head, spreading like an inkblot. All forgotten when I walk.

I recall once watching the summer Olympics on TV and taking a keen interest in competitive walking. Earnest young athletes traipsing toward gold. They looked absurd. Walking is not a sport. The phrase "competitive walking" makes about as much sense as "competitive meditation." In our Age of the Accessory, walking is one of the few unadorned activities still available to us, one that, as author Rebecca Solnit points out, remains "essentially unimproved since the dawn of time."

Walking is democratic. Barring a disability, anyone can walk. The wealthy walker has no advantage over the impoverished one. Rousseau, despite his literary success, always saw himself as "the son of a worker," what we now call blue-collar. People like that didn't ride in fancy carriages. They walked.

They walked as I do now: attentively, one step at a time, relishing the sturdiness, and the springiness, too, of serious earth.

In late October 1776, Rousseau was navigating a narrow Parisian street, on his way home after a long walk, when, as the biographer Leo Damrosch relays, "a nobleman's carriage came hurtling toward him, flanked by a huge, galloping Great Dane. He was unable to dodge in time, the dog bowled him over, and he fell hard on the cobblestone street, bleeding profusely and unconscious." Rousseau likely suffered a concussion and neurological damage. He never recovered fully. Less than two years later, Jean-Jacques Rousseau returned from his morning walk, collapsed, and died.

By all accounts, he died a happy man. Toward the end of his life, his walking had taken on a softer, more sanguine quality. There are still traces of the usual self-pity ("So here I am alone on the earth") and of the paranoia ("The ceiling above my head has eyes, the walls around me have ears") but gone is the neediness. He no longer walked to flee or to find or to make a philosophical point. He simply walked.

Rousseau's legacy is vast. It includes Hallmark cards, Hollywood tearjerkers, heart-shaped emojis, and tell-all memoirs. If you've ever said, "I need a good cry," you can thank Rousseau. If you've ever said, "Use your imagination," you're being Rousseauvian. If, in the heat of an argument, you've actually uttered the words "I don't care if it makes no sense, it's how I *feel,*" Rousseau is your man. If you've ever answered heartbreak with a long and angry walk, Rousseau. If your spouse has ever dragged you on a ten-mile trek on a damp, cold day, because "it will be good for you," you can thank, or curse, Rousseau. Because of him, we think and feel differently, and we think about our feelings differently.

If Descartes was the modern era's philosopher of the head, Rousseau was its philosopher of the heart. He elevated the passions and made feelings acceptable, not on par with reason, but close. This wasn't easy. During Rousseau's time, the Age of Reason, imaginative thinking was suspect. Two centuries later, no less a rationalist than Albert Einstein declared that "imagination is more important than knowledge."

It's tempting to dismiss Rousseau as a tree-hugging Luddite who would like to see us all hunting and gathering again and fighting over the good rock, next to the fire. That is not what he had in mind. Rousseau wasn't advocating a return to the cave but a realignment with nature. A better cave. He foresaw environmental issues decades before the industrial revolution and centuries before California freeways.

Rousseau's naturalism was never intended as a prescription. It was a thought experiment. What if, Rousseau posited, we peel away the layers of artifice society has applied liberally, like so much rouge, and reveal a more authentic self? Lurking beneath the prim insurance executive lies a rabble-rouser and inside every office worker a mountaineer, itching to break free.

I step out of Rousseau's old room on the island that is no longer an island and shield my eyes from the sun. I have a choice: rush to catch the water taxi back to town or walk. I decide to walk.

I walk alone. I walk with intention. I let my mind wander, but not too far. I'm getting good at this. *No, that is pride speaking. Silence that voice. Connect with the earth. That's better.*

I find a rhythm. I sense my surroundings—the birds singing, the satisfying crunch of gravel underfoot. I walk, and walk some more. My legs ache. My feet grow sore. Yet, still, I walk. It hurts, and it feels good.

I'm making good progress now. How many steps, I wonder? Reflexively, I twist my wrist and am about to check my Fitbit when I stop myself. I inhale deeply, greedily, like a diver coming up for air.

Somewhere along the path, I sense a subtle but definite shift in my . . . my what? My consciousness? No, it's my heart. The expectations freeloading in my mind—of "getting" Rousseau, of making progress in my philosophical investigations—melt away. I walk but it doesn't feel like I am the one doing the walking. I'm all verb, no subject.

The Jewish theologian Abraham Heschel described the Sabbath as a "sanctuary in time." Walking is a sanctuary in motion. The peace we experience with each step adheres, and it conveys. Portable serenity.

The pain evaporates. With each step, I feel less burdened, more buoyant, as if someone had inflated my shoes. I sense the seriousness of the earth, and its lightness, too. Step. Step.

As the sun bows low in the sky, I grow aware of a peculiar presence, as if my feet were grazing a large and benevolent creature. It's not anything I can name, this presence, yet I know, and with unaccustomed certainty, that it is older than old, bubbling up from a long ago time, before words.

4.

How to See like Thoreau

11:12 a.m. On board Amtrak's Acela, Train No. 2158, en route from Washington, D.C., to Boston.

I am seated in the Quiet Car. We Quiet People eye each other approvingly and, of course, silently. We're comrades in an undeclared war, entrenched in our own private Dunkirk, taking enemy fire, the odds not good, but holding firm. The Quiet Car is civilization at its most civilized, a bulwark against the barbarian raucousness that lies beyond.

It's a futile attempt, judging by the conductor's half-hearted reprimand of a couple of wayward passengers violating the "library-like atmosphere" that Amtrak has decreed. In our hearts, we Quiet People know the battle is already lost. Besides, whatever quiet prevails here is strictly an exterior phenomenon. Inside our heads, the decibel levels are off the charts. That's the thing about lives of quiet desperation. They're only quiet on the outside.

None of this matters, not now, when I have a small library of books, as well as my reassuringly analog notebook and pen. Suddenly the train lurches and my pen, a Japanese beauty crafted of stainless steel, a sublime union of aesthetic and ergonomic perfection, is gone.

I search under the seat, around the seat, in the seat. I get down on all fours and poke inside the surprisingly complex seat mechanism. This last contortion attracts a few sideways glances, but no reprimand, for I have been careful to conduct these maneuvers at the prescribed decibel levels.

I do not find my pen. Uncharacteristically, I do not care. The rhythmic motion of the train—not rocking, exactly, more like that of a rusty seesaw—quiets my mind while the scenery floats by: puffy white clouds smeared across the late-spring sky, the wide Susquehanna River, the posh seaside towns of Connecticut and Rhode Island. All this I see. Or at least I think I do. Spend enough time reading philosophy and soon you're not sure of anything.

Some are born Thoreau, others achieve Thoreau. Most have Thoreau thrust upon them.

Henry David Thoreau was thrust upon me in ninth grade. I couldn't follow him, nor would I if I could. As I said, I am no woodsman. My life is not a model of simplicity. And while I do have reclusive tendencies, I prefer to do my recluding in a hotel room, not a tiny cabin without plumbing or decent Wi-Fi. I promptly exiled *Walden* to the Siberia of my brain, where it joined *Moby-Dick, The Brothers Karamazov,* and integral calculus.

A few weeks before my journey to Concord, I stumbled upon a *New Yorker* article about Thoreau. It was called "Pond Scum" and, as you can imagine, did little to rehabilitate the Hermit of Concord in my mind. The story's author, Kathryn Schulz, opens the piece by painting a picture of a coldhearted, misanthropic crank. Then she takes the gloves off.

But as the commuter train pulls into Concord Station, just as it did during Thoreau's day, I resolve to maintain an open mind. If I've learned anything from my philosophical investigations, it's that first impressions are often wrong. Doubt is essential. It is the vehicle that transports us from one certainty to another. Slowly, making all local stops.

I've arrived in Concord with a plan. This chapter will be called "How to Live Alone like Thoreau" or "How to Live Simply like Thoreau" or, given the hypocrisies revealed in "Pond Scum," perhaps "How to Pretend to Live Simply and Alone While Sneaking Off to Your Mom's for Homemade Cookies like Thoreau." His experiment in isolation wasn't so isolated after all.

I take one step inside the Concord Free Public Library and see it's not a typical small-town library. How could it be? Concord is not a typical small town. "The biggest little place in America," as the novelist Henry James called it, played a pivotal role in the Revolutionary War—the shot heard round the world was heard here first—and, later, the Transcendentalist movement that birthed, among others, Henry David Thoreau.

Thoreau was born in Concord and, except for his time at Harvard and a brief (and unhappy) stint in New York, lived his entire life here. Thoreau loved Concord. Friends tried to convince him to see Paris, but he demurred. Even when he did travel, to Maine and Canada, he took Concord with him. "I carry Concord ground in my boots and in my hat—and am I not made of Concord dust?"

The Concord library, like all good ones, provides plenty of reading nooks. I step into one called the Transcendentalist Cove. The movement's giants, frozen in marble, look down on me. There's Emerson and Alcott and, of course, Thoreau. The bust is later Thoreau, bearded and owlish. It's a kind face. Or is that a mask, concealing a dark, pond-scummy interior?

Thoreau's favorite books, on display here, offer a few clues. Like Marcus, Thoreau was a wisdom scavenger. "I do not the least care where I get my ideas, or what suggests them," he wrote. Thoreau read the ancient Greeks and Romans, but also sampled more exotic fare: *The Analects of Confucius*, the *Bhagavad Gita*. Forager extraordinaire, he was among the first Western philosophers to mine Indian and Chinese sources. Good philosophy, like a good lightbulb, brightens the room. Where the bulb was manufactured, how much it cost, its wattage, its age, the science behind it—none of this matters as long as it illuminates the room. Illuminates *your* room.

Thoreau turned east for the usual reason: personal crisis. The year was 1837. He had just been fired from his teaching position at a Concord school for refusing to administer corporal punishment, as was the practice of the day. He was broke and directionless. Then he stumbled across a book, one thousand pages long and with a title to match: *A Historical and Descriptive Account of British India.* Thoreau slogged through it, and unearthed gems. These ideas, at once alien and familiar, wormed their way into his mind. "To some extent, and at rare intervals, even I am a yogi," he wrote to a friend.

Thoreau, I think, was less yogi and more *sannyasi.* In Hindu tradition, a *sannyasi* is someone who, having discharged his familial obligations, relinquishes all material goods and retreats to the forest to pursue a purely spiritual life.

I turn a corner, and nearly collide with Leslie Wilson, curator of special collections. She is tall and trim, with alert, searching eyes. I like her. I like how she has lived with Thoreau for decades, yet not tired of him. I like how her admiration for the man hasn't slipped into sycophancy.

Leslie tells me she regularly fields inquiries from the many "pilgrims, groupies, and crackpots" who swarm to Walden Pond every day, the irony of crowding into a temple of solitude apparently lost on them.

There's nothing special about Walden, she tells me. "It's a mosquito-ridden swamp-hole." She elongates "swamp-hole," letting the words loiter on her tongue, savoring the delicious blasphemy. "There's nothing magical about this place."

To believe otherwise is to miss Thoreau's point. Places are special to the extent we make them so. Don't come to Walden, Thoreau would chide his twenty-first-century groupies. Find your own Walden. Better yet, *make* your own Walden.

Leslie disappears to a nearby safe, where she retrieves a piece of paper sheathed in plastic. It is the original manuscript of Thoreau's essay "Walking." The handwriting is expansive, with a wildness to it. Thoreau loved that word. "In wildness, there is preservation of the world," he said. It's often misquoted as "wilderness," but that's not what he meant. Wilderness exists out there. Wildness resides inside us. Wildness is strong and willful.

I examine the manuscript more closely, and notice the revisions.

How Thoreau, for instance, changed "early in the afternoon" to "early in the *summer* afternoon." A small change, but for Thoreau, the small mattered. It mattered not because he was fastidious, though he was that, but because in the details he found, if not God, certainly a mother lode of beauty.

I broach the subject of "Pond Scum" with Leslie, deploying diplomatic skills usually reserved for mentioning tax audits or genital warts. Yes, she's read it. Everyone in Concord has. The article was unfair, but not inaccurate, she says. Thoreau was "not an easy guy to warm up to," she tells me, in classic New England understatement.

Henry David Thoreau, hero of *Walden*, beloved icon of American lore, apostle of environmentalism, giant of letters, was something of a jerk. Everyone who knew him said so. Thoreau possessed "a certain iron-pokerishness, an uncompromising stiffness in his mental character," said Nathaniel Hawthorne. Others were less kind. "Thoreau was literally the most childlike, unconscious and unblushing egotist it has ever been my fortune to encounter in the ranks of manhood," said Henry James Sr., father of Henry James the novelist and William James the philosopher.

The harshest criticism centered on Thoreau's alleged hypocrisy. There he was pretending to live alone in the woods, self-sufficient, while sneaking off to his mom's for pie and laundry service.

It's true. Thoreau wasn't nearly as isolated at Walden as many believe. He regularly made the half-hour walk into town, not only for Mom's home cooking but to visit the local post office or coffee shop. So was *Walden* a ruse? Have ninth graders nationwide been hoodwinked?

I don't think so. Thoreau never claimed to have severed all ties with society. He doesn't conceal his forays into town, or the visitors he received at his cabin. (*Walden* contains a chapter called "Visitors.") As one Thoreauvian tells me, *Walden* isn't a book about a man living in the woods. It's a book about a man living.

As for Thoreau's purported crankiness, guilty as charged. But that does not diminish the value of his wisdom. If crankiness disqualified a thinker, all of philosophy would be contained in a pamphlet.

I tell Leslie about my practical approach to philosophy, and ask what "how-to" question she thinks Thoreau addresses. I'm expecting the usual "How to live alone" or "How to live simply."

"How to see," she says, without hesitation.

"How to see?"

Yes, she says. All the rest—the simple living, the solitude, the naturalism—were in service of something larger: vision. Thoreau teaches us how to see.

I did not see this coming. I will investigate, I assure her.

"Good," she says. "Have you read Thoreau?"

Oh yes, I say. Not only *Walden*, of course, but also his essays and even his obscure first book, *A Week on the Concord and Merrimack Rivers.*

"Not bad," she says, as if praising a toddler who's mastered Curious George. "But if you want to understand Thoreau, you need to read his journals."

I promise her I will. Only later do I discover what I've gotten myself into.

Everyone who met Thoreau commented on his appearance. Some remarked on his nose, prominent and Roman, "a sort of interrogation mark to the universe"; others his mouth, "uncouth and somewhat rustic"; or his hands, "strong and skillful." Others remarked on Thoreau's eerily acute senses, like his keen ear ("He could hear the most faint and distant sounds") and acute sense of smell ("No hound could scent better").

But Thoreau's eyes made the biggest impression. No two people saw them alike. "Strong serious blue eyes," said one Concord resident. "Piercing eyes, like an owl's," recalls another. "Enormous eyes . . . [that] frightened me dreadfully at first," recalls a third.

Thoreau's vision was legendary. At a glance, he could estimate the height of a tree or the weight of a calf. He'd reach into a bushel of pencils and, by sight alone, grab exactly a dozen. He had a knack for finding buried Indian arrowheads. "There is one," he'd say, kicking it up with his foot.

When it comes to the senses, philosophers are, as usual, divided. One school, known as the Rationalists, mistrusts the senses. Only our intellect, and the innate knowledge it contains, can lead us out of the cave and into the light. The Rationalist Descartes famously said *Cogito, ergo sum.* "I think, therefore I am." Another school, the Empiricists, believe our senses can indeed be trusted, and it is only through them that we come to know the world.

Thoreau refused to get twisted in such epistemological knots. Trustworthy or not, our senses are all we've got, he argued, so why not use them as best as we can? His was an outside-in philosophy.

Thoreau is considered a Transcendentalist, a member of a philosophical movement that can be summed up in four words: faith in things unseen. Thoreau, though, possessed an even stronger faith in things *seen.* He was less interested in the nature of reality than the reality of nature. Was there more to the world than meets the eye? Probably, but what does meet the eye is plenty miraculous, so let's start there. Thoreau valued vision even more than knowledge. Knowledge is always tentative, imperfect. Today's certainty is tomorrow's nonsense. "Who can say what *is*? He can only say *how* he *sees.*"

How exactly do we see? Most of us subscribe to the photographic model of seeing. We believe our eyes capture images from the world like a camera, then relay these images to our brain. Our eyes "photograph," say, the coffee mug in front of us.

It's a nice model. It is also wrong. Seeing is less like photography and more like language. We don't see the world so much as converse with it. *What is that? Looks like a coffee mug, you say? Let me check my database and get back to you. Yep, it's a mug.* We don't see the mug in front of us. We tell ourselves it is there. The coffee mug sends electromagnetic waves, nothing more, to our eye and brain. From that raw data, we create information, then meaning—in this case, that the object in front of us is called a "coffee mug."

Sometimes we create meaning too quickly. Maybe what looks like a coffee mug is something else entirely. Quick to define objects and people, we risk blinding ourselves to their uniqueness. Thoreau guarded against this tendency. "Let me not be in haste to detect the *universal law*," he tells himself. "Let me see more clearly a particular instance of it." Postpone defining what you see and you will see more.

Thoreau slowed the process to a crawl. He elongated the gap between hypothesis and conclusion, between seeing and seen. Time and again, he reminds himself to linger. "We must look for a long time before we can see," he said.

Seeing is subjective. The scientist's detached "view from nowhere" was not a vista that interested Thoreau. For something to be truly seen, it must be seen from somewhere by someone. "Your observation, to be interesting, i.e. to be significant, must be *subjective*," he wrote.

It's impossible *not* to take beauty personally. A blood-red sunset. An ink-black night sky specked with countless stars. Personal verdicts, all of them. As the philosopher Roger Scruton said, "A world that makes room for such things makes room for you."

For Thoreau, seeing and feeling were intertwined. He couldn't see something if he didn't feel it. How he felt determined not only how he saw but *what* he saw. For him, seeing was not only emotive but also interactive. When he saw, say, a rose, he corresponded with it and, in a way, collaborated with it. I realize that sounds odd, a tad unhinged. Many artists, though, describe a similar phenomenon: When they look at an object, they sense it looking back at them. They can't all be nuts.

Read the journals. Leslie Wilson's words lodge in my brain like a bad Top 40 song you can't shake. Thoreau kept a journal most of his adult life, some two million words spanning fourteen volumes.

When I screw up my courage and turn to the first volume, I'm overcome with dread, and flash back to ninth-grade English class. As I read, the dread lifts, replaced by relief, and, ultimately, delight. In his journals, Thoreau comes alive in a way he doesn't in *Walden*. This is Thoreau at his most honest, and vulnerable. "I never know, and shall never know, a worse man than myself," he writes at one point.

We tend to think of Thoreau as—how do I say this diplomatically?—a wuss. Reading his journals set me straight. The pages reveal a virile Thoreau. Philosopher as action hero. He walks, skates, swims, tastes fermented apples, chops wood, sounds ponds, surveys lots, paddles upriver, builds houses, plays the flute, juggles, shoots (he was an expert marksman), and, on at least one occasion, stares down a woodchuck. He did all these activities to see better. "It needs the doing hand to make the seeing eye," he said.

Thoreau wasn't afraid to get his hands, or any other body part, dirty. In one journal entry, he describes immersing himself in a swamp up to his chin, feeling the cool mud against his skin, embracing the scum.

As I wade deeper into the journals, I hear echoes of Marcus and his *Meditations.* Like Marcus, Thoreau is having a conversation with himself. We, the reader, just eavesdrop. I hear Socrates, too. They are not obvious doppelgängers, these two. Centuries separate them. Thoreau wrote more than two million words, Socrates not a single one. Yet they are philosophical brothers.

Like Socrates, Thoreau led an examined life, one conducted with a "fearless self-inspection." Like Socrates, Thoreau vacillated between terrific velocity and utter stillness. He walked four miles a day but could also, as one neighbor recalls, "sit motionless for hours, and let the mice crawl over him and eat cheese out of his hand."

Both Socrates and Thoreau asked a lot of impertinent questions, which annoyed people. Both were pains in their respective eras' asses. Useful irritants. Both paid a price. Athens put Socrates to death. Concord panned Thoreau's writing.

Like Socrates, Thoreau believed all philosophy begins with wonder. He expresses this idea many times, in many ways, but my favorite is this simple line from *Walden*: "Reality is fabulous." I love the way Thoreau sounds less like a philosopher and more like an awestruck teen. Maybe they're not so different.

The Concord dust Thoreau wrote about so lovingly has today been efficiently hoovered from view. Twenty-first-century Concord is a cute-as-a-button New England town, with curated wine shops, precious cafés, and, on warm spring days, bicyclists in peacock colors astride their pricey rides. The sort of town where Thoreau, with his shabby clothes and undisciplined mane, would draw searching, albeit discreet, glances.

I have to give Concord this: it wears its history well. Everything is low-key. New England understated. Even the local Rite Aid and Starbucks sport tasteful, temporally appropriate architecture.

The town's most famous son gets his due, of course. There is a Thoreau Street and a Thoreau School and a fitness center called, yes, the Thoreau Club. There is no Thoreau Water Park or Thoreau Wax Museum.

June 20 is the summer solstice. A good day, I figure, to contemplate the art of seeing. If we really are children of the light, then today is our birthday.

I wake early in order to . . . what? To be Thoreau? No. That's neither possible nor advisable. But I figure by tracing the arc of his day, I might, for a moment, see the world through his eyes.

Thoreau, unlike Marcus, was a morning person. He savored those first moments of consciousness, that "debatable ground between dreams and thoughts," and liked to quote this line from an ancient Indian text, the Vedas: "All intelligences awake with the morning."

Bathing in the pond at dawn, Thoreau then dove into his "morning work," reading and writing. He might refine a rough journal entry, or polish a chapter. The physical sensation of a hand moving across a page was for Thoreau, the occasional yogi, a kind of meditation.

Notebook and pen in hand, I devote my morning work to some nagging questions about Thoreau. What did he see in seeing? How did he manage to see so much? I stare at these questions for a long time. They stare back, mute. We're at an impasse. So I do what Thoreau did when his muse absconded. I close my notebook and lace my walking shoes.

Every day, usually in the afternoon, Thoreau walked the Concord countryside. Like Rousseau, he couldn't think clearly unless his legs were moving. While Rousseau embarked on reveries, Thoreau sauntered. (He loved that word.) He sauntered in order to shake the village and return to his senses.

Thoreau didn't need a destination when he sauntered, but I do. In a blatant act of civil disobedience, I decide to ignore Leslie Wilson's warning about visiting that overcrowded swamp-hole otherwise known as Walden Pond. I unfurl the little map of the trail leading from Concord to the pond. It's less than two miles. Thoreau's cabin in the woods was more of a cabin on the outskirts of a vibrant little town. I cut Thoreau some slack. A book called *Walden, or a Life in a Cabin Not Very Far at All from Civilization* lacks commercial appeal.

I'm loading my backpack, a sleek urban model that Thoreau would never own, when I decide to do something out of character. I tuck my smartphone into the desk drawer and step outside without it.

It takes only a few minutes for the withdrawal symptoms to manifest: clammy skin, increased heart rate. It's not that I feel naked without my phone. Naked I could handle. I feel as if I've departed on my walk without my liver or some other vital organ. Yet I soldier on.

I see why Thoreau liked to saunter here. The air is soft and cool, in repose. The ground feels plush underfoot. I'm reminded of what Thoreau's friend John Weiss said of him: "He walked as if a great deal of surmising went on between the earth and him." Not as much surmising goes on between the earth and me—small talk, really—but I soon find my stride. I'm determined to channel Thoreau's visual acumen.

What I see first is a blur, approaching rapidly. The blur is wearing a denim bandanna and white earbuds. Arms pistoning, muscular legs pumping, she is the picture of efficiency. She is not sauntering.

I arrive at a body of water called Fairyland Pond and sit on a nearby bench. I look but I don't see. "Go not to the object; let it come to you," Thoreau chides, in that covertly critical way of his. "Pond scum," I mutter.

It's not working. I see nothing but hear everything: the whine of a propeller plane high overhead, the whoosh of a passing car from a road nearby. Twenty-first-century sounds. I owe my acute sense of listening to my years as an NPR correspondent. There I learned to hear what others might not. Everything has a sound. Even a seemingly dead-quiet room, if you listen hard enough. "Room tone," audio engineers call it. I wonder: Is sensory acuteness transferable? Can I convert my keen ear into a keen eye?

The phantom vibrations in my pocket, emanating from where my phone should be, have dissipated. I become aware of a stillness. I experience a moment of what I believe is commonly called "peace."

Then the mosquitoes strike. Some snipe at me, while others, more aggressive, dive-bomb. They're annoying. I decamp and continue my amble. I'm contemplating Thoreau's imperviousness to distraction when I slip on a wooden plank and nearly fall. That was close. I stop and regroup. I make a conscious effort to see, clearly and honestly, what nature proffers. To my surprise, this attempt works. I spot a robin hopping on a telephone wire. At least, I think it's a robin. It could be an oriole or a towhee or God knows what other species. Does it matter?

Thoreau didn't necessarily think so, and he knew his birds. Knowledge of the supposed robin can amplify the pleasure of viewing it, but it can also detract. An ornithologist may know the biological rationale for a peacock's colorful plume but not appreciate its beauty. "I begin to see objects only when I leave off understanding them," says Thoreau. Jaded eyes see little.

Thoreau cultivated an "innocence of the eye." He never lost the child's sense of wonder. He couldn't pass a berry without picking it. "He is a boy and will be an old boy," Ralph Waldo Emerson said of his friend. Like Socrates, Thoreau valued a thoroughly conscious ignorance and suggested, only half-joking, that he form a Society for the Diffusion of Useful Ignorance.

Humans have been creating beauty far longer than they've been explaining it. Homer knew nothing of literary theory. The unknown artists who adorned the caves of Lascaux some seventeen thousand years ago would flunk an art history class. Better to see beauty than understand it.

The mosquitoes have, thankfully, dispersed, and the ambitious runner is long gone. The bird, though, is still hopping on the wire, and shows no sign of tiring. Good for him, I think, but Walden Pond awaits. I decide to move on.

After a few steps, I stop myself. Why the rush? It's my visual hypothesis mechanism at work. My brain posits that a creature—quite possibly a robin—is hopping on a telephone wire. In a fraction of a second, my brain accepts this supposition and files a report: *Bird, probably a robin, doing something cute and birdlike. Yeah, nature. You're a regular John Muir. Can we get going now?*

I force myself to linger, as Thoreau did. "You must walk sometimes perfectly free—not prying nor inquisitive—not bent upon seeing things." Thoreau could easily spend an hour watching a painted tortoise lay her eggs in moistened sand or a sail fluttering in the wind. He once spent an entire day watching a mother duck teach her ducklings about the river, later delighting children with his duck tales. But what children find wonderful, adults often find peculiar. A farmer named Murray recalls seeing Thoreau standing motionless, staring into a pond.

> I stopped and looked at him and I says, "Da-a-vid Henry, what air you a-doin'?" And he didn't turn his head and he didn't look at me. He kept on lookin' down at that pond, and he said, as if he was thinkin' about the stars in the heavens, "Mr. Murray, I'm a-studying—the habits—of the bullfrog!" And there that darned fool had been standin'—the livelong day—*a-studyin'*—the habits—of the *bull-frog*!

It's not easy to see slowly like Thoreau. Vision is the speediest sense, far faster than, say, taste. There is no visual equivalent of "savoring." (We can say our eyes "lingered" on an object, but that lacks the sensuousness of "savor.")

I am a lazy seer. I expect the subject of my gaze to do all the work. *Dazzle me, scenery. Be beautiful, damn it!* When the subject—be it the Alps or a Monet—inevitably falls short of my unreasonable expectations, I assign blame to it, not me. Thoreau thought otherwise. The person attuned to beauty will find it in a garbage dump while "the fault-finder will find fault even in paradise."

I reach a clearing in the woods: the site of Thoreau's cabin at Walden. A wrought-iron fence encircles the spot, marked by a pile of stones. (The cabin itself is long gone.) An engraving informs me, "Beneath these stones lies the Chimney Foundation of Thoreau's Cabin: 1845–1847."

The site of history's greatest experiment in voluntary solitude is, naturally, crowded: a woman clutching a large Starbucks cup and shouting into her cell phone, a group of Chinese tourists maneuvering their long camera lenses like artillery before snapping photos of the rocks. They're messing with my solitude, with my Thoreauvian moment. I want them to leave, but they don't.

That's unfair, I know. They have as much a right to be here as I do. It's like traffic. When we're stuck in it, we gripe about "all this traffic," ignoring the fact that we're part of the traffic, part of the problem.

A middle-aged couple is staring at the stone markers. I can tell the man, in particular, is enthralled. He's muttering something about how much he admires Thoreau.

"What are you going to do," says his wife, teasing, "go live in the woods?"

The man, chastised, grows silent. No, he's not going to live in the woods. He is going to steer the minivan home, unload the luggage, and resume his life of quiet desperation.

This is the problem with Thoreau. What he did was impractical. We can't drop everything and live in the woods, not even with Mom's home cooking nearby. We have bills to pay and recitals to attend and conference calls to join. Then again, Thoreau never suggested we do as he did. *Walden* was meant as a wake-up call, not a prescription.

I saunter a bit farther and spot another inscription. These words, from *Walden,* are perhaps Thoreau's most famous: "I went to the woods because I wished to live deliberately, to front only the essential facts of life, and see if I could not learn what it had to teach, and not, when I came to die, discover that I had not lived."

I like it, but would make one small edit. I'd change "live" deliberately to "see" deliberately. I don't think Thoreau would object. Seeing was the point of his experiment. All the rest—the solitude, the simplicity—were means to this end.

Thoreau saw too much. It exhausted him. "I have the habit of attention to such excess that my senses get no rest, but suffer from a constant strain," he writes in his journal.

We think of our senses as antennae, scanning the environment and plucking information. They are more like filters, sifting through the jumble of noise for the few relevant signals, lest the flood of sensory data overwhelm us. We are built to, as Thoreau put it, receive "our portion of the infinite," and not a drop more.

Seeing is deliberate. It's always a choice, even if we don't realize it. Proper seeing, says Thoreau, requires "a separate intention of the eye." It's all about the angles. No one played them better than Thoreau. Change your perspective and you change not only how you see but *what* you see. "From the right point of view, every storm and every drop in it is a rainbow."

Thoreau observes Walden Pond from every conceivable vantage point: from a hilltop, on its shores, a boat on its surface, and underwater. He viewed the same scene by daylight and moonlight, in winter and summer.

Thoreau rarely stared at anything directly. He looked with the side of his eye. There's a physiological basis for this. In dim light, we can detect objects best by looking at them from the side. Thoreau may or may not have known that. He did know from experience.

Determined not to get stuck in a visual rut, he altered his perspective. Sometimes only the slightest shift, "a hair's breadth aside from our habitual path or routine," revealed new worlds. On a cold December day in 1855, Thoreau spotted a pine grosbeak, "unusually far south for the winter," only because he had chosen a different path.

Sometimes he took more drastic steps. He'd bend over and peer through his legs, marveling at the inverted world. (Thoreau was big on inverting; he even flipped his name, changing it from David Henry to Henry David.) Turn the world upside down, and you see it anew.

I find a relatively secluded spot along the pond and, checking first to make sure no one is watching, try this maneuver myself. I bend over and peer between my legs. Sky and earth flip. Blood rushes to my head. I feel dizzy. I stand up straight, and sky and earth return to their proper positions. Maybe I'm not doing this properly.

No, I'm missing the point. Thoreau's stellar vision wasn't merely technique, a fun-pack of optical tricks. It was a function of character. He considered the perception of beauty "a moral test." Beauty is not in the eye of the beholder. It is in his heart. We can't improve our vision without improving ourselves. The dynamic works both ways. Not only does who we are determine what we see but what we see determines who we are. As the Vedas say, "What you see, you become."

Leslie Wilson was right. Sure, it's a fine pond, tree-lined and with water that glistens in the solstice light. But it is just a pond. Not necessarily the most peaceful, either. As I walk along the shoreline, I hear the rumble of a passing train, just as Thoreau did in his time. His life coincided with the rapid growth of the railroad. From his cabin, he could hear the whistle of the locomotive "sounding like the scream of a hawk sailing over some farmer's yard."

Thoreau was conflicted about this newfangled technology. On the one hand, the raw power of the locomotive awed him. Yet he feared the railroad disrupted familiar rhythms. Farmers who once gauged time by the sun now set their clocks to the 2:00 p.m. train from Boston. Walden Woods was stripped of trees, fuel for the wood-fired engines. "We do not ride on the railroad," Thoreau concludes. "It rides upon us."

I arrive at the Walden Pond Visitors Center, and find a to-scale replica of Thoreau's cabin. It's nicer than I imagined. A proper A-frame, with a woodstove, a desk, a trapdoor that leads to a root cellar, chairs (for visitors), a small but comfortable bed, and a large window with southern exposure. Not Versailles, but no dump, either.

A park ranger named Nick is leading a tour. It's clearly not his first, but a genuine enthusiasm for Thoreau animates what might otherwise be a canned spiel. I've noticed this about Thoreauvians. There's something about Henry (Thoreauvians always call him Henry) that discourages the sort of reflexive cynicism that typically accompanies excessive familiarity.

Nick wraps up his prepared remarks, then solicits questions. They come rapid-fire.

"How much did the cabin cost to build?"

"Twenty-eight dollars, twelve and a half cents. The nails were the most expensive."

"What did he do all day?"

"He read and he wrote."

"Why did he do it?" asks one teenager, incredulous, as if Thoreau had embezzled millions or joined a dangerous cult instead of living in the woods for a couple of years.

"It was an experiment in simplicity," says Nick the Ranger. "Plus, he was twenty-eight years old. He needed to get away from Mom and Dad." The teenager, judging by his nodding head, clearly likes this answer.

Thoreau did live simply, growing some of his own food. He lived off the grid before there was a grid. The point, though, wasn't simplicity for its own sake. Thoreau, student of the East, was undergoing a kind of purification. Cleansing his lens of perception.

French philosopher Michel Foucault wrote of the need to make ourselves "susceptible to knowing." Thoreau, adrift at Walden, made himself susceptible to seeing. He knew we see best when unencumbered, when nothing comes between us and the light. Thoreau compared himself to a mathematician who, confronting a difficult problem, disembarrasses it of the extraneous and cuts to the heart of the equation.

Thoreau was superficial. I mean that in the best possible sense. The superficial gets a bum rap. It's often used synonymously with "shallow," but they are different. Shallow is a lack of depth. Superficial is depth diffused. Our portion of the infinite spread thin, but very wide.

"Why have we slandered the outward?" wondered Thoreau. "The perception of surfaces will have the effect of a miracle to the sane sense." This explains why Thoreau didn't stare. He glanced. His eyes alighted on various objects, first here, then there, like a bumblebee in search of pollen. A "sauntering of the eye," he called it.

Humans glance for the same reason other animals sniff: it's how we probe our surroundings. Glancing also reveals unexpected wonders. The words "surface" and "surprise" share a linguistic root.

Glancing is our natural state. Our eyes are rarely still, even when we think they are. They make rapid jumps, called saccades, pausing briefly in between. Our eyes typically move at least three times per second: roughly 100,000 times per day.

The glance is helpful. It comes in handy when cooking a three-course meal, or flying an airplane. A number of years ago, I earned my private pilot's license. I've forgotten much from those days, but one technique stuck with me: the instrument scan.

"Don't stare!" my instructor barked. "Scan!"

Altimeter. Airspeed indicator. Artificial horizon. Rest the eyes on each for a second or two, then move on. Keep your eyes, and your attention, moving. Pilots get into trouble when they fixate on one instrument. Stare at the altimeter and your heading drifts. Focus on heading and your airspeed strays. Scan, scan, scan. It's a valuable lesson. We see more by scanning than staring.

I resume my walk along Walden Pond's sandy shoreline. Signs warn of steep drop-offs and hazardous swimming conditions. Walden isn't the perfect pond, but something need not be perfect, or even functional, to be beautiful. Thoreau regularly saw beauty in nature's imperfections. Gazing at Walden on a calm September afternoon, he notices the water is perfectly smooth save for a few motes speckling the surface. While others might see blemishes, Thoreau saw something "pure and beautiful like the imperfections in glass." In *Walden,* he describes encountering a horse carcass rotting near his cabin, and finding it not repulsive but oddly reassuring. Beautiful, even. Nature's wisdom at work.

I've been thinking about Thoreau's admonition to find my own Walden. I didn't care for the real Walden. Too many mosquitoes and tourists. Not enough air-conditioning, or coffee. Yes, my own Walden. But where?

The next day, I put that question to Jeff Cramer, curator of collections at the Walden Woods Project. A fit man, with shaved head and neatly trimmed beard, Jeff was a late convert to Thoreau. He was working at the Boston Public Library in a comfortable job when he picked up and moved to Concord.

Jeff has earned his Thoreauvian cred. I trust him. I like him, too, especially when he reveals his favorite Thoreau quote (this from a man who edited *The Quotable Thoreau*). "If I am not I, who will be?"

I want to be I, really I do, but a better, less melancholy I. A Thoreauvian I, with Thoreauvian eyes. I want to learn how to see and where. For me, a place person, the two are inseparable. How is where. Where is how.

"Let's see," says Jeff. "You could cross over the North Bridge and cut through the woods on the left and . . ."

"Woods? As in trees and bugs?"

"Well, yes."

"Any other suggestions?"

"You could go to the South River Bridge and rent a canoe."

"Canoe, as in boat?"

"Uh, yes."

"Any other suggestions?"

"Sleepy Hollow is very peaceful."

"You mean the cemetery?"

"Yes."

"What else have you got?"

"Let's see. You could go to Starbucks."

"I'm listening."

"And take *Walden* and maybe some pages from his journal, and observe."

"Starbucks? Really?"

"Yes. It's Thoreau's words that matter. He was inspired by all this land around us. It helped make Thoreau who he was, but it won't make you who you are."

I like this idea. Back in Thoreau's time, Concord also had a coffee shop, and Thoreau was a regular. Besides, if Thoreau's wisdom is portable, as all true wisdom is, then surely it's just as useful sipping an overpriced beverage as it is roughing it in the woods. The heck with Walden. I'm going to Starbucks.

I wake early and pack a Thoreau kit—*Walden,* his essay "Walking," a collection of letters to a spiritual seeker named William Blake, selections from his journal. (I'm nearly finished.) I saunter to Concord's one Starbucks.

It is appropriately Concordian, the lighting a bit softer than most, the furniture a bit more refined. It is still a Starbucks, though, the way Walden is still a pond.

I order a simple coffee, plop down in a big leather chair, and crack open Henry. "Beauty is where it is perceived," he tells me. Even here, in Starbucks? I look around but find no beauty. My reflex is to blame my surroundings, my Walden.

I catch myself. Don't be so passive. If you don't see beauty, create some. Use your imagination. Heighten your senses.

This works, but, again, the wrong sense responds. My acoustic reflex kicks in, and I hear beauty everywhere: the gentle hum of an air conditioner, the musical clink of ice cubes, giggling baristas, beeping cash registers, the singsong call of "Venti Green Iced Tea!" and, off in the distance, sirens.

I take Thoreau's advice—"all faculties in repose but the one you are using"—and focus exclusively on the visual. Sure enough, I see. I see a young father, sunglasses perched on forehead, muscular arms swinging, cradling his infant son. At the milk and sugar station, I notice how people dance with one another. One step forward, one step back. *Excuse me, oh, I'm sorry, pardon my reach, no, pardon mine.* I notice how people wait for their order from varying distances. Some crowd the barista, while others give her space. Some people stand still, while others fidget.

Scan, scan, scan. I see the muscular dad again. He's placed his son on a table and is rocking him back and forth. I wonder if that is wise. Scan. A girls' softball team, in uniforms of blue, white, and orange, high-fiving their coach. Scan. The man next to me, reading Montaigne. He sees I'm reading Thoreau, and nods approval, discreetly, of course. Concord is the Quiet Car of New England.

Minutes, then hours pass. The muscular dad leaves. So does the softball team, and the man reading Montaigne. Yet I'm still here, glancing. I deploy other Thoreauvian techniques. I change my position, standing by the door for a while, sauntering over to the coffee bar, cocking my head sideways. I consider inverting my head between my legs but decide against it. Even here, in Thoreauville, that is going too far.

Hours later, the man who was reading Montaigne returns. He spots me in the same chair, with the same books, and says, "You've been here entirely too long."

"Actually," I say, looking up, with fresh eyes, "not nearly long enough."

It's true. I need more time. While I see more clearly here, in my own private Walden, I do not have a visual epiphany, the "single expansion" Thoreau achieved. I am disappointed, but take solace in the words of—who else?—Henry David Thoreau. Seeing requires not only time but distance, he tells me. "You cannot see anything until you are clear of it."

5.

How to Listen like Schopenhauer

2:32 p.m. On board Deutsche Bahn, Train No. 151, en route from Hamburg to Frankfurt.

Trains make human noises. Locomotives snort and whistle and, occasionally, belch. The railway cars whine and squeak and protest.

Deutsche Bahn, German Rail, muffles these sounds. There is no need for a Quiet Car. It is a given. Everything about my train whispers discretion. Not only the hushed atmosphere but the wood panel lining the cars, the coffee served in real mugs, not Styrofoam.

I sip my coffee, and survey the understated German countryside. A train heading in the opposite direction passes, its whistle piercing the silence. The sound increases in pitch as the train approaches, then decreases as it passes. Or does it?

The whistle hasn't really changed pitch. It is an auditory illusion known as the Doppler effect. The motion of the train has conspired with my susceptible brain to make it sound as if the whistle's pitch had changed. I had misperceived reality.

What if all of life is like this? What if the world is an illusion? Some 2,400 years ago Plato posed just such a question. In "The Allegory of the Cave," he asks us to imagine prisoners chained inside a cave, facing a stone wall. They have been inside the cave from birth and are unable to move and therefore cannot see each other or even themselves.

All they can see are shadows cast on the wall. They're unaware that they're looking at shadows. The shadows are the only reality they know.

Philosophy, Plato suggests, enables us to escape the world of shadows and discover its source: the light. We don't always see the light. Sometimes we hear it.

I wake to an unexpected quiet. Tired from the long train ride, I'm tempted to remain under the covers, Marcus-style. Somehow I muster the willpower to extract myself and head to breakfast. Afterward, I walk, like Rousseau, mindful of each step, only to discover Frankfurt's streets empty on this, a weekday. I promptly retreat to the hotel and ask questions, like Socrates.

"Where is everyone?"

"A national holiday," replies the concierge. "Didn't you know?"

I can hear Thoreau scolding me. *Look. Observe. See the world with the eye of a child and the mind of a sage. Open your eyes, man!*

I need to regroup. My intended destination, the Schopenhauer Archives, is closed, but surely other establishments are open.

Apparently not. Europeans take holidays seriously. I pass shuttered shops and cafés and must have walked a mile before finding an open coffee shop, an outlier. A good one, too, judging by the beans procured from exotic locales and the serious, artisanal expressions of the baristas.

I order the Sumatran pour-over, which is prepared with an attention to detail usually reserved for neurosurgery and weddings. When I ask for milk, the barista purses his lips and suggests—discreetly, of course—that adding milk to this exquisitely roasted, naturally nonacidic, perfectly balanced Beverage of the Gods would constitute an affront to all that is good and beautiful in the world.

Of course, I say. Wouldn't dream of it.

I wait until he leaves, presumably to educate another customer, before pouring a splash of milk. I find a table outside and read the first page of Arthur Schopenhauer's collected essays.

Darkness arrives, and looks like it will be staying awhile. Pessimism infuses each page, every word, much like the hint of chocolate infusing my coffee, only more bitter. Schopenhauer makes no attempt to conceal his glumness. It's right there in the essay titles: "On the Suffering of the World" and "On Suicide," for instance.

Don't blame philosophy for his pessimism. His gloomy outlook manifested at a young age, long before he read Plato or Descartes. At the age of seventeen, while touring Europe with his parents, he concluded, "This world could not be the work of an all-good being, but rather that of a devil who had summoned into existence creatures, in order to gloat over the sight of their agony." A few years later, embarking on his philosophy career, he writes to a friend: "Life is a wretched business. I have decided to spend it trying to understand it."

Schopenhauer's pessimism didn't temper with age. If anything, it grew, congealing into a black hole of despair. "Today it is bad, and day by day it will get worse—until at last the worst of all arrives," he writes. All of us are careening headlong toward a "total, inevitable, irremediable shipwreck." I put the book down and sigh. It's going to be a long day. I order another cup of Sumatran and soldier on.

We are living in the "worst of all possible worlds," the philosopher of pessimism informs me. Any worse, and it wouldn't exist. Which wouldn't be so bad. "Life is happiest when we perceive it least," he writes.

I pause for air, and light. There is none. I swear I can feel Schopenhauer's dark shadow hovering over me. I focus my eyes and see an older woman wearing baggy, wrinkled pants and missing more teeth than she has. She is clearly homeless, or nearly so. She gestures to the other chair at my table and says something in German. Whatever she says does not contain any of the four German words I know. Thinking on my feet, I conclude she has asked to borrow the chair. "*Ja, bitte*," I say, deploying—with aplomb, I might add—two of my four German words.

Making assumptions in your native tongue is ill-advised. Making assumptions in a foreign language you do not speak is just stupid. She did not ask to borrow the chair. She has asked if she can sit in the chair and speak with me, speak *at* me. For a long time. She talks and talks, and I nod and nod, tossing out the occasional "ja, ja."

It's a one-sided conversation. I pick up dribs (no drabs). She is an *oma,* or grandmother (my third German word). The rest is static.

I'm hoping she'll exhaust herself but she's not even slowing down. What would Socrates do? He would converse, of course, but how?

A waiter brings her a coffee—clearly, on the house. She expresses gratitude effusively. Gratitude is a universal language, one expressed with the eyes, the entire body, more than with words.

Schopenhauer, the philosopher of pessimism, didn't dismiss the possibility of gratitude—and compassion. We experience the world as separateness but, Schopenhauer believed, echoing Eastern mystics, this perception is an illusion. The world is one. When we help another person, we help ourselves. We feel the pain of others the way we feel the pain in our finger. Not as something foreign, but as part of us.

My visitor is still talking, even as she drinks her coffee. I decide to listen. I can't understand, but I can listen.

Listening mattered to Schopenhauer. Listening to music, that "universal language of the heart," as he called it. Other kinds of listening, too. Listening to your intuition, above the din and noise of the world. Listening to other voices, speaking foreign tongues, for you never know where wisdom lurks. And, yes, listening to those who suffer. Despite his misanthropy and chronic grumpiness, Schopenhauer valued compassion, even if he demonstrated it more to animals than to his fellow humans.

Listening is an act of compassion, of love. When we lend an ear, we lend a heart, too. Good listening, like good seeing, is a skill, and like all skills, it can be learned.

The woman seems to appreciate my attentiveness, judging by the smile fanning across her toothless mouth. Eventually she gets up to leave. We say good-bye, *tschüss.* German word number four.

Schopenhauer wasn't the first, or last, pessimistic philosopher, but he was in a league of his own. What distinguishes Schopenhauer is not his broodiness but the philosophical edifice, the metaphysics of misery, he constructed to explain it. There have been many pessimistic philosophers, but only one true philosopher of pessimism.

It's all laid out in his opus, *The World as Will and Representation*, a title only a philosopher could love. Completed while still in his twenties, it was, he said, "the product of a single thought." That thought required 1,156 pages to explicate. I cut Arthur some slack. It is a very big thought. The opening sentence is a doozy: "The world is my idea."

This is not, for once, Schopenhauer's arrogance speaking. It's his philosophy. He's not suggesting he is author of the world but, rather, that we all construct reality in our minds. His world is his idea, and your world yours.

Schopenhauer was an Idealist. In the philosophical sense, an Idealist is not someone with high ideals. It is someone who believes that everything we experience is a mental representation of the world, not the world itself. Physical objects only exist when we perceive them. *The world is my idea.*

I realize this concept sounds odd, possibly delusional, but it is not so far-fetched, I think. Nigel Warburton, a contemporary philosopher, uses the analogy of a giant movie hall, with everyone in separate screening rooms, watching the same film. "We cannot leave because there is nothing outside," he says. "The films are our reality. When no one is watching the screen, the projector light is switched off but the films keep running through the projector."

Idealists don't believe only our minds exist (that is known as solipsism). The world exists, they say, but as a mental construct, and only when we perceive it. To use a different analogy, think of your refrigerator light. Whenever you open the door, it's on. You might conclude that it is always on, but that would be a mistake. You don't know what happens when the door closes. Likewise, we don't know what exists beyond our mind's capacities of perception.

Every day, as we go about our lives, we experience this mentally constructed, or phenomenal, world. It is real—the way the surface of a lake is real. But just as the glassy surface isn't the whole lake, the phenomenal world represents only a fraction of reality. It fails to account for the depths.

Those depths, Idealists like Immanuel Kant believe, lie beyond sensory perception, but are every bit as real as the unseen lake bed. More real, in fact, than the fleeting sensory phenomena we typically experience. Philosophers have given this unseen reality various names. Kant called it the noumenon. Plato called it the world of Ideal Forms. For Indian philosophers, it is Brahman. Different names but the same idea: a plane of existence that remains unknown to us as we rush to work, binge-watch Netflix, and, in general, go about our business in the world of shadows.

Schopenhauer subscribed to this world-beyond-this-world notion but added his own intriguing and, naturally, dark twist. Schopenhauer, unlike Kant, believed the noumenon was a single, unified entity, and one we can access, albeit indirectly. It suffuses all humans and animals, and even inanimate objects. It is purposeless and striving, and it is unrelentingly, unapologetically evil.

Schopenhauer called this force the "Will." It's an unfortunate name, I think. By Will, Schopenhauer doesn't mean willpower, but, rather, a kind of force or energy. Something like gravity, only not as benign. He writes:

> Its desires are unlimited, its claims inexhaustible, and every desire gives birth to a new one. No possible satisfaction in the world could suffice to still its craving, set a final goal to its demands, and fill the bottomless pit of its heart.

Two observations. One, the Will sounds an awful lot like my college girlfriend. Two, those shafts of light are looking more remote.

Will is endless striving. Will is desire without satisfaction. The preview but never the movie. Sex but never climax. Will is what makes you order a third Scotch when two was enough. Will is that grinding sound in your head that, while occasionally muffled, is never silenced, even after the fourth Scotch.

It gets worse. The Will is destined to harm itself. "At bottom," says Schopenhauer, "the Will must live on itself, since nothing exists besides it, and it is a hungry will." When a lion sinks its teeth into a gazelle it is sinking its teeth into its own hide.

One day, Schopenhauer, an amateur zoologist, caught wind of a newly discovered genus of ant discovered in Australia. *Myrmecia*, or the Australian bulldog ant, has a much-deserved reputation for viciousness. It grips its prey in its powerful jaws, then repeatedly stings it with a deadly venom. When the bulldog ant is cut in two, its biting head engages in a fierce battle with its stinging tail. "The battle may last a half hour until they die or are taken away by other ants," notes Schopenhauer.

It is not malice or masochism that compels the ant to devour itself, but the Will. The ant is no more capable of resisting the Will, Schopenhauer thought, than the coffee mug in my hand right now is capable of resisting gravity should I release my grip. Like the bulldog ant, we are author and reader of our own cruelty, victim and perpetrator, fated to consume ourselves, slowly, after suffering for a long time.

Don't despair, says the philosopher of gloom. We can escape the black hole that is the Will by "shaking off the world." There are two ways to do so. Option one: lead an ascetic life, fasting for days at a time, meditating for hours, and remaining celibate. I skip ahead to option two: art. That's better. Art is not only pleasurable, he says. It is liberating. It offers a reprieve from the ceaseless striving and suffering that is the Will.

The arts accomplish this feat by, in effect, catapulting us free of ourselves. When creating, or appreciating, a work of art, we lose the sense of separateness that Schopenhauer, as well as the Buddha, says lies at the root of all suffering. Art, says Schopenhauer, "takes away the mist." The illusion of individuality dissolves and "thus we are no longer able to separate the perceiver from the perception, but the two have become one, since the entire consciousness is filled and occupied by a single image of perception."

This merging of subject and object happens, says Schopenhauer, without the aid of reason, or curators. Aesthetic delight needn't occur at an art museum or concert hall. It can happen anywhere. Walking down a familiar street, you see something—a mundane object like a mailbox, a fire hydrant, objects you've seen many times before. This time, though, you see it differently, as philosopher Bryan Magee explains: "It is as if time had stopped, and only the object existed, standing before us unencumbered by connections with anything else—just simply there, wholly and peculiarly itself, and weirdly, singularly thingy."

During these aesthetic moments, we aren't distressed but neither are we happy. Such distinctions—happy, sad—vanish. We have shaken off the world, and with it such false dichotomies. We become a mirror to the object of art, what Schopenhauer calls the "clear eye of the world."

There's a catch, naturally. This aesthetic moment is fragile, fleeting. The instant we become aware of it, the Will reenters our consciousness and "the magic is at end."

Schopenhauer received little recognition during his lifetime and, even in death, can't get any respect. There is no Schopenhauer museum. The philosopher's worldly possessions are housed at a local university, out of sight. I emailed the curator and explained my interest in Frankfurt's forgotten son.

A few days later, I receive a reply from one Stephen Roeper. He is courteous and cheerful and, I get the distinct impression, more than a little surprised. Not many visitors come calling on Arthur these days.

The next morning, appropriately rainy and dreary, I walk the few blocks to the university. I step into a drab, utilitarian building—and promptly get lost. I approach a young woman behind the counter.

"Schopenhauer?" I say—or, rather, ask, as if the name itself constitutes a metaphysical question. She nods grimly. The mere mention of the philosopher of pessimism has soured her mood, or so I imagine. It's difficult to distinguish a sullen German from a happy German. There are, I'm sure, subtle changes in facial muscles and ocular motion, but these lie beyond the ken of an outsider like me.

I push a buzzer, and a few seconds later, a slight, pleasant, and shy man materializes. Stephen Roeper is mustached with a receding hairline, clear blue eyes, and a rosy complexion that reminds me of a tipsy cherub.

We step into a large room. It smells of old books and disinfectant. As we walk, Schopenhauer looks down at us from the walls. On every square inch is a portrait, and one or two photographs, of Schopenhauer in different stages of life, from a boyish fifteen-year-old in Hamburg to the septuagenarian sage of Frankfurt.

For a man who boldly declared "the world is my idea," Arthur Schopenhauer felt oddly ill at ease in it. Like Rousseau, he thought of himself as homeless, even when at home. A philosophical untouchable, he was living proof that the only fate worse than being criticized is being ignored. For most of his life, his books went unread, his ideas unloved. He failed to win a Danish philosophy prize even as the sole entrant. Only in the last few years of his life did he achieve a modicum of recognition.

In one of the many ironies that was his life, Schopenhauer, whose philosophical ideas would influence Freud, had a very Freudian childhood. Mother issues explain a lot. Johanna Schopenhauer had high aspirations—literary and social—and raising a young child didn't factor in those plans. She soon tired of "playing with my new doll," as she put it, and spent the rest of Arthur's childhood alternately ignoring and resenting him. "A very bad mother," Schopenhauer later wrote.

Schopenhauer's father, a successful merchant, wasn't much better. In one letter, he urges his son to improve his handwriting by capitalizing properly and curtailing those fancy flourishes. In another, it's young Arthur's posture that draws his father's ire. "Your mother expects, as I do, that you will not need to be reminded to walk upright like other well-raised people," he wrote, adding, with a twist of the parental knife, "and she sends her love."

The elder Schopenhauer groomed his son to take over the family business. He even chose the name "Arthur" because it sounded international. Arthur's social skills, though, were lacking, much to his father's frustration. "I wish you learned to make yourself agreeable to people," he sniffed in one letter.

Arthur never did learn. He alienated nearly everyone he encountered. He could be charming when he wanted, but he rarely wanted. He remained a bachelor throughout his life and, with the exception of a brief friendship with Goethe, had no real companions—other than his beloved poodle, named Atman, the Sanskrit word for soul. Schopenhauer displayed a warmth toward Atman he never could muster for people. "You, sir," he affectionately chided the poodle whenever he misbehaved.

Schopenhauer enlists another animal—the porcupine—to explain human relations. Imagine a group of porcupines huddled on a cold winter's day. They stand close to one another, absorbing their neighbor's body heat, lest they freeze to death. Should they stand too close, though, they're pricked by a needle. "Tossed between two evils," says Schopenhauer, the animals approach and retreat, again and again, until they discover "the proper distance from which they could best tolerate one another."

The Porcupine's Dilemma, as it's now known, is our dilemma, too. We need others to survive, but others can hurt us. Relationships demand constant course corrections, and even the most skilled navigators get pricked now and then.

Stephen Roeper reaches into a large rectangular box and retrieves a rusting fork and spoon. Schopenhauer carried them, as well as a drinking cup, whenever he dined out. He didn't trust restaurant hygiene, nor much of anything else. He avoided barbers, fearful they'd cut his throat. He suffered from anxiety and occasional panic attacks.

Stephen reaches into another box and retrieves a cylindrical object. An ivory flute. A gift from the elder Schopenhauer to his son. I pick it up. It possesses a pleasing weightiness, a solidity, as well as that vaguely creepy quality that adheres to the possessions of the dead. Touching it feels like an intrusion, a violation. I can almost hear grumpy Schopenhauer snapping at me. *Get your grubby paws off my flute!*

The flute was Schopenhauer's companion throughout his adult life, in bad times and worse. Every day, just before noon, he sat down and played *con amore*, with love. Schopenhauer liked Mozart but adored Rossini, and would roll his eyes heavenward whenever the Italian composer's name was uttered. He had all of Rossini's music arranged for the flute.

Schopenhauer's joyous flute playing prompted his admirer-turned-critic Friedrich Nietzsche to question his pessimism. How could someone who played the flute every day, and with so much joy, so much love, be a pessimist? Schopenhauer didn't see the contradiction. The world is indeed suffering, a colossal mistake, but there are reprieves. Slivers of joy.

No sliver is more joyous than art. Art—*good* art—is not an expression of emotion, Schopenhauer believed. The artist is not conveying a sentiment but, rather, a form of knowledge. A window into the true nature of reality. It is a knowledge beyond "mere concepts," and therefore beyond words.

Good art also transcends the passions. Anything that increases desire increases suffering. Anything that reduces desire—reduces willing, as Schopenhauer puts it—alleviates suffering. When we behold a work of art, we are not craving anything. This is why pornography is not art. It is the exact opposite of art. Pornography's sole purpose is to stir desire. If it fails to do so, it's considered a failure. Art aims for something higher. If the only reaction we have to a still-life of a bowl of cherries is hunger, the artist has missed the mark.

Schopenhauer devised a hierarchy of aesthetics. Architecture occupies the bottom rung, while theater (tragedy, in particular, of course) the top. Music does not appear on the ladder. It is its own category.

The other arts speak of mere shadows, says Schopenhauer. Music speaks of the essence, the thing-in-itself, and so "expresses the innermost nature of all life and existence." An image of heaven, even a secularized version, may or may not include paintings and statues. We take it as granted that there will be music.

While language is man-made, music exists independent of human thought, like gravity or thunderstorms. If a trumpet blares in a forest and there is no one to hear it, it still blares. Music, Schopenhauer once said, would exist even if the world did not.

Music is personal in a way the other arts are not. You may not have a favorite painting, but you probably have a favorite song. My thirteen-year-old daughter is experimenting with different musical genres, discovering what she likes and what she doesn't. She isn't forming her "musical identity." She is forming her identity. Period. The music we choose to listen to says more about us than the clothes we wear or the cars we drive or the wine we drink.

Music reaches us when nothing else can. A ray of light in the darkness. William Styron, in his memoir on depression, *Darkness Visible,* describes how he was contemplating suicide when he heard a soaring passage from Brahms. "The sound, which like all music—indeed, like all pleasure—I had been numbly unresponsive to for months, pierced my heart like a dagger, and in a flood of swift recollection I thought of all the joys the house had known: the children who had rushed through the rooms, the festivals, the love and work."

Music is therapy. Listening to music speeds cognitive recovery after a stroke, several studies have found. Patients in minimally conscious, or even vegetative states, showed healthier brain activity when listening to a favorite song.

I recognize the benefits of music intellectually, but can't seem to make the leap to a more intimate knowledge. I suffer from a kind of musical apathy. As a teenager, I never collected albums or compiled mixtapes. I attended concerts rarely, only when coerced by friends. To this day, entire genres of music remain foreign to me. I am not opposed to music. If played, I enjoy it, though not as much as I enjoy a good Scotch or a good bag. This lack of musical appreciation has always struck me as odd, given my love of sound and the spoken word.

There's an old joke we like to tell at NPR.

"Why is radio better than television?"

"Because the pictures are better."

There is something primal about oral storytelling. We humans have been listening to stories far longer than we've been reading them. Sound matters. The written word excels at conveying information, the spoken word at conveying meaning. The written word is inert. The spoken word is alive, and intimate. To hear someone speak is to know them. This explains the popularity of NPR, podcasts, and audio books. It also explains why my mother insists on phone calls, not emails, each Monday.

Working for NPR as a foreign correspondent, I learned to appreciate the rich and varied texture of sound. The singsong call of a Delhi street hawker, the cacophony of a Tokyo pachinko parlor. What intrigued me most, though, was the sound of the spoken word. The human voice is nature's greatest lie detector, and I soon learned to gauge a speaker's sincerity within seconds. Politicians are the least sincere not only because of their gutless vocabulary but also their tone of voice. Cautious and falsetto. Even a child can recognize the voice of someone selling something. *Especially* a child.

Why can't I translate this intuitive feel for sound to the world of music? Perhaps I don't know enough about music, or perhaps the limited knowledge I do possess is tripping me up, preventing me from hearing this universal language of the heart.

My friend John Lister is an aficionado of both classical music and German philosophy. Plus, he lives in Baghdad, where he works for a relief agency. For security reasons, John is confined to his hotel for days at a time. John has a lot of time on his hands. The perfect correspondent.

I fire up my laptop and ask John if his knowledge of music enhances his enjoyment or interferes with it. How can I learn to appreciate music? I hit send.

A few hours later, a lengthy reply lands in my inbox. I scan John's email, which runs to several pages, and am silently grateful for both his erudition and the surplus time he has on his hands.

"So these are all tough questions," writes John, then proceeds to tackle them as if they weren't tough at all. Knowledge of music, he says, enhances your enjoyment of it. "It may give you specific insights into the music that you might not otherwise have and it might prevent you from becoming so captivated by the tonal beauty that you see music as only an aesthetic experience."

Music doesn't have a single home. It "hovers between two worlds."

(I can practically hear Schopenhauer murmuring his assent.) Different types of music, John continues, require different kinds of listening. Wagner is easy. "The music is sensuous to the point of being like a drug rush." Beethoven and Mahler and Brahms are trickier. "You feel that you are trying to understand what another person is trying to communicate directly to you. Wagner talks to you *about something*. Beethoven, Mahler, and Brahms talk to you. That is the difference."

There's another, more practical, reason to know something about musical structure, John explains. It disciplines the ear. You know what to listen for, so the mind is less likely to wander.

Schopenhauer thought a lot about the wandering mind. We view the world in a calculating, mercenary way, he said. The Amsterdam stockbroker intent on closing a deal is oblivious to the world around him; the chess player does not see the elegant Chinese chess pieces; the general doesn't see the beautiful landscape as he makes his battle plan.

We must have a different, less transactional, relationship with music. We must experience it from a disinterested perspective. Disinterested but not *uninterested*. There is a difference. To be uninterested in a piece of music is to be apathetic toward it. To be disinterested is to harbor no expectations, make no demands of the music, yet remain open to the possibility of aesthetic delight. A Buddhist would say we are not attached to the music but nor are we detached from it. A Christian mystic would say we maintain a "holy indifference" toward it. The idea is the same. True listening demands we postpone judgment. When we listen like this, hearing without judging, says Schopenhauer, we "feel positively happy."

I read that and am stunned. This is the first time I've seen Schopenhauer use the word "happy." A glint of light.

Music is not what I think it is, Schopenhauer tells me. It does not convey emotion. It conveys the essence, the container, of emotions without the content. When we listen to music, we perceive not a particular sadness or a particular joy but sadness itself and joy itself—"the extracted quintessence of these feelings," says Schopenhauer. Sadness by itself isn't painful. It is sadness *about something* that hurts. This is why we enjoy watching a tearjerker or listening to a Leonard Cohen song. Less invested in the drama, we experience the emotion itself, unmoored, and can appreciate the beauty in sadness.

For Schopenhauer, slow melodies are the most beautifully sad. "A convulsive wail," he calls them. Samuel Barber's *Adagio for Strings* is a good example. I listen to it whenever I'm feeling sad. It is not an act of self-indulgence, a wallowing in my misery, but, I think, something more noble. The music matches my mood, validates it, yet also enables me to distance myself from the source of my sadness. I can taste sadness without swallowing it, or being swallowed by it. I can savor the bitterness.

Schopenhauer, I suspect, invited misfortune to validate his pessimism. A tributary of masochism runs through his life. In Berlin, during a brief stint as a professor, he insisted on scheduling his lectures at the same time as his bête noire, Friedrich Hegel, that "repulsive and dull charlatan and unparalleled scribbler of nonsense." Hegel was a philosophy rock star, Schopenhauer an unknown. Predictably, Schopenhauer attracted fewer than five students. He would never teach again.

Schopenhauer would be surprised—outraged, really—to see his worldly possessions housed in an *institution*. He despised academia, with its rigid rules and "petticoat philosophers." He preferred the life of a feral philosopher and, thanks to his father's inheritance, could afford to lead one. No need to grind lenses at an optician's shop like Spinoza, or teach undergrads like Kant.

I share Schopenhauer's melancholy but not his pessimism. There's a fundamental problem with his glumness: it presupposes perfect knowledge, something we humans are incapable of possessing. We may suspect we are living in the "worst of all possible worlds," but do we know for sure? Pessimism requires a certainty I lack, and for that I am grateful.

Consider the parable of the Chinese farmer. One day, the farmer's horse ran away. That evening, the neighbors stopped by to offer their sympathies.

"So sorry to hear your horse ran away," they said. "That's too bad."

"Maybe," the farmer said. "Maybe not."

The next day the horse returned, bringing seven wild horses with it. "Oh, isn't that lucky," said the neighbors. "Now you have eight horses. What a great turn of events."

"Maybe," said the farmer. "Maybe not."

The next day the farmer's son was training one of these horses when he was thrown and broke his leg. "Oh dear, that's too bad," said the neighbors.

"Maybe," said the farmer. "Maybe not."

The following day, conscription officers came to the village to recruit young men for the army, but they rejected the farmer's son because he had a broken leg. And all the neighbors said, "Isn't that great!"

"Maybe," said the farmer. "Maybe not."

We lead telephoto lives in a wide-angle world. We never see the big picture. The only sane response is, like the Chinese farmer, to adopt a philosophy of maybe-ism.

Good philosophers are good listeners. They listen to many voices, no matter how strange, for you never know where wisdom might be hiding. Arthur Schopenhauer found it concealed in an ancient, alien text.

The year was 1813. Still on speaking terms with his mother, Schopenhauer joined one of her regular salons. Among the attendees was a scholar named Friedrich Majer. His specialty, new and suspect at the time, was Eastern philosophy. He showed Schopenhauer an obscure magazine, the *Asiatic*, and told him of an Indian text called the Upanishads. Schopenhauer was instantly fascinated.

Today we take it for granted that Eastern philosophies and religions are a source of great wisdom, as any visit to a bookstore attests, but that was not the case in Schopenhauer's time. Buddhism and Hinduism were virtually unknown in the West. It would be another three decades before a copy of the *Bhagavad Gita* made it to Thoreau's cabin at Walden. Academics knew little about Eastern philosophy, and denigrated what they did know. All the literature of India and Arabia, the British politician Thomas Macaulay infamously said, "equaled a single shelf of a good European library."

Schopenhauer was different. He devoured these teachings, mesmerized by their "superhuman conceptions." He was hungry. Every evening, without fail, he read several passages of the Upanishads. It was, he said, "the most profitable and sublime reading that is possible in the world; it has been the consolation of my life and will be that of my death."

Later, he'd study Buddhism, declaring it the greatest of all religions. He kept a statue of the Buddha in his Frankfurt study. Some biographers call Schopenhauer "the Buddha of Frankfurt," but he was no monk. While he developed a deep and, at the time, rare understanding of Buddhism, he did not practice what he knew. He did not meditate. He did not renounce worldly pleasures. He enjoyed gourmet cuisine and expensive clothes and remained sexually active throughout his life, once remarking that "the sexual organs are the true center of the world."

Western philosophy, some say, is myopic, blind to the wisdom of others. A rigidly exclusive club of dead white, and only white, men. There's some truth to this charge, but look more closely at the fabric of Western philosophy and you see Eastern threads running throughout. As far back as Epicurus's time, in 350 BC, East and West were conversing, even if they didn't always listen to one another. Centuries later, the conversation resumed. Not only Thoreau and Schopenhauer, but others, too. Nietzsche, Heidegger, and William James were intimately familiar with the wisdom of India and China. This wisdom seeped into their philosophy.

I'm warming to Schopenhauer. The prince of darkness, the philosopher of pessimism, is a master stylist, a joy to read. His writing is crisp and lively, almost poetic. He is the most readable of the German philosophers (admittedly, a low bar, but Schopenhauer clears it easily). No philosopher, says Schopenhauer scholar Bryan Magee, is "more with you, almost tangibly and audibly present when you read them."

True, he was a wounded soul, perhaps more than most, but that is a difference of degree, not kind. We all have a little Schopenhauer inside us. We're all wounded. Only the size and shape of the wounds differ.

Schopenhauer is not an easy man to like—"a nasty piece of work," says one biographer—but he is an easy man to admire. A lover of art and music, he developed one of philosophy's most profound, and beautiful, theories of aesthetics, and influenced generations of artists and writers. Tolstoy and Wagner kept portraits of the philosopher in their studies. The Argentinian writer Jorge Luis Borges learned German so he could read Schopenhauer in the original. Comedians love Schopenhauer, confirming suspicions about the darkness that lurks behind humor.

While other philosophers attempted to explain the world out there, Schopenhauer was more concerned with our inner world. We can't know the world if we don't know ourselves. This fact strikes me as incredibly obvious. Why do so many philosophers—otherwise intelligent folk—miss it? Partly, I think, it's because it's easier to examine the external. We're like the proverbial drunk looking for his keys in a lighted alleyway.

"Did you lose them here?" asks a passerby.

"No. I lost them over there," he says, pointing to a dark parking lot.

"Then why are you looking here?"

"This is where the light is."

Not Schopenhauer. He searched where it is darkest. You might disagree with his gloomy outlook or bleak metaphysics, but you can't ding him for half measures. He is all in. A heroic philosopher.

Every fetish suggests an equal and opposite revulsion, and every passion a complementary annoyance. And so it was with Schopenhauer. His intense love of music begot a corresponding loathing of noise.

"Knocking, hammering and banging have been throughout my life a daily torment to me," he writes in his essay "On Din and Noise." He especially disliked the "sudden sharp crack" of a whip against the side of a horse, a sound "which paralyzes the brain, tears and rends the threat of reflection, and murders all thoughts." I wonder if Schopenhauer, lover of animals, was feeling the horse's pain.

At night, he jumped at the slightest noise and reached for the loaded pistol he always kept at his bedside. In Frankfurt, he wrote to the theater manager, urging him to do something about the racket: control the crowd, install cushioning on the doors and hinged seats, *anything*. "The Muses and the audience will be grateful to you for improving matters," he wrote.

For Schopenhauer, noise was more than an annoyance. It was a barometer of character. One's tolerance for noise, he believed, is inversely proportional to his intelligence. "Therefore, when I hear dogs barking unchecked for hours in the courtyard of a house, I know what to think of the inhabitants."

I'm with Schopenhauer. My train of thought is rickety, easily derailed. Even the sound of a ticking clock can upend my concentration. My wife's hair dryer, an evil little fucker called the Bio Ionic PowerLight, has been known to sabotage an entire day. And don't get me started on leaf blowers.

Recent research reveals the insidious effect noise pollution has on our physical and mental well-being. According to one study published in the *Southern Medical Journal,* noise pollution can lead to "anxiety, stress, nervousness, nausea, headache, emotional instability, argumentativeness, sexual impotence, changes in mood, increase in social conflicts, neurosis, hysteria, and psychosis." Another study found that the roar of planes taking off and landing causes our blood pressure to spike, heartbeat to race, and stress hormones to release—*even while sound asleep*.

Schopenhauer would find confirmation but little pleasure in these studies, for they fail to account for another, more insidious type of noise: mental. Mental noise does more than disturb. It masks. In a noisy environment, we lose the signal, and our way. Some 150 years before email, the cluttered inbox worried Schopenhauer.

In his essay "On Authorship," the philosopher foreshadows the mind-numbing clamor that is social media, where the sound of the true is drowned out by the noise of the new. "No greater mistake can be made than to imagine that what has been written latest is always the more correct; that what is written later on is an improvement on what was written previously; and that every change means progress."

We make this mistake every time we click mindlessly, like a lab rat pulling a lever, hoping for a reward. What form this reward will take we don't know, but that is beside the point. Like Schopenhauer's hungry readers, we confuse the new with the good, the novel with the valuable.

I am guilty of this. I'm constantly checking and rechecking my digital vital signs. While writing this paragraph, I have checked my email (nothing), opened my Facebook page (Pauline's birthday, must remember to send her a note), placed a bid for a nice leather backpack on eBay, checked my email again (still nothing), ordered a disturbingly large quantity of coffee, upped my bid for that backpack, and checked my email again (still nothing).

The encyclopedia was the Internet in Schopenhauer's day, and nearly as seductive. Why puzzle over a problem when the solution is readily available in a book? Because, answers Schopenhauer, "it's a hundred times more valuable if you have arrived at it by thinking for yourself." Too often, he said, people jump to the book rather than stay with their thoughts. "You should read only when your own thoughts dry up."

Substitute "click" for "read" and you have our predicament. We confuse data with information, information with knowledge, and knowledge with wisdom. This tendency worried Schopenhauer. Everywhere he saw people scrambling for information, mistaking it for insight. "It does not occur to them," he wrote, "that information is merely a *means* toward insight and possesses little or no value in itself." I'd go a step further. This excess of data—noise, really—has negative value and diminishes the possibility of insight. Distracted by the noise, we don't hear the music.

I'm walking back to my hotel, having left Stephen Roeper and the sad Schopenhauer Archives to fend for themselves in this, "the worst of all possible worlds."

Strolling along Frankfurt's leafy boulevards, the air soft and pliant, it doesn't feel that way. It's a pleasant evening, the sort Schopenhauer favored for his afternoon constitutionals. I listen to the street sounds, garbled Teutonic resonances, and to my own inner voice. I'm alarmed to discover that it, too, is muddled. Schopenhauer was right. Fill your head with the ideas of others and they'll displace your own. I make a mental note to evict these uninvited voices.

Back in my room, I decide, out of boredom or reflex (or some perverse combination), to log on. I'm clicking away, mindlessly, when it dawns on me: the Internet is Schopenhauer's Will made manifest in the digital age. Like the Will, the Internet is omnipresent, and purposeless. It is always striving, never sated. It devours everything, including our most precious resource: time. It offers the illusion of happiness but delivers only suffering. As with the Will, the Internet offers two ways to escape its clutch: the path of the ascetic and that of the aesthete. Meditation or music.

I choose music. Rossini, naturally. I pour a hot bath and a Scotch. Taking a swig of the single malt, I close my eyes, and listen. I follow the melody the way the Dalai Lama must follow the news, disinterested but not uninterested. Attentive yet not reactive. I let the music wash over me, as warm and soothing as the bathwater. Sound without words. Emotion without content. Signal without noise.

This, I realize, is what Schopenhauer saw in music: not a respite from the world but an immersion in another, richer one.

PART TWO

NOON

6.

How to Enjoy like Epicurus

7:35 p.m. Somewhere in Montana. On board Amtrak's Empire Builder, en route from Chicago to Portland, Oregon.

We travel to escape the tyranny of habit. We humans, though, are lost without structure and, after two days on board Amtrak, I'm craving just that. I read, and I think. I read about thinking and I think about reading. I rearrange my roomette, moving luggage from nook to cranny then back to nook again. For hours I position myself at the stern of the train and, peering out a small window, watch the world retreat, like a movie that's perpetually ending but never does. Mostly, I wait for a chirpy Amtrak voice, Miss Oliver, beckoning me to the dining car.

Nothing says structure like food. Meals are the girders that hold the day upright. Without them, time collapses onto itself and gravity increases exponentially, like in a black hole. This is a scientific fact.

Dining while stationary is pleasurable enough, but my enjoyment increases exponentially when in motion. There is something wonderfully decadent about the combination of dining and moving. At least there once was.

In 1868, George Pullman inaugurated the first dining car. He named it the Delmonico, after the famous New York restaurant. Fine dining had taken to the rails.

The menu, printed on silk, offered dozens of choices, including oysters and Welsh rarebit. All served on fine china, naturally, and complemented with a bottle of Chateau Margaux or perhaps a sparkling Krug.

A *New York Times* correspondent wrote breathlessly of his 1869 journey on board a Pullman from Omaha to San Francisco. He adored the antelope steak ("The gourmet who has not experienced this—bah! What does he know of the feast of fat things?") and swooned over the mountain brook trout (cooked in a sauce "piquante and unpurchaseable"). All served, he notes, on "tables covered with snowy linen."

I consider my Amtrak food and regret having missed the golden age of railway dining by a good century. My linen is not snowy. My china is not fine. There are no bumpers of sparkling Krug, though, to be fair, my Diet Coke does fizz a bit. My entrée—allegedly seared shrimp over rice pilaf—does not make me swoon. It is edible, yes, but not gourmet.

All philosophers, like all teenagers, are misunderstood. It comes with the territory. None is more misconstrued, more unjustly maligned, than the great philosopher of pleasure, Epicurus.

Born in 341 BC, on the island of Samos, Epicurus turned to philosophy at a young age, and for the usual reasons: an abundance of questions and a deep suspicion of the answers adults gave him. He studied the greats—Heraclitus and Democritus in particular. Soon he amassed his own students, drawn to his charming and accessible teaching style. He often used colorful, shocking language. Like Socrates, Epicurus was a practitioner of Crazy Wisdom. People needed to be shaken out of their trance, and by any means necessary.

Epicurus hopped around the Greek world, living briefly in Colophon (now Turkey) and on the island of Lesbos, before settling in Athens, at the age of thirty-five. There he purchased a house outside the city walls. Encircled by a large wall, it contained a lush garden. The perfect place, he thought, to found a school, and a community. Instantly popular, it eventually became known simply as *Kepos*. The Garden.

Gardens and philosophy go together well. Voltaire, the darling of the French Enlightenment, said "we must cultivate our garden." The seventeenth-century English writer and gardener John Evelyn agreed, adding that the "air and genius of gardens" lend themselves to "philosophical Enthusiasms."

I love that phrase. The world needs more philosophical enthusiasts. Not students of philosophy, and God knows not experts, but enthusiasts, with all of the unabashed gusto the word implies. Gardens, sequestered from the noise of the world, lend themselves to such philosophical enthusiasms.

Gardens require tending. So do our thoughts. Someone who thinks is not a philosopher any more than someone who putters about in his backyard is a gardener. Both pursuits—gardening and philosophy—require an adult's disciplined commitment combined with a child's easy joy.

Both pursuits represent an attempt to create, not impose, order out of chaos while retaining a hint of wildness, à la Thoreau, and a dash of mystery, too. The gardener collaborates with nature. Dresses it up, as Voltaire said. The gardener does her bit, planting and shoveling and weeding but, ultimately, the fate of her garden lies elsewhere. It rests with the natural processes—and, yes, the magic—that unfolds within the garden walls. Philosophy contains its own magic, provided you do the hard work.

Places matter. They are repositories of ideas. That's why I travel, and why I am here now, in Athens, searching for traces of Epicurus and his garden. It won't be easy. Archaeologists, with all the tools and smarts at their disposal, have yet to pinpoint its precise location. Yet this does not dampen my philosophical enthusiasm. You needn't know what you're looking for in order to find it. Gumption is the best navigator.

After a few wrong turns, I find my first landmark: the *Dipylon*, or

Double Gate. Once the main entrance to Athens, it was the largest gate of the ancient world. The centuries have shrunk the gate to a low stone wall—not unlike, I imagine, the one in Philadelphia where Jacob Needleman and Elias sat and experienced questions.

In olden times, a city's walls demarcated two worlds. To step outside the city walls was to make a statement, and to take a chance, as Rousseau knew so well. Today, the neighborhood outside the Double Gate occupies a netherworld: that fleeting interval between the formerly sketchy and the currently unaffordable. Auto repair shops abut trendy cafés. I stop and listen, as Schopenhauer would. A rhythmic banging emanates from the auto shops, pop music from the cafés. Laughter, too. People seeking pleasure, just as they did in Epicurus's time, and long before.

I pause at a small clearing between two not-yet-hip concrete buildings. I notice a few scrappy plants sprouting from the concrete. Not a garden, exactly, but close enough. I try to imagine the scene some 2,500 years ago.

The streets back then were crowded. I can picture a young woman among the throng. Her name is Themista, the history books tell us. As a woman, life is difficult even in the best of times. And these are not the best of times. Nothing seems certain anymore. Alexander's death upended the world. The old order has collapsed and a new one has yet to take its place.

I can picture Themista venturing outside the city gates, taking a chance, when she spots a walled compound. On one side is an odd inscription: "Stranger, your time will be pleasant here. Here the highest good is pleasure."

Themista is intrigued. This sounds much more inviting than Plato's Academy, not far from here. There a more foreboding sign greets visitors: "Let no one ignorant of geometry enter here." She steps across the threshold and finds not only a garden but a small farm, and a welcoming atmosphere.

Epicurus's choice of a walled garden, in a relatively remote location, was no accident. In a sharp break with the Stoics and other philosophical schools, he urged his followers to avoid "the prison of business affairs and politics." Political bonds, Epicurus thought, reduced your self-sufficiency, and amounted to outsourcing your happiness. His motto was *Lathe Biosas*. "Live in obscurity." Such reclusiveness was as controversial then as it is today. Those who withdraw from the world are always suspect. We mock the recluse to the extent we feel threatened by him.

Epicurus broke with tradition in other ways, too. While most schools accepted only male citizens of Athens, Epicurus welcomed freed slaves and women, like Themista, to whom he dedicated several works.

Not surprisingly, a walled-off community that welcomed people not normally welcome and advocated a life devoted to pleasure raised suspicions. Rumors of orgies and lavish feasts circulated. Epicurus, it was said, vomited twice a day due to overindulgence and "for many years he was unable to get out of his sedan chair."

The rumors were unfounded. The Garden resembled a monastery more than a brothel. Life was communal, with little privacy. "Let nothing be done in your life, which will cause you fear if it becomes known to your neighbor," said Epicurus. Few of his followers seemed to mind that prohibition. They had nothing to hide.

Like others I've encountered on my journey, Epicurus was a philosopher of the body as well as the mind. The body, he believed, contains the greatest wisdom.

Epicurus was an Empiricist. We know the world, he believed, through our senses and only our senses. The senses may not be perfect, but no other reliable source of knowledge exists, and anyone who tells you otherwise is either deluded or selling something.

Epicurus honed his own senses. He was a keen observer of human behavior. He surveyed Athens, and everywhere he saw people who had enough: enough food, enough money, and certainly enough culture. Why weren't they happy?

Epicurus approached this mystery like a physician treating a patient with unexplained symptoms. Philosophy, he said, should be dispensed like medicine for the soul. The first four of his *Principal Doctrine*s are known as the *tetrapharmakos*, the "Four-Part Cure." Like medicine, philosophy must be ingested at regular intervals, and at prescribed dosages. Like medicine, there are potential side effects: dizziness, disorientation, and, occasionally, manic episodes.

The medical approach was no accident. Epicurus lived during the peak of therapeutic philosophy. During the time, an era known as the Hellenistic Age, people chose a school of philosophy with the same ardent deliberation people today choose a spouse or a wireless plan. The stakes were high. You weren't making an academic choice, Princeton over Stanford. You were making a life choice that would shape your character, and therefore your destiny.

The schools were combination university, health club, self-help seminar, and, in the case of Epicurus, hippie commune. Teachers focused on ethics. Derived from the Greek word for "character," ethics was the study of the good life: *eudaimonia*. Some philosophers thought only the gods and the blessed few could achieve this elevated state of happiness. Epicurus thought anyone could. Meditate on these teachings "night and day," he told his students, and you will "live like a god among men."

Examining the sickly body politic of Athens, Epicurus posited a simple diagnosis: we fear what is not harmful and desire what is not necessary. What do we fear the most? he asked. The gods and death. (Presumably taxes were not a major stressor in ancient times.) He had answers for both. The gods, he said, exist but couldn't care less about human affairs. Why should they? They're too busy being gods. For Epicurus, the gods were like celebrities. They lead enviable lives, free of worries, always able to get a reservation.

As for death, Epicurus tells us to relax. Yes, *dying* can be painful, Epicurus acknowledges, but such pain is self-limiting. It won't last forever. Either it subsides, or you die. Either way, there's nothing to fear.

I find this idea, like much of Epicurus's philosophy, sound in theory but problematic in practice. I don't fear the gods, but the prospect of nonexistence freaks me out. I suspect it always will.

Relax, says Epicurus, *and enjoy*. He advocated pleasure as "the beginning and the end of the happy life," adding provocatively: "I do not know how I shall conceive of the good if I take away the pleasure of taste, if I take away sexual pleasure, if I take away the pleasure of hearing, and if I take away the sweet emotions that are caused by the sight of a beautiful form."

No wonder Epicurus was so maligned. Pleasure is suspect. It resides in the shadows, behind closed doors. When we speak of "secret" or "hidden" pleasures, we're acknowledging the shame attached to this most basic of human instincts.

Epicurus thought otherwise. He considered pleasure the highest good. Everything else—fame, money, and even virtue—mattered only to the extent they furthered pleasure. "I spit upon the honorable and those who vainly admire it," he wrote, in his typically provocative style. Pleasure is the only thing we desire for its own sake. Everything else, even philosophy, is a means to that one end.

The primacy of pleasure, Epicurus said, was self-evident. What does a child respond to? Pleasure and pain. You don't need to teach her that fire is hot and candy tasty; she knows it. Seeking pleasure and avoiding pain is as natural, and automatic, as breathing.

Epicurus defined pleasure differently from the way most of us do. We think of pleasure as a presence, what psychologists call positive affect. Epicurus defined pleasure as a lack, an absence. The Greeks called this state *ataraxia*, literally "lack of disturbance." It is the absence of anxiety rather than the presence of anything that leads to contentment. Pleasure is not the opposite of pain but its absence. Epicurus was no hedonist. He was a "tranquillist."

Some psychologists take exception with Epicurus's focus almost exclusively on pain relief. "Happiness is definitely something other than the mere absence of all pain," sniffs the *Journal of Happiness Studies.* Before reading Epicurus, I would have agreed. Now I'm not so sure. If I'm honest with myself, I recognize that what I crave most is not fame or wealth but peace of mind, the "pure pleasure of existing." It's nearly impossible to describe such a state in terms other than that of absence.

Avoiding pain is sound advice—I'm all for it—but isn't it an awfully thin basis for a philosophy? Not if you're in pain, Epicurus thought.

Imagine you've fallen from a horse and broken your leg. A doctor is summoned and promptly offers you a bowl of grapes. What's wrong? The grapes are pleasurable, aren't they?

This absurd situation is the one many of us find ourselves in, Epicurus believed. We scoop trivial pleasures atop a mountain of pain, and wonder why we're not happy. Some of us suffer the sharp shock of physical pain, others the dull ache of mental pain or the I want-to-die pain of a broken heart, but pain is pain, and we must address it if we hope to achieve contentment. "We are only born once—twice is not allowed," he said. Every human life, Epicurus believed, is the fortuitous product of chance, a swerve in atomic motion, a miracle of sorts. Shouldn't we celebrate that?

I decamp from the site of what may or may not have been the Garden, and retreat behind the walls of an inviting café. I order a Mythos beer and contemplate the many pleasures of Epicurus. He didn't merely celebrate pleasure. He dissected it, developing an entire taxonomy of desire.

At the top of the ladder were the "natural and necessary" desires. A glass of water, for instance, after a trek through the desert. Next came "natural but not necessary" desires. A glass of simple table wine after drinking the water after trekking across the desert. Finally, at the bottom of the pyramid, are desires that are neither natural nor necessary, what Epicurus calls "empty" desires. A pricey bottle of champagne after imbibing the table wine after drinking the water after trekking across the desert. These empty desires cause the most suffering, Epicurus thought, since they are difficult to obtain. "It is better for you to lie upon a bed of straw and be free of fear, than to have a golden couch and an opulent table, yet be troubled in mind."

I sip my beer—natural but not necessary—and take silent inventory of my various desires. I don't like what I find. I devote energy—too much, I know—chasing mirages. I devote a lot of energy to bags. I love bags (satchels, mainly, but also backpacks and briefcases) and, like all loves, this one consumes me. Epicurus would take one look at my outsize bag collection (I have a problem) and declare it, at best, a natural but not necessary desire. Yes, we need something to carry our stuff, but we don't need fifty-four bags of various vintages and leather-and-canvas configurations. A simple rucksack will do.

Not only are there different kinds of pleasures, Epicurus says, but they operate at different speeds. Here he differentiates between static and kinetic pleasures. The act of slaking our thirst with a glass of chilled water is a kinetic pleasure. The sated feeling—the lack of thirst—we experience afterward is a static pleasure. Or, put another way, drinking is a kinetic pleasure, having drunk a static one.

We typically think of kinetic pleasures as the most satisfying, but Epicurus didn't see it that way. Static pleasures are superior, for we seek them for their own sake. They are ends, not means. "I find full pleasure in the body when I live on bread and water," said Epicurus, "and I spit upon the pleasures of plush living not for their own account, but because of the discomforts that follow them."

What exactly are the discomforts that follow, say, a five-course meal at the French Laundry? Epicurus is speaking of physical sensations—indigestion, a hangover—but mostly about another, insidious kind of pain: the pain of not-having. You enjoyed the Pacific Wild King Salmon Terrine—the pleasure was real—but now it is gone and you crave it again. You have outsourced your happiness to the Salmon Terrine—and to the fisherman who caught it, the restaurant that serves it, the boss who cuts your paycheck so you can afford it. You are now a Salmon Terrine junkie, your happiness dependent on regular hits of the stuff. All because you have mistaken an unnecessary desire for a necessary one.

Take heart, says Epicurus. Nature has you covered. She has made the necessary desires easy to obtain and the unnecessary ones difficult. Apples grow on trees. Teslas don't. Desire is nature's GPS, guiding us toward the highest pleasures and away from the empty ones.

We are supposedly living in a golden age of pleasure. So many tantalizing options lie only a click away: gourmet food, memory-foam mattresses, kinky sex, gadgets galore. Pleasure decoys, all of them, Epicurus would say. Like any good decoy, they look real, and so we take aim. If we fail to hit the target, we blame ourselves for poor marksmanship and reload.

Stop aiming at decoys, counsels Epicurus. Better yet, stop shooting altogether. "Not what we have but what we enjoy constitutes our abundance," he says, noting that, with the right mind-set, even a small pot of cheese can convert a simple meal into a lavish feast.

Beyond a certain point, Epicurus believed, pleasure cannot be increased—just as a bright sky cannot get any brighter—but only varied. That new pair of shoes or smart watch represents pleasure varied, not increased. Yet our entire consumer culture is predicated on the assumption that pleasure varied equals pleasure increased. This faulty equation causes needless suffering.

Not only does the variety of pleasure matter less than we think, so does its duration. A twenty-minute massage isn't necessarily twice as pleasurable as a ten-minute one. You cannot double tranquility. You're either at peace or you are not.

This philosophy may not sound like much fun, but it was. The Epicureans, ensconced behind the garden walls, lived a simple life but one punctuated by lavish feasts. They knew that luxury is best enjoyed intermittently, and welcomed whatever goodness came their way. Epicureanism is a philosophy of acceptance, and its close cousin, gratitude. When we accept something, truly accept it, we can't help but feel gratitude.

I recently met a young psychologist named Rob, who, I think, embodies the Epicurean ethos, even if he doesn't know it. Rob and I spent three days hiking in the otherworldly wilderness that is southern Utah as part of an experiment into the health benefits of nature. (I was the guinea pig.)

One day, I noticed Rob's water bottle, sleek and ergonomic, eliciting in me a nearly baglike thrill.

"Where did you buy it?" I asked Rob.

"I didn't buy it," he replied. "It happened at me."

A lot happens at Rob. Not only water bottles but coffee mugs, flashlights, and other items. After our expedition, Rob and I exchanged emails, and he informed me: "A new coffee mug happened at me about an hour ago as I crossed campus; it is fairly fancy and came, for some unfathomable reason, in its own box. I have placed it in my office along with five other mugs, eight water bottles, a protein shaker, and two headlamps, all of which also happened at me. If this doesn't abate soon, I'll be able to retire early and just open up a gift shop."

Rob's attitude is pure Epicurus. If goodness comes your way, enjoy it. Don't seek it. Good things come to those who don't expect good things to come to them. Rob doesn't expend energy hunting for these baubles. They simply happen at him. When they do, he is grateful.

In the centuries that followed Epicurus's death, Epicurean gardens sprang up across the Mediterranean. They attracted large and devoted followings and, unlike other schools, had low attrition rates. Many entered the garden; few fled.

Those outside the garden walls threw stones. The Stoic teacher Epictetus called Epicurus a "foul-mouthed bastard." Epicureanism, with its ethos of principled pleasure, threatened other schools of philosophy, and especially a popular new religion: Christianity. Eventually, the Church prevailed. For many centuries, Epicureanism all but disappeared.

Then, in 1417, an intrepid scholar named Poggio Bracciolini, scouring southern Europe for lost treasures from antiquity, discovered the single remaining copy of *On the Nature of Things*, an Epicurean treatise by the Roman poet Lucretius. In 1473, it became one of the first books printed on the newly invented mechanical press.

Epicurus's ideas—about pleasure and simplicity and the good life—found a receptive new audience, from France to the American colonies. In 1819, a retired Thomas Jefferson declared, "I too am an Epicurean." In a letter to a friend, he expands. "I consider the genuine (not the imputed) doctrines of Epicurus as containing everything rational in moral philosophy which Greece & Rome have left us."

Jefferson was less familiar with the teachings of the Buddha, but the similarities with Epicurus are striking. Both men identified desire as the root of all suffering. Both identified tranquility as the ultimate goal of their practice. Both saw the need for a community of like-minded thinkers: the garden for Epicurus, the sangha for the Buddha. And both men apparently liked the number four. The Buddha had the Four Noble Truths, Epicurus the Four-Part Cure.

These similarities might be more than coincidental. Two of Epicurus's early influences, Democritus and Pyrrho, traveled to India and encountered Buddhist schools there. Perhaps Epicurus had learned of the Buddha's teaching. Or perhaps both men, journeying by different routes, arrived at the same destination.

Today the Garden has, like nearly everything else, migrated online. This is where I find Tom Merle. I wasn't looking for Tom. He happened at me.

Tom is a capital-*E* Epicurean—adhering to the philosopher's original principles—living in small-*e* epicurean Napa, California, where the word is synonymous with culinary indulgence. How does he reconcile these upper- and lowercase existences? That is the first question I jot down in my notebook. Questions, though, are like M&M's, or bags: it's impossible to have only one. Before long, I've filled a dozen pages in my notebook. Epicurus, the apostle of simple living, would not approve.

All my questions, I realize, distill to this: How can a dead Greek dude, prone to cursing and spitting, who lived in a garden and preached a life of radical simplicity, possibly be relevant in today's complex, high-tech world?

I've traveled halfway around the world, from Athens to Napa, in order to meet Tom for an early lunch. I let him choose the venue, partly because it's his town, but mostly because I'm curious which way he tilts, epicurean or Epicurean. He suggests we meet in the center of town, then walk to the restaurant.

Tom is seventy-three years old but looks a decade younger. He is wearing dark sunglasses, which he never removes, even in the shade, and a silk shirt adorned with colorful wine bottles. Tom is clearly comfortable in his tanned skin. I like him. As we walk, I make small talk, asking about life in Napa.

Tom likes living here, though he tires of the covert preening, the glut of beautiful people—and the utter lack of grit.

Grit is important, I agree. Never trust a place without grit.

Tom steers us to a little café. The menu is simple and inexpensive. Capital-*E* Epicurean. I order a sandwich called "Settin' the Woods on Fire," intrigued by the prospect of Oaxaca cheese and reminded of something I had read about Thoreau. He and a friend accidentally set a sizable parcel of Walden Woods on fire, much to their chagrin.

"Do you want anything to drink with that?" asks the woman who takes our order.

I look at my watch: 11:00 a.m.

"Is it too early for wine?" I ask.

Tom and she exchange a knowing glance. *We've got a tourist on our hands.* In Napa, it is never too early, or too late, for wine.

I order a pinot noir that Tom recommends. We settle into a table outside, the sun warm, the sky a flawless California blue. No grit in sight. A Tesla floats by.

As we wait for our food, I dive into my question—which, when I wasn't looking, multiplied again into *questions.*

How did you find Epicurus, I ask Tom, or did Epicurus find you?

Tom explains that he's always been an "idea person." He dabbled in philosophy as an undergraduate, but it wasn't until later, as a graduate student, that he dove deep. It was the 1960s. A good time to be an idea person.

Tom read Spinoza and Kant and others but was drawn to Epicurus and his focus on pleasure. "To me, pleasure is so all-encompassing—even more so than happiness," he tells me, between sips of wine.

Tom never tires of correcting the record on Epicurus. The philosopher was no foodie, and would be appalled to find a culinary website named after him. He valued the simple life. The low-hanging fruit tastes the best.

I wonder aloud how Tom reconciles the idea of simple living with the reality of living in Napa, a place where the low-hanging fruit is likely a pampered grape bound for a two-hundred-dollar bottle of Merlot and a simple roof over your head can easily set you back a cool million.

It's not easy, concedes Tom, but it's possible. You need to do the math.

I wince at the mention of math. For me, math and geometry are right up there with the gods and death in the fear department. I would never have stepped foot in Plato's Academy, with his strict entry requirement.

All pleasures are good, and all pain bad, explains Tom, but that doesn't mean we should always choose pleasure over pain. Certain pleasures might lead to future pain and thus should be avoided. The pain of lung cancer outweighs the pleasure of smoking. Likewise, certain pains lead to future pleasure and thus should be endured. The pain of the gym, for instance.

As odd as it may sound, we can reason our way to pleasure, Epicurus taught. If we are unhappy, it is not because we are lazy or flawed. We have simply miscalculated. We have failed to deploy prudence, "sober reasoning," when appraising pleasure and pain.

Tom is constantly doing the math, "checking his pleasure," as he puts it. Does the benefit of a given pleasure outweigh the pain exacted?

A few days ago, explains Tom, he noticed that a play he hoped to see was coming to San Francisco. Should he go? On one side of the ledger was the pleasure of watching the performance, but he weighed that against the pain of the ticket price and the agony of California freeway traffic. In the end, Tom decided, that yes, in this case the pleasure outweighed the pain. He bought the tickets.

"Very few things are unadulterated pleasures," he says. "That's why this philosophy is perfect for me. I'm a very indecisive person."

I, too, am flummoxed by choice. Oddly, it is not life's big decisions—Which career should I pursue?—that stump me but the small ones: Should I order the Guatemalan or Sumatran coffee? At the root of my indecisiveness, I realize, is fear. The fear of making the wrong choice. Choosing the good instead of the best.

As Tom and I sip our Pinot Noir, I'm beginning to see the appeal of Epicureanism. Yet something continues to nag: *ataraxia,* the lack of mental disturbance that Epicurus considered the highest good. It seems like such a passive form of pleasure. What is wrong with actively satisfying desires? I ask Tom.

"Consider this french fry," he says, waving one in the air as if it were a wand.

"Okay," I say, not sure where he is going with this.

"If you have a desire for french fries, it starts with a pain. An absence of the item. A craving. A seeking. An itch."

"So the pleasure is the scratching of the itch?"

"Right, but it is not something you ever reach because there will always be other pains, others itches that you have to scratch."

This sounds awful, this endless cycle of itching and scratching. I'm getting itchy just thinking about it. We get a taste of caviar and it is pleasurable, which is good, but then we crave caviar again, and this is problematic. The caviar will never taste as good as the craving hurts. What began as a pleasure ends as pain. The only solution is to minimize those desires.

Inevitably, the conversation swerves to wine. I assume Tom, denizen of Napa, is something of a wine snob. I am wrong. Tom Merle, resident of Napa, amateur oenologist, stakeholder in a catering firm called "Splendor in a Glass," drinks Two-Buck Chuck. The wine, by Charles Shaw, sells for two dollars a bottle, and sells well.

"Really, Tom? The cheap stuff?"

"It's table wine, and it's not bad. To spend thirty-five dollars on something that is consumed, swallowed, then gone, is nuts. There's a reason Charles Shaw is successful. Two-Buck Chuck is decent wine. It's what I call 'good-enough wine.' "

"Good enough?"

"Yes. I would say good enough is good enough. It leaves you time for the more important parts of life. Besides, nothing is enough for the man to whom enough is too little," says Tom, channeling Epicurus.

I stop mid-sip. How much is enough? I've rarely stopped to ask that question. I've always assumed the answer is "more than I have now." It turns out that "more" is a moving target. Psychologists call it the "hedonic treadmill." This quirk of human nature explains why that third crème brûlée never tastes as good as the first or second. It explains why the new car that thrilled us on the test drive bores us after a month on the road. We acclimate to new pleasures, rendering them neither new nor quite as pleasurable.

We're particularly susceptible to what I call Just-a-Bit-More-ism. We don't need a lot more—money, success, friends—in order to be happy. Just a bit more. When we get that bit more, we recalibrate and calculate we need . . . just a bit more. We don't know how much is enough.

Good enough doesn't mean settling. Good enough isn't a cop-out. Good enough represents an attitude of deep gratitude toward whatever happens at you. Not only is the perfect the enemy of the good but the good is the enemy of the good enough. Follow the creed of good enough for long enough and something remarkable happens. The "enough" drops away, like a snake sloughing its skin, and what remains is simply the Good.

Epicurus considered friendship one of life's great pleasures. "Of all the things which contribute to a blessed life, none is more important, more fruitful, than friendship," he said. Friends, he added, are essential during meals, like the one Tom and I are enjoying. To eat and drink without a friend is "to devour like the lion and the wolf."

Epicurus's emphasis on friendship seems to contradict his pleasure-first principle. Genuine friendship, after all, means sometimes placing a friend's pleasure above your own. Doesn't that throw off the hedonic calculus? No, says Epicurus. Friendship, taken as a whole, alleviates pain and promotes pleasure. Whatever pain is associated with friendship is more than offset by its pleasures.

It dawns on me that Tom and I are having an Epicurean moment. A simple meal, paired with a good-enough wine. The luxury of friendship, and time. The pleasure of painlessness, of *ataraxia*. I register my agreeable state of mind but don't dwell on it, lest I fall prey to the Pleasure Paradox. Happiness contemplated is happiness lost.

As we say good-bye, I ask Tom if he can recommend a coffee shop. I'm hoping he suggests a quirky local place where dedicated staff lovingly craft each cup. A special place.

"There's a Starbucks down the road," he says.

I am disappointed, but stop and ask myself, "What would Epicurus do?" He would go to Starbucks, of course. So I do.

It is not quirky. It is not staffed by loving baristas. It is not special. It is good enough.

In other words, perfect.

7.

How to Pay Attention like Simone Weil

8:24 a.m. Wye Rail Station, United Kingdom, waiting to board the Southeastern Limited bound for Ashford. Total travel time: seven minutes. Total waiting time: nine minutes.

It is early, and the station is lovely. The simple wooden building, little more than a glorified shack, exudes an air of warmhearted community and quiet efficiency. A small bulletin board informs me the local book club is meeting next Thursday and it would be nice if I brought potato salad or maybe some scones. A nearby sign declares Wye an "area of outstanding natural beauty." And it is. Endless meadows and rolling hills, emerald green.

I sit in the small waiting room and let the wonderful absurdity of that term sit with me. Waiting room. A room built for the sole purpose of engaging in the nonactivity of waiting. I rock on my heels. I glance at my watch. Eight more minutes. I survey the small library, really just a few shelves of well-thumbed paperbacks.

I glance at the small departures board. Seven more minutes. I fidget. I pace. I finger my ticket: Wye to Ashford, Return Journey. I prefer that to the American "round-trip." A round-trip sounds bloated and pointless.

I check the departures board again. Six minutes. I sigh. What to do with a parcel of time like this? Too short to accomplish anything meaningful, yet too long to blink away. I know, six minutes is nothing. But it adds up. I read in the *Daily Telegraph* that the average Briton spends over the course of his or her lifetime six months standing in line.

Six months is not a speck. Six months is the bulk of a pregnancy. Six months is a short marriage, or a long fling. Six months is a good chunk of a life. And that's only the time spent queuing. We also wait for a pot of water to boil, a doctor to see us, a website to download, a customer service representative to pick up already, a pot of coffee to brew, a toddler to fall asleep, a traffic jam to clear, the right word to materialize, our daughter who is never, ever this late getting home to walk through the front door, popcorn to pop, ice cubes to freeze, snow to melt.

Six minutes. If I had more time, I'd read. I've packed some appropriate literature for my short train ride. A collection of haikus and Seneca's essay "On the Shortness of Life." Some two thousand years later, Ferris Bueller, on his day off, echoed Seneca: "Life moves pretty fast. If you don't stop and look around once in a while, you could miss it."

Speed breeds impatience. Our capacity for waiting diminishes in inverse proportion to the velocity of life. Why is the Internet connection so slow? Where is my pizza already? Impatience is a greediness for the future. Patience is a generous attitude toward time.

The dot in the distance grows steadily larger until at last the Southeastern locomotive edges into tiny Wye station, and I step aboard with coiled alacrity. Settling into my window seat, I am about to glance at my watch when I stop myself. Instead, I look out the window, and I wait.

The train accelerates, each passing second bringing me a smidgeon closer to Ashford, the final resting place of a philosopher who thought a lot about waiting and about time and who, in one of those sad ironies that seem to befall philosophers disproportionately, was granted so little of it herself.

Philosophy doesn't coddle. It challenges. It makes demands. The best philosophers are the most demanding. Socrates demands we question assumptions, especially our own. Marcus Aurelius demands we honor our duties.

Simone Weil's entreaty is simpler but no less difficult. She demands we pay attention. Not any sort of attention, either. Weil's notion of attention is unlike any I've encountered.

I'm looking at a black-and-white photograph of Simone Weil. She's in her early twenties, I guess. I first notice her jet-black hair, thick and unruly, then the glasses, almost comical in their chunkiness. She is all hair and glasses, I think.

Then I notice the eyes. Dark and steady, they simultaneously exude warmth and a fierce, preternatural wisdom. These are wounded eyes. Serious eyes. Thoreauvian eyes. Everyone remarked on them. One friend recalled "her piercing look through the thick glasses." Another was struck by how "in her presence all 'lies' were out of the question . . . her denuding, tearing and torn gaze would grasp and render helpless the person she was looking at."

She is dressed in a capacious, unflattering outfit, consistent with the complete disregard for fashion she displayed throughout her life. She wore shabby clothes, always black, and flat-heeled shoes. "A real ragamuffin," recalled one friend. "A medieval hermit," said another.

The philosopher of attention didn't want any directed at her. She wanted to see but not be seen. Whether riding a train or working on a factory floor, her goal was anonymity—"merging into the crowd and disappearing among them, so that they show themselves as they are," she said. Yet she always stood out. How could she not? Intellectual. Awkward. Jewish.

Weil was born in Paris in 1909 to a fiercely secular and highly intellectual family. From a young age, she found solace, and inspiration, in books. By age fourteen, she knew much of Blaise Pascal's *Pensées* by heart. She read works in the original Sanskrit and Assyro-Babylonian. ("Such a ridiculously easy language!" she told a friend.) She could go for days at a time without food or sleep.

While she excelled at school, she never valued knowledge for its own sake. "The only serious aim of schoolwork is to train the attention," she said. That single word—attention—would come to possess her. It was the thread that held her sprawling philosophy, and her life, together.

The ability to pay attention is, along with the ability to walk upright and open pickle jars, what makes us human. Every brilliant scientific discovery, every great work of art, every kind gesture, traces its source to a moment of pure, selfless attention.

Attention matters. More than anything else, it shapes our lives. "For the moment, what we attend to is reality," said the American philosopher William James. Something only exists for us if we attend to it. This is not a metaphor. It is a fact. As many studies reveal, we do not see that to which we don't pay attention.

The quality of our attention determines the quality of our lives. You are what you choose to pay attention to and, crucially, *how* you pay attention. Looking back at your life, which memories bubble to the surface? Maybe it's something big, like your wedding day, or maybe something small, that unexpectedly kind exchange with the person standing behind you on the ridiculously long post office line. Chances are, though, it's moments when you were most attentive. Our lives are no less and no more than the sum of our most rapt moments. "The highest ecstasy," said Weil, "is the attention at its fullest."

During these rare moments, we enter a state of mind—a state of being—that Weil calls "extreme attention" and psychologist Mihaly Csikszentmihalyi calls "flow." When in a state of flow, you shed any semblance of self-consciousness, and experience an altered perception of time and a heightened sense of reality. Everything seems more real than real. Unlike so much in life, flow is "a condition so rewarding as to be sought out for its own sake," says Csikszentmihalyi.

People immersed in flow are not self-absorbed, for there is no self to be absorbed. No musician, only music. No dancer, only dancing. Here is how an avid sailor describes being in flow. "One forgets oneself, one forgets everything, seeing only the play of the boat with the sea, the play of the sea around the boat, leaving aside everything not essential to that game." You don't need to sail the Atlantic or climb Everest to experience flow. You just need to pay attention.

Given the importance of attention, you'd think philosophers would be all over it. But they've paid scant attention to attention. Maybe they find the subject too obvious, or too opaque. Maybe they're simply too distracted.

Over the centuries, a few philosophers have sat still long enough to weigh in. René Descartes, the father of modern philosophy, saw attention as a kind of intellectual divining rod, a tool that enabled us to distinguish between dubious ideas and "clear and distinct" ones that lie beyond doubt. The philosopher who famously said "I think, therefore I am" also said, in so many words, *I pay attention; therefore I am able to transcend doubt.* Not as catchy, I admit, but probably more accurate.

As the turn of the twentieth century approached, the subject of attention was, ironically, in a fractured state of chaos. Some thinkers even concluded (as some still do) that attention does not exist. As the British philosopher Francis Bradley wrote, "There is no primary act of attention, there is no specific act of attention, there is no one kind of act of attention at all."

Nonsense, said William James, wading into the chaos. "Everyone knows what attention is. It is taking possession of the mind, in clear and vivid form, of one out of what seems several simultaneously possible objects or trains of thought." James, predicting the hazards of multitasking, warned that attention demands not only focusing on some aspects of reality but ignoring others.

Our current conception of attention dates to 1958. That's when a British psychologist named Donald Broadbent posited the "filter model" of attention (also known as the "bottleneck model"). The world floods our senses with data, like a fire hose. Our brain's ability to process this data is limited, so it deploys attention as a means to prioritize all that information, to control the fire hose.

It's a compelling theory, one that intuitively seems to make sense.

Attention, we assume, is like a bank account we draw down, or a hard drive with limited capacity. We've all experienced that sensation of being overwhelmed by too much information. So much bombards us that nothing sticks. Several studies have found we routinely overestimate our ability to multitask.

Yet history is replete with those whose capacity for attention far exceeded the norm. Napoleon and Churchill, for instance, could juggle multiple tasks and conversations fluently. Our capacity for attention is not finite, concludes Alan Allport, an experimental psychologist at Oxford University. "No such upper bound has been identified, either generally or within specific processing domains." As Rousseau reminds us, often what we consider natural, "the way things are," is really the way things are *here* and *now*. A local truth masquerading as a universal one.

A sickly toddler, Simone Weil grew into a sickly young adult. At age thirteen, she began to suffer acute, debilitating headaches that would torment her throughout her life. At times the pain was so bad she'd wedge her head in a pile of pillows. Her birdlike appetite didn't help. She would go days without eating, and may have suffered from anorexia.

The Weils were a family of germophobes. (A bacteriologist was a close family friend, which didn't help.) Weil's mother insisted her children wash their hands several times a day, open doors with their elbows, and never kiss anyone. Not surprisingly, Simone Weil grew into an adult who flinched at the thought of physical contact. She once signed a letter to a friend, "Affectionate and bacilli-free kisses."

Brilliant as she was, Weil felt overshadowed by her wunderkind brother, André, who would go on to become one of Europe's greatest mathematicians. Clearly, her parents had wished for a second genius son. They sometimes referred to Simone as "Simon" and "our son number two."

From a young age, Weil experienced the pain of others as if it were her own. At age six, as World War I raged, she announced she was forsaking sugar because "the poor soldiers at the front didn't have any."

Later, as a young adult, she refused to heat her apartment, out of sympathy for the workers who couldn't afford heating fuel. She insisted on sleeping on hard floors. For a while, she worked in a vineyard harvesting grapes and in a factory, doing the most tedious assembly line work. "The affliction of others entered into my flesh and my soul," she wrote.

Weil broke into tears upon hearing news of a famine in China. This deeply impressed fellow philosopher Simone de Beauvoir. "I envied her for having a heart that could beat right across the world," she recalled. The two Simones, giants of twentieth-century French philosophy, and women in what was, and to an extent still is, very much a boys' club, met in 1928 in the courtyard of the Sorbonne. They did not get along.

Weil's radical empathy helps explain her radical views on attention. She didn't see it as a mechanism, or a technique. For her, attention was a moral virtue, no different from, say, courage or justice, and demanding the same selfless motivation. Don't pay attention to be more productive, a better worker or parent. Pay attention because it is the morally correct course of action, the right thing to do.

There's a name for attention at its most intense and generous: love. Attention is love. Love is attention. They are one and the same. "Those who are unhappy have no need for anything in this world but people capable of giving them their attention," writes Weil. Only when we give someone our attention, fully and with no expectation of reward, are we engaged in this "rarest and purest form of generosity." This is why the attention denied by a parent or lover stings the most. We recognize the withdrawal of attention for what it is: a withdrawal of love.

In the end, our attention is all we have to give. The rest—money, praise, advice—are poor substitutes. So, too, is time. Giving someone your time but not your attention is the cruelest fraud of all. Children know this instinctively. They can smell bogus attention a mile away.

Pure attention is not easy, Weil concedes: "The capacity to give one's attention to a sufferer is a very rare and difficult thing; it is almost a miracle; it *is* a miracle." Our first impulse when confronted with suffering is to turn away. We make excuses. We're busy. I've been known to cross the street to avoid earnest solicitors raising money for a no-doubt worthy cause. When I spot one, clipboard in hand, smile lighting her face, I shrink, ashamed not by my cheapness but, rather, my attentional impotence, my inability to look suffering in the eye.

It doesn't take much, says Weil. A simple five-word question can soften a heart, and change a life: "What are you going through?" These words are so powerful, says Weil, because they recognize the sufferer, "not only as a unit in a collection, or a specimen from the social category labeled 'unfortunate,' but as a man, exactly like us, who was one day stamped with a special mark by affliction."

There's a busy intersection near my home in Silver Spring, Maryland, where on most days, but especially on Sundays, an elderly African American man named Chip stands on the traffic island. He rests his thin frame on a walking stick, Styrofoam cup in one hand, cardboard sign in the other. It says simply, "Chip." No story. No pitch. Just his name.

I see Chip now, but for a long time I didn't. Not until my daughter, ten years old at the time, pointed him out. Now whenever we pass that intersection, she chirps, "There's Chip!" and insists I give him a dollar or two.

True attention entails not merely noticing the Other but acknowledging him, honoring him. Nowhere is this more essential than in medicine. An overworked ER doctor can notice when a patient is in pain, treat the pain and its underlying cause, yet never give the patient his or her attention. The patient, consciously or not, feels cheated.

My mother is not happy with her cardiologist. Technically, he is proficient. He went to all the right schools. Yet he lacks the capacity for attention. "I get the feeling I could drop dead in front of him and he wouldn't care," she told me one day. She is looking for a new cardiologist. A more attentive one.

I am at London's St. Pancras Station. It is glorious. All glass and light and promise. The station, like many, was built with two distinct purposes in mind: functional and aesthetic. "*Mi-usine, mi-palais.*" Half factory, half palace. After the success of London's Crystal Palace Exhibition in 1851, cities began building the main hall of railway stations out of glass and steel, while constructing the fronts of cut stone.

The result was a Janusian edifice, an architectural paradox bound to make you think. No wonder Wittgenstein said the only place where one can tackle philosophical problems is the railway station. The train station is philosophy made manifest in stone and steel. The station's dual allegiances, to art and commerce, remind us that it's sometimes necessary to hold two paradoxical thoughts simultaneously. *The station is a factory; the station is a palace.* Both statements are true. Neither negates the other.

My favorite station is Antwerp Central. If train stations are cathedrals, Antwerp is St. Peter's. With its soaring ceilings and polished marble, the station elicits the same sublimity I've experienced in other great buildings, that sensation of being diminished and enlarged at the same time. A train station is where I am at my most attentive.

I love all train stations, even the ugly ones. They don't get much uglier than New York's Penn Station, a rat-infested cavern of dingy, low-ceilinged halls. But as a student of human quirks I can't help but marvel at the strange boarding custom. Station officials don't announce a departing train's platform number until just a few minutes ahead of time. Until then, passengers, clutching boarding passes and lattes, wait anxiously. Some try to guess the gate and, like a roulette player betting it all on 32 Red, stake their claim. Others, in a display of learned helplessness, stare at the floor, forlorn.

Rail stations, even bad ones, pulse with life in a way that airports, even good ones, do not. They are training grounds for attention. This has been true from the beginning. One painting, from 1862, captures the vivacity of the rail station. Called simply *The Railway Station,* by William Frith, it depicts a frenzied scene, or *scenes,* unfolding on the platform. Porters, young ruddy-skinned men, haul huge suitcases onto trains. A passenger adjusts the collar on one of his two dogs. A wedding party, complete with bridesmaids, prepares to board. Two Scotland Yard detectives arrest a criminal. A bearded man in a fur coat, a Venetian nobleman, haggles over his cab fare.

Viewing the painting, my attention fragments. Splinters. That is the nature of attention, right? It is like a feral cat, a wild savanna lioness that must be "captured," not by us but by outside agents, like Scotland Yard detectives cuffing a fugitive. Maybe, maybe not.

Today's St. Pancras Station features no Venetian noblemen or Victorian bridesmaids. Yet currents of energy still pulse through its departures hall and through the ticket counters and cafés. There is nothing stationary about a train station. Everyone is in motion.

Everyone but me. I have planted myself at a little coffee shop. I order an overpriced espresso and find a seat that overlooks the action.

I reach into my bag, a waxed canvas and leather beauty, and retrieve a collection of Weil's writing. I turn to her essay "Reflections on the Right Use of School Studies with a View to the Love of God." It's a curious title. Weil was profoundly, if unconventionally, spiritual, and she frames many of her ideas in religious terms. Her work resonated with Pope Paul VI. But you needn't be a pope or religious at all to appreciate Weil's wisdom. No less an unbeliever than Albert Camus called her "the only great spirit of our time." He spent an hour meditating in her Paris apartment before boarding the plane for Stockholm to accept the Nobel Prize for literature.

The essay is short, only eight pages, but it takes me a long time to read it. I start and stop, then start again. Each reading produces a different shade of meaning, like a crystal that appears as different colors, depending on how the light strikes it. The essay is arresting, demanding. Weil begins by telling me I know nothing. Attention is not what I think it is.

Attention is not concentration. Concentration can be coerced—*listen up, class!*—while attention cannot. Observe what happens to your body when you concentrate. Your jaw tightens, your eyes narrow, your brow furrows. Weil found this sort of muscular effort ridiculous.

Concentration constricts. Attention expands. Concentration tires. Attention rejuvenates. Concentration is focused thinking. Attention is thinking suspended. "Above all our thought should be empty, waiting, not seeking anything but ready to receive in its naked truth the object that is to penetrate it," Weil writes. If that statement isn't perplexing enough, Weil goes further, declaring that "all errors arise from a lack of passivity."

Really? Isn't it an *excess* of passivity that bedevils? That is certainly what our culture teaches. We assume the active person is paying attention and the passive one is somehow clueless.

No, says Simone Weil. Attention is not something we do so much as consent to. Less weight lifting, more yoga. "Negative effort," she called it. Genuine attention, she believed, is a kind of waiting. For Weil, the two are virtually the same. "We do not obtain the most precious gifts by going in search of them but by waiting for them." The opposite of attention is not distraction but impatience.

Don't seek solutions. Wait for them. The more you scan your brain for the "right" word, the more it eludes you. Wait for it, though, and it will come. Eventually.

Speed is the enemy of attention. Of all the indecencies she witnessed on the factory floor, the greatest, Weil thought, was the violation of the workers' attention. The conveyor belt moved at a velocity "incompatible with any other kind of attention since it drains the soul of all save a preoccupation with speed."

We pay attention only to what we consider worthy of our attention. On one level, this mental triage is necessary, lest our lives become, in the words of William James, "a bloomin' buzzin' confusion." But it comes at a cost. By triaging too quickly, too impulsively, we risk overlooking precious gems.

Just as we often rush to judgment, so, too, do we rush to attention. We latch on to an object or idea too quickly, and pay a price: a flash of beauty, or an act of kindness, not seen. That's why, says Weil, it's important to maintain a state of unknowing, of unthinking, for as long as possible. This requires patience, something scarce during Weil's time and even more so today.

Weil paid great attention to matters most of us consider trivial. Handwriting, for instance. In high school, relays her friend and biographer Simone Pétrement, Weil decided to reform her "sloppy, almost careless, scrawled handwriting." She worked at it tirelessly, attentively, despite headaches and frequently swollen and painful hands. Her scrawl grew "progressively less rigid and more supple and, finally, attained the pure, beautiful script of her last years."

Patience is a virtue. It is also good for you, as the latest research shows. Patient people are happier and healthier than impatient ones, studies find. Patient people are more likely to act rationally. They have better coping skills.

Patience, though, doesn't strike us as a lot of fun. The English "patience" comes from the Latin *patiens*, for suffering, endurance, forbearance. The Hebrew *savlanut* is a bit cheerier. It means both patience and tolerance. Tolerance for what? For suffering, yes, but also tolerance for the rejected parts of our selves. People impatient with others are rarely patient with themselves.

I am not a naturally patient person. Mine is a mercenary mind. It always wants something, ideally something big: the Big Idea, the Big Break, the Big Breakfast. Like a stealthy alcoholic whom no one suspects, I am able to conceal my impatience from others. Usually. Sometimes people see through me. Like the Dutch messiah I met in Jerusalem.

I was working on a story for NPR about "Jerusalem Syndrome." That's a malady that afflicts some visitors to the Holy Land. They arrive sane enough but soon are convinced they are Elijah or Lazarus or some other biblical figure. It's more common than you'd think.

I had heard of a hostel in Jerusalem's Old City that for some reason attracted people suffering from Jerusalem Syndrome, so that's where I headed and, sure enough, where I met the Dutch messiah. A balding, middle-aged man, unremarkable in appearance, he explained, as if relaying that day's weather forecast, that the messiah will be coming soon. "And he is a Dutch man, like me," he said.

That was it. I had it. That was the tape cut I knew I was going to use. I kept listening and recording but my mind had checked out; it had bagged its prey. The Dutch messiah, sensing my inattention, suddenly stopped talking and stared at me. "You," he said, slowly, accusingly, "are an impatient man."

His words stopped me cold. He was right. I had seen him not as a fellow human being, or potential messiah, but as a tape cut. Ego food. A piece in a story that would, I hope, win me accolades. I had what I needed from him and, as far as I was concerned, our transaction was over. Not for him, though. I'm fairly certain he didn't view it as a transaction at all. From his perspective, we were engaged in a conversation, a mutual exchange of attention, and I was being stingy.

All disputes stem not from a misunderstanding per se, but a "category error." It's not that the two sides see the same problem differently. They see two different problems. Where one person sees an inefficient loading technique that fails to maximize the cleansing power of the high-performance dishwasher, another person sees a swipe at his core competency and, by extension, his masculinity. This is how wars and hissy fits begin.

The Dutch messiah's words stung because until then I had prided myself on my attentiveness. Eyes trained, ears cocked, I was on the lookout for the compelling character, the emotive tape cut, or the resonant bit of ambient sound that would add auditory texture to my story. I was concentrating but not paying attention. I knew what I was looking for before I found it. I was caught up in my own desire. That's always dangerous.

Weil warned against the sort of mercenary impatience I displayed in Jerusalem, and of another kind, too. An intellectual impatience, born from insecurity, that grasps at ideas, even bad ones, the way a drowning man will grasp even a sword. All our mistakes, says Weil, "are due to the fact that thought has seized upon some idea too hastily, and being prematurely blocked, is not open to the truth."

We see this dynamic at work in people eager to hook the Big Idea, one they hope will transform them from mere thinker to Thought Leader. More interested in packaging ideas than pondering them, they release their Big Idea into the world before it has ripened.

These aspiring Thought Leaders don't want to do the hard work attention demands. Attention is hard not the way judo or archery is hard. It's hard the way meditation, or parenting, is hard. It's hard the way waiting for a train is hard. Attention is not a skill we acquire, like knitting or fencing. It is a state of mind, an orientation. We don't so much learn attention as turn toward it. This pivot only happens when we pause, like Socrates, and get out of our own head. "Decreation," Weil calls it.

I prefer Iris Murdoch's term: "unselfing." The British novelist and philosopher describes one such moment of unselfing. She was looking out her window, feeling anxious and resentful due to a perceived slight earlier in the day, when she spotted a hovering kestrel. "In a moment everything is altered," she says. "The brooding self with its hurt vanity has disappeared. There is nothing now but kestrel. And when I return to thinking of the other matter it seems less important."

All inattention is a form of selfishness. We've decided that whatever is happening in our heads is more interesting, more important, than what is happening in the rest of the universe. That's why narcissists are so inattentive. Their attention is bottled up, stagnant. Attention is our lifeblood. It needs to circulate. To hoard attention is to kill it.

Sometimes endings reveal more than beginnings. I suspect this was the case with Simone Weil. The final months of her life were like a movie fast-forwarded. There was the prodigious, heroic output, the kindness shown and received, the collapse, and the inevitable, ambiguous end.

All of this played out in England, during the height of World War II. I grow obsessed with Weil's London days, with the city she loved, the people she met, and with the giant question mark that hangs over her death.

Simone Weil's life was measured not in coffee spoons but train tickets. In June 1940, she and her parents boarded the last train out of Paris, one step ahead of Hitler's troops. For a while she taught philosophy to railroad workers. She spent her most productive years in London, where she'd read and think while riding the Tube.

That is where I am now, too, the Central Line, to be precise, the last leg of my journey that began at St. Pancras. In my pocket is the ingenious Tube map. A triumph of simplicity, it dates to 1931. That's when

Harry Beck, a technical draftsman working for the Underground's signals office, paid attention. Beck knew the old map was flawed. It superimposed the subway lines over a city road map, which confused people, and showed the station distances to scale, which further confused people. No one cared how far apart the stations were or which streets lay above their heads. They wanted to know how to get from one station to another, and where to change lines. Yet they found themselves ensnared in the sort of cognitive trap that Sherlock Holmes warned about: "What was vital was overlaid and hidden by what was irrelevant."

Beck, working in his spare time, created a new map, one modeled on an electrical schematic. Beck's map made reality look a bit neater and simpler than it is, with stations equidistant, and lines meeting at neat 45- or 90-degree angles. The Beck map enthralled the public, and remains essentially unchanged today. Beck succeeded because he paid attention. He thought like a passenger and not just like an engineer.

At each stop, the subway car exhales some passengers, inhales others. In. Out. In. Out. "Please Mind the Gap," chimes the recorded announcement in a chipper English accent. Riding the Tube is a wonderful way to practice paying attention. There's an endless carousel of people to watch: wide-eyed tourists, narrow-eyed bankers, eyeless panhandlers. The air is ripe with linguistic fragments: a French gerund, an Italian participle, an American exclamation. Much competes for your attention, we'd say, but that's not right. It is not a competition so much as a wild collaboration.

I steer my attention, as if guiding a spotlight, and shine it on the woman sitting directly across from me. She is wearing patterned floral pants and a look of fierce concentration as she tackles a crossword puzzle in the tabloid floating on her lap. She nods her head rhythmically while waving her pen like a conductor's baton, or a french fry. She is focused, but is she paying attention? No, Simone Weil would say, she is not.

When the train reaches my stop, Holland Park, I mind the gap, and head for the exit. I am not so much walking as surfing, swept along by the crowd. I try to pay attention but my velocity precludes that. Speed is the enemy of attention. Stepping out of the station, I blink away the sudden sunlight and struggle to regain my bearings.

Transitioning from subterranean to terrestrial life is always tricky. There's that moment of disorientation, of not knowing where you are and, oddly, who you are, either: respectable terrestrial being or sketchy denizen of the underworld? Strangers look at you, or so you imagine, sizing you up, unsure whether you belong here, in the light.

Eager to confirm my surface credentials, I start walking. Where exactly I don't know, but forward momentum is essential. The neighborhood, not far from Notting Hill, is London cozy. I pass cafés where you can spend an entire day nursing a single coffee and bookshops lovingly curated and stubbornly defying the laws of economics by their continued existence. A Pakistani man is selling flowers.

I turn the corner onto Portland Road and walk a few yards until I reach No. 31. A fresh coat of white paint adorns the front door. Otherwise, it is indistinguishable from the other town houses on the block. No sign. No engraved placard. Simone Weil's admirers apparently don't extend to London's guardians of historical sites. I can't say I'm surprised. The "philosopher of margins and paradoxes," as one biographer called her, never expected, nor wanted, fame.

Weil lived on the second floor, which she rented from one Mrs. Francis, a widowed schoolteacher with two small children. Weil took a liking to the boys, helping the younger one, John, with his homework. He'd curl up by the front door, waiting for "Miss Simone."

Weil loved her little room, with its view of tree branches during the day and the stars at night. She loved London, too, and she loved the British, full of humor and kindness. "Especially *kindness,*" she wrote in a letter to her parents, who had sought refuge in New York. "People's nerves are tense, but they control them out of self-respect and a true generosity toward others. . . . I tenderly love this city with its wounds." A wounded soul in a wounded city, I think, as I watch a young couple ring the door next to No. 31, a bottle of wine in hand.

Weil's day job was with the Free French movement, a ragtag group of French exiles working to liberate their nation from Nazi occupation.

Weil earned a reputation as a tireless worker—and serial dreamer. "She was boiling with ideas," recalls her friend Simone Pétrement. Her quixotic schemes included parachuting into occupied France and leading a frontline nursing squad ("women of tenderness and cold resolution"). She labored over the details of her plan, and even bought a parachutist helmet and an aviation manual. Not everyone shared her enthusiasm. "But she is mad!" Charles de Gaulle exclaimed when he read of one of her schemes, none of which came to pass.

When she wasn't dreaming, she was writing, and writing. In just four months she cranked out eight hundred manuscript pages, plus countless letters. She rarely slept more than three hours a night, often working until dawn. The pace took a toll on her already frail health. She ate less, coughed more. Her headaches grew worse. She worried she was going insane.

On April 15, 1943, she failed to show up for work. Worried, a friend hurried to No. 31 Portland Road. He found Weil on the floor, unconscious. She was rushed to Middlesex Hospital, where doctors determined she was suffering from tuberculosis.

She was extremely weak, barely able to lift a spoon, but somehow continued to read and write. The doctors insisted she slow down. She ignored them. "The steadiness of her writing, even in her last letters, is astonishing and presupposes an extraordinary act of will," says Pétrement.

Simone Weil didn't like the dreary urban view from her hospital window. It saddened her. The doctors agreed country air would help, and in August 1943 she was transferred to a sanatorium in the bucolic town of Ashford. She supervised the packing of her most precious books: Plato, Saint John of the Cross, the *Bhagavad Gita*.

At the sanatorium, she remained lucid, her serious eyes as bright and probing as ever. Her physical health deteriorated, though, no doubt exacerbated by her refusal to eat anything substantial. She never told her parents about her illness, an act of either duplicity or compassion, I'm not sure. She ended her last letter to them with a cheery "*Au revoir*, darlings. Heaps and heaps of love." In the evening of August 24, shortly after receiving a visiting colleague, she slipped into a coma. Five hours later Simone Weil was dead. She was thirty-four years old.

The cause of death, concluded the attending physician, was "cardiac failure due to degeneration through starvation." That report caught the notice of a few local papers. "French Professor Starves Herself to Death," said one headline. "Death from Starvation" another. The medical verdict has been disputed ever since. Some say Weil took her own life; others insist she did not.

Seven people attended her funeral, mostly friends and colleagues from the Free French movement. A priest, due to officiate, never showed up. He missed his train, a lapse of attention that Simone Weil, bighearted as she was, surely would have forgiven.

The seven-minute train ride from Wye to Ashford is over in a flash. I couldn't tell you what I saw or heard or thought. My attention needs more than seven minutes to come online. Before I know it we're pulling into Ashford. I exit the station and, after walking a few blocks, join the High Street. It's a pleasant pedestrian walkway lined with cafés and secondhand shops.

Walking farther, savoring the sun's rare appearance, I notice a man paying close attention to something on the pavement. As I inch closer, I see that he has a brush in one hand and is grooming a dog. How cute, I think.

I look more closely, more attentively, and see that it is not a real dog. It is a sand dog. A dog made of sand. So expertly has he fashioned the curve of its tail, the folds of flesh above its snout, the wrinkles etching its neck, that I had mistaken it for a sentient canine.

"How long did that take you?" I ask.

What a silly question, I later realize. Attention is not measured in minutes or hours. (Better fifteen minutes of pure attention, said Weil, than eight hours of lazy, diluted attention.) I could have asked the man other, more salient questions. How did he shut out the distractions around him and focus on the sand dog? How did he persevere when the wind smudged a paw, or the shifting sands collapsed an ear? Yet I did not ask these questions. It's easier to probe the quantity of attention than the quality. We measure what is easiest to measure, not what matters most.

I walk along Canterbury Road, which, despite the fabled name, is a busy thoroughfare with trucks whizzing by. I come to an intersection and spot a sign: "Simone Weil Boulevard." The description on an adjacent placard is insultingly brief, describing her as a "French authoress and philosopher who died in Grosvenor Sanatorium."

I climb a small hill, then enter Bybrook Cemetery. A woman and her elderly mother arrive. They've brought flowers and a wind chime, which they hang from a nearby tree.

"It's beautiful, isn't it?" says the daughter. I'm not sure if she's referring to the musical chime or the flowers or the azure sky or perhaps the way one can find joy in the most unexpected of places, even a cemetery, if one pays close enough attention. No matter. It is the quality of our attention, not its object, that counts.

A trim man carrying more flowers arrives. Her father, I presume. They all sit on the ground in front of a grave marker and enjoy an impromptu picnic.

There's a story here, and I know it is not a happy one. How unhappy I don't learn until later when, after they'd left, I approach the grave site. Only then do I notice how small it is and how the tombstone is fashioned in the shape of a teddy bear. Many physical objects trigger strong emotions, but nothing, absolutely nothing, tears a heart asunder more quickly and thoroughly than a tombstone shaped like a teddy bear.

I find Simone Weil without looking for her. Strolling through the cemetery grounds, I look up and there she is.

The plot is well maintained, though I notice a few flowers are dying and the wind has toppled a small plastic flowerpot. Hers is a simple tombstone, indistinguishable from the others except the dates are in French. *3 Février 1909, 24 Août 1943.*

Resting on the ground is a framed photograph of Weil. It's the same one I had seen before. The same unruly hair and chunky glasses and knowing eyes. And something else, something I had missed before: a slight arcing of the lips into the suggestion of a smile. What explains this proto-smile? I wonder. Perhaps the photographer had cracked a joke, or perhaps Weil had just received word of her acceptance to the prestigious École Normale.

There's another possible explanation. Perhaps the photographer had captured Simone Weil in a moment of extreme attention, of flow, and her reaction, the natural and indeed only reaction to such a state, was to forget for a moment the torturous headaches and the genius brother and the coming war, and smile.

We lose objects suddenly but experience the loss gradually. It takes time to accept that your car keys or wallet or heart is not merely misplaced but has crossed that invisible yet no less precipitous line that separates objects we possess from objects we once possessed. Nonexistence terrifies us. It takes time to register.

"Loss" is a short but menacing word. The Napoleon of nouns. Unless preceded by "weight," it is almost always negative. That's why we don't just experience a loss. We *suffer* a loss. Someone struggling, in work or love, is said to be "lost." When retracing the arc of a nation, or a life, historians demarcate a specific point in time beyond which "all was lost."

Losses come in different sizes, though not in small. They start at medium and ascend from there. They come in different flavors, too. Some losses are painful, some devastating, some merely inconvenient. A few are ironic. Losing a notebook while writing a chapter about paying attention, for instance.

I loved that notebook. I still recall when I first laid eyes on it. It was at a chic little stationery store in Baltimore on a warm spring day. I was drawn to its clean aesthetics and muted colors, its robust cover, so solid and reassuring, the soft-to-the-touch pages complemented with not one but three—three!—of those little ribbons that mark your place.

My reaction to losing the notebook is disproportionate. I know this intellectually, but to know something intellectually only is not to know it at all. I take a deep breath and examine my reaction. Where is it coming from? I've lost things before and have not reacted this way. In college, I once lost an entire week and hardly missed a beat. Why has this one missing notebook tipped me into a tailspin?

Because it was not just a notebook. Thoughts committed to paper represent a record of our mind at its most attentive. These rapt moments are fragile things, sand dogs on High Street, and, once lost, nearly impossible to recover. It's easier to retrieve a lost diamond than a lost thought. Which is why I must—*must!*—find my notebook and restore the past.

A surefire way to increase your fondness for something, anything, is to lose it. As my search turns up dry, the missing notebook grows not only in aesthetic excellence but editorial brilliance as well. By day two of my search, I'm convinced the thoughts contained within its covers, recorded during my trip to England, are unequaled in astuteness and originality. By day four, I declare the notebook the Most Precious Notebook in the World. Ever. More precious than Da Vinci's Codex Leicester or Hemingway's cahiers.

I look in the obvious places (cabinets, bookshelves) and the less obvious ones, too (refrigerator, litter box). Nothing. I double and triple my efforts. I retrace my steps. I look in the same desk drawer, three, four, five times.

My behavior alarms the dog and freaks out the cat, who has, wisely, gone to ground. My daughter declares the entire episode "literally the most annoying thing in the world."

It is not only the notebook's absence that smarts but the act of losing it, and what that lapse of attention says about me. Nothing good, I've decided. (There's a word for people who chronically lose things: losers. The most damning of labels.) The memoirist Mary Karr lost a notebook recently but had the good editorial sense to do so on a boat captained by a sultry Greek named Dionisos and his "freewheeling, tequila-soaked heart." I lost mine in the kitchen while putting away boxes of Ellio's frozen pizza and Honey Nut Cheerios. No tequila. No Dionisos. Only regret and self-loathing.

At a loss (*that* word again), I turn to Simone. Desperate times, I tell myself, opening one of her books. She looks at my predicament and offers a simple diagnosis: I don't really want to find my notebook. I want to possess it. I am consumed with desire, and desire is incompatible with attention. To desire something is to want something from it, and that clouds our vision.

We think the problem rests with the object of our desire when in reality it is the subject—the "I"—that is the problem. It might appear that by craving something you are paying attention to it, but this is an illusion. You are engrossed in your *desire* for the object, not the object itself. A heroin addict doesn't crave heroin. He craves the experience of having heroin, and the concomitant relief of not *not* having heroin. Freedom from mental disturbance, *ataraxia*, is what he wants.

I return to Simone. "What could be more stupid than to tighten up our muscles and set our jaws about virtue, or poetry, or the solution of a problem? Attention is something quite different."

I loosen my muscles and turn the page.

"The cause is always that we have wanted to be too active; we have wanted to carry out a search."

This confounds me. Annoys me, too. Of course I want to carry out a search, Simone! How else am I going to find my notebook but by searching for it?

I take a deep breath and read on. It's important, Weil continues, "to draw back before the object we are pursuing. Only an indirect method is effective. We do nothing if we have not first drawn back."

I draw back, retreating to the basement and the large-screen TV that beckons like a truckload of opium. Not good. I've drawn back too far. I have succumbed to resignation. Despair in disguise.

My problem, says Weil, is that I have yoked action to results. Life doesn't work that way, nor does attention. An attentive life is a risky one. Results are not guaranteed. We don't know where our attention will lead, if anywhere. Pure attention, the kind Weil advocated, is untainted by external motives such as impressing your friends or advancing your career. The person who applies his full attention to something—

anything—makes progress "even if his effort produces no visible fruit," says Weil.

She's right, I know, but we live in a world that celebrates visible fruit. The more visible and the fruitier the better. Is it possible to live like Simone Weil, invested in the moment yet indifferent about future rewards? Can I raise my daughter, lovingly and attentively, and not care whether she pursues a career as a neurosurgeon or as a barista? Can I enter a writing contest and not care if I win? Can I let my notebook go?

I pause the insanity and gain a speck of perspective. I lost a notebook. Big deal. Hemingway lost an entire collection of short stories. Or, to be precise, Hemingway's wife, Hadley Richardson, lost an entire collection of Hemingway's short stories. It was 1922 and she was en route from Paris to Switzerland to meet her husband. She had just boarded the train at Gare de Lyon station, but she had a few minutes before it departed so she decided to buy a bottle of mineral water. When she returned to the train, the suitcase—and Hemingway's manuscript—were gone.

Hemingway is known for his minimalism, but this was too much even for him. He fell into a funk. Yet, in the end, Ernest persevered, and became Hemingway.

A few years earlier, a young British officer named T. E. Lawrence was changing trains in Reading, England, when he lost the manuscript of his memoir, *Seven Pillars of Wisdom*. Handwritten, it was his only copy.

Lawrence had survived the Arab revolt of 1916 and the battle of Aqaba, traveled by camel across the Sinai Desert, yet the lost manuscript nearly did him in. Eventually, he rallied, holing up in an unheated Westminster loft and rewriting the book from memory.

I read these tales of lost manuscripts and recall Simone Weil's words. "We do not obtain the most precious gifts by going in search of them but by waiting for them." She's right. I must wait.

If this book were a Steven Spielberg movie, this would be the moment when I miraculously find my lost notebook and realize it was right under my nose the whole time. Sadly, this book is not a Spielberg movie. Its fealty lies with the truth, not the box office, and the truth is I never did find my notebook. I will never know what wisdom it may or may not have contained. So I let it be. I let it go.

Is this progress? Perhaps, but that's not a word Simone Weil used often. There is no progress to make, no prizes to win. There is only waiting.

And so I wait, willingly and with more patience than I imagined possible, for waiting is its own reward.

8.

How to Fight like Gandhi

11:02 a.m. At Baroda House, headquarters of India's Northern Railways. Attempting to obtain a ticket on the Yoga Express, from New Delhi to Ahmedabad. Odds of success: not good.

When I first heard of the Yoga Express, I knew I had to ride it, and was prepared to contort myself to get a ticket. To be clear: my yoga practice is strictly theoretical. "Yoga Express" appealed to me. It suggests a fast track to enlightenment. Then there is the train's destination: Ahmedabad, the city where Mahatma Gandhi, my philosopher-hero, established his first ashram on Indian soil and from where he launched his famous Salt March, a pivotal moment in the struggle for India's independence.

A train journey of a thousand miles begins with a single reservation. Obtaining one on Indian Railways is a process that, since its inception in 1853, has meant enduring hellish queues and navigating a bureaucratic maze. In the digital age, hell has migrated online. It takes me a good three hours to create an account, only to discover the Yoga Express is fully booked. I add my name to the wait list and download an app to track my progress. I quickly move up from number 15 to 8 and then number 1. Promising.

My friend Kailash consults a travel agent who says, "No problem." A friend of his who works for Indian Railways also says, "No problem." The obvious conclusion: big problem. In India, nothing is final until it's final, and not even then. Every ending is a beginning. Every finale contains a tacit *to be continued.*

Number one sounds impressive, I realize. But this is India, a country that invented the concept of zero and is on speaking terms with infinity. What is a number? It is maya, illusion. As the ancient Stoics observed, if you're drowning it matters not whether you're one hundred feet underwater or one foot. Drowning is drowning. The wait list is the wait list.

"Why don't you fly to Ahmedabad?" asks Kailash. It's quicker and easier than the train, and only slightly more expensive.

He's right, but I cannot fly. Gandhi didn't fly. Not once. He took trains, and so will I. Gandhi firmly believed the means matter more than the ends. Not whether you win or lose but how you fight. Not where you go but how you get there. I will not fly. I will take a train. I will take the Yoga Express.

The situation, I decide, calls for drastic, analog measures. Before long, I am in the office of a railway official, one Mr. Singh, a trim, balding man wearing wire-rimmed glasses and a sour expression. I hurriedly explain my predicament. Can he help?

It's a rhetorical question. I know Mr. Singh can help. In India, power is directly proportionate to office size. Mr. Singh is clearly a man of power. I count no fewer than three separate sitting areas; the ceiling touches the heavens. With a stroke of his pen, a click of his keyboard, he could secure me a seat on the Yoga Express.

"It's complicated," he says, as if we were discussing integral calculus and not a train reservation. A certain number of seats are set aside for VIPs, he explains. "And VVIPs, too," he adds.

I am tempted to resort to violence, but restrain myself. Gandhi would not approve. Violence harms the perpetrator as well as the victim, he said, and I don't want to harm myself, not yet.

I try charm instead. I explain my lifelong fascination with Gandhiji, using the honorific suffix, and how I believe his ideas remain relevant today.

The pain on Mr. Singh's face grows. I can see him weighing his options: risk disappointing a foreigner, a guest (one with a keen interest in Gandhiji, no less), or risk the wrath of a member of Parliament or some other uppity bigwig.

I never stood a chance. Go to the Foreign Quota Office at New Delhi Railway Station, he says. They can help, he assures me. We both know they cannot.

I thank Mr. Singh for his time, and walk down the hallway to the thick sludge of particles that passes for air in New Delhi. My quest for a seat on the Yoga Express has ended. Or, to put it in Indian terms, it has begun.

I am walking to the subway station with my friend Kailash. The air is fresh today, he tells me, freshness being relative in this, one of the world's most polluted cities. The air quality is in the "hazardous range," though slightly less hazardous than yesterday.

We pass two men sweeping the street with rattan brooms, kicking up a cloud of dust, as if Delhi needed more of that.

"Better wear your mask," says Kailash.

I reach into my pocket and fumble for the flimsy black-and-gray cloth mask that, the clerk assured me, would protect my lungs. It cost the equivalent of $1.50. I am skeptical.

Gandhi would be alarmed but not surprised by the sorry state of India's alleged air. More than a century ago, he warned of the dangers of industrialization. India's future, he said, lies with her villages, not her cities. From a coldly economic sense, he was wrong. India's cities are booming, its villages impoverished. You can breathe in the villages, though.

We pass a small group spread across a blanket, right on the sidewalk. A girl, not more than six years old, is looking at a book. She is barefoot and covered in a layer of grime. Two young adults are pointing to the book and speaking to her in Hindi.

"Tutors," explains Kailash. The girl is a beggar. She's never seen the inside of a school, so these volunteers bring the school to her. Gandhi would approve of this selfless act. That's the thing about India. Just when you're ready to write it off you stumble across unexpected kindness and your faith is restored.

We step into a Delhi Metro station. It's like entering another world. Everything is shiny and new and clean. "Delhi's lifeline," Kailash says proudly. We're about to step onto a departing train but I hesitate. It's awfully crowded. Should we wait for the next car?

"No," says Kailash. "It will be just as crowded. Office hours."

I point out that today is Sunday.

"India," says Kailash, as if that explains all, which it does.

We squeeze on board, and I hear the chipper words I haven't heard since London. "Please Mind the Gap." In India, the gaps are wider and more treacherous. Extra mindfulness is required.

Mohandas K. Gandhi wasn't ambivalent about much. Except trains. When two American women asked him if it's true he opposed railways, he replied, "It is and it is not."

On the one hand, Gandhi saw the railroad as just another way for Britain to keep India under her thumb. And, like other philosophers I've encountered, he was wary of excessive speed. "Is the world any the better for quick instruments of locomotion?" he asked. "How do these instruments advance man's spiritual progress? Do they not in the last resort hamper it?" Yet it was his travels by rail, almost always in third class, that enabled him to crisscross India, touching lives and rallying masses.

One train journey changed Gandhi's life, and the course of history. It was 1893. Gandhi had arrived in South Africa only a week earlier. His law firm dispatched him from Durban to Pretoria to handle an important case. They booked him a first-class ticket for the overnight journey. When the train reached Maritzburg station, a white passenger entered the compartment, took one look at Gandhi, and summoned the conductor, who insisted Gandhi move to third class.

"But I have a first-class ticket," Gandhi said.

"That doesn't matter," replied the conductor. No "coloreds." Gandhi refused to leave. A policeman removed him from the train.

It was a bitterly cold night. Gandhi's overcoat was in his luggage, which he was too proud to request. So he shivered, and pondered. Should he retreat to India or remain in South Africa and fight injustices like the one he had just experienced?

By dawn, he had his answer: "It would be cowardice to run back to India without fulfilling my obligation. The hardship to which I was subjected was superficial—only a symptom of the deep disease of color prejudice. I should try, if possible, to root out the disease and suffer hardships in the process." In that moment, he chose a path, one that, despite bumps and swerves and occasional collisions, he remained on for the rest of his days.

Decades later, when the American evangelist John Mott asked Gandhi to describe the most creative experiences of his life, he pointed to the train incident in South Africa. It's telling he equated a moment of quiet resolve with creativity. Some biographers have noted Gandhi's lack of interest in the arts. He rarely read a novel, or went to the theater or an art gallery. He did not possess Thoreau's eye for beauty, or Schopenhauer's ear for music. In London, he enrolled in a dance class but soon discovered he had no rhythm.

It would be a mistake to conclude Gandhi was not creative. He was, only not in the usual way. Gandhi's paintbrush was his resolve, his canvas the human heart. "Real beauty," he said, "is doing good against evil." All violence represents a failure of imagination. Nonviolence demands creativity. Gandhi was always searching for new, innovative ways to fight.

We exit the subway station and are promptly lost. Kailash asks a rickshaw *wallah* for directions but walks away unsatisfied. We stroll a few more yards and find a policeman. He is wearing a mask, a serious one with vents. Mine doesn't have vents. I calculate the damage being done to my lungs while Kailash asks the policeman for directions.

The policeman suggests a direction opposite to the rickshaw *wallah*'s. Kailash, still not satisfied, asks a third person for directions. "I never ask one person," he explains. "I always ask two or three." Life in India demands constant triangulation. Gandhi, great experimenter that he was, knew this better than most.

We enter the grounds of the old Birla House, as close to home as the peripatetic Gandhi had. The house—more of a compound—belonged to a friend, the wealthy industrialist G. D. Birla.

A familiar peace descends on me. I've been here before many times, though I have trouble finding it each time. I am drawn to it, as I am to Gandhi, for reasons I can't articulate. I like the wide expanse of lawn, the white stone markers, shaped like feet, Gandhi's feet, and the verandas where I can picture the Mahatma, a young seventy-eight years old, wearing his big straw hat and white dhoti, hunched over a letter he was writing or playing with one of his grandchildren or helping steer the shaky ship that was infant India.

Some places are sanctified by acts of superhuman achievement—the Bodhi tree under which the Buddha achieved enlightenment, for instance—while others are consecrated by terrible acts of violence. Gettysburg. Normandy. Birla House falls into the latter category. Here Gandhi took his last step, breathed his last breath.

On the last day of his life, Mahatma Gandhi woke at 3:30 a.m., as he always did. He brushed his teeth, using a simple twig, like most Indians. It was a cold January morning. His grandniece and assistant, Manu, wrapped him in a shawl, covering his bony shoulders. He drank a glass of lemon and honey followed by his daily serving of orange juice. His diet was simple, and salubrious. He wanted to live a long life—to the age of 125, he said—and he wanted to purify himself. The fight is only as effective as the fighter. "How can a damp matchstick kindle a log of wood?" he said.

Kailash often accompanies me to Birla House. He is, as I said, a friend, but that wasn't always the case. For a while, Kailash was my servant.

I realize those words sound harsh to Western ears, but it's true; "servant" is what others called Kailash, and what he called himself.

We met many years ago, in 1993. I had just arrived in India, as NPR's Delhi correspondent. Everything about it was frenzied and raw. I needed a place to live, but the apartments I saw were either too pricey or too noisy or prone to attack by flying cockroaches the size of small birds.

Finally I found a flat with heavy wooden doors and a terrace that overlooked a pleasant street. The landlord, an imperious man with tufts of wiry black hair sprouting from his left ear, pointed out the apartment's features, including Western-style toilets, air-conditioning, and, he added matter-of-factly, a "servant."

A few days later, the servant loped upstairs and reported for duty. He was skinny, alarmingly so, with mahogany skin and sharp features. His name was Kailash, and he was eleven years old. I was prepared for cultural differences in India, but not this. I started downstairs to confront the landlord, but Kailash stopped me. Stay, he said or, rather, gestured; he didn't speak a word of English. I rationalized if Kailash, an orphan, didn't work for me, he'd work for someone else, and who knows how that person would treat him? Washing my hands of Kailash seemed like a cop-out.

And so every afternoon Kailash climbed the stairs and knocked on my door. He was, truth be told, not much of a cleaner: he didn't remove the dirt; he just rearranged it. But he was naturally kind, honest, and, it turned out, a wizard with temperamental laptops and printers.

Kailash picked up English by eavesdropping on me and my wife. Before long he was parroting colloquialisms like "I'm history" and "Get outta here." Over time, he told us his story: how his parents died years ago, how much he loved cricket, and how the landlord beat him if he didn't cook the chapatis properly.

I'm not sure when we decided to help, but it didn't cost much to hire a tutor, and soon Kailash was in school for the first time in years. Later, when we moved to another apartment, Kailash moved with us. He was, technically, still our employee, but at some point he began referring to us as his parents. This made me uneasy, yet there was no denying our new roles.

I always imagined my relationship with Kailash would follow a linear, screenplay trajectory. Orphaned Indian boy has fateful meeting with bighearted American; boy struggles to overcome disadvantaged youth; boy perseveres and is eternally grateful for bighearted American's help. But more than a decade after I left India, Kailash and I were stuck in the second act.

Thanks to my quarterly wire transfers, Kailash lived in a tiny apartment in Delhi that was too cold in the winter and too hot in the summer. His main companion was a Pomeranian named Envy. When he told me he had turned down a job serving tea, an opportunity he would have jumped at before meeting me, I was angry but not surprised. I had raised his expectations, dangerous in a country of more than a billion restive souls.

My Indian friends watched from the sidelines, skeptical of my efforts. "You're thinking like an American," they said, as if it were a mental illness. "Kailash is from a lower class, a lower *caste*. He can only go so far. Face the facts."

They're right, I told myself, trying to come to terms with the possibility that this Indian orphan and I would be tethered for life. Yet I couldn't shake the naïve idea that one day Kailash would float free into a life of his own making.

And he has. The trajectory proved more jagged than the Hollywood version, but the ending just as happy. Kailash now lives in a ramshackle neighborhood with middle-class aspirations. He is a husband, and a father. A landlord, too. He owns a two-story building. He and his family live on the top floor. On the ground floor he's opened a small stationery store called Emma's, named after his daughter. He sells notebooks and pens and Gandhi wallets. Kailash and I are no longer tethered financially. Our bond is made of sturdier stuff.

On this, an unseasonably warm December day, we walk under a white marble colonnade that leads to the spot where Gandhi died.

Kailash knows of my Gandhi obsession. He finds it touching and, I suspect, a bit odd. Most Indians know Gandhi the way most Americans know George Washington: a hazy father figure whose name is uttered with reverence and whose image graces the money in their wallet.

As we pause for a moment, cooling off and absorbing the quiet beauty of Birla House, Kailash turns and asks, "Why do you like Gandhiji so much?"

I'm not sure how to answer. I concede my interest in Gandhi makes little sense. I am not Indian. I am not an ascetic. I do practice nonviolence, but inconsistently, and with passive-aggressive undertones. Gandhi was a leader of his people. I lead no one, not even my dog, Parker, who answers to a higher power: food. Gandhi's worldly possessions, at the time of his death, could fit in a small shoulder bag. Mine require considerably more space, and I'm still shopping. Yet Gandhi spoke to me, and I listened.

During my three years living in India, Gandhi seeped into my brain. How could he not? His image, if not his ideas, was everywhere: on the money, in office buildings. Even the phone company's offices featured a photo of Gandhi using a telephone, the enormous receiver dwarfing his small head.

Mohandas K. Gandhi was many things: barrister, vegetarian, sadhu, experimenter, writer, father of a nation, friend of all, enemy of none, manual laborer, failed dancer, stretcher-bearer, meditator, mediator, gadfly, teacher, student, ex-convict, humorist, walker, tailor, timekeeper, rabble-rouser. Most of all, he was a fighter. Gandhi fought the British and he fought bigotry, among foreigners and among his own people. He fought to be heard. His biggest fight, though, was the fight to change the way we fight.

Eventually, yes, Gandhi imagined a world without violence, but he was realistic enough to know that was unlikely to happen soon. In the meantime, we must learn how to fight better.

Think of the married couple that boasts how they "never fight." When you hear of their divorce, you're not surprised. Fighting, done properly, is productive. Both sides can arrive not only at a win-win solution but something more: a solution that neither would have found had they not fought in the first place. Imagine a soccer match that ends in a tie but with the field greener and healthier than before the game. Gandhi saw fighting not as a necessary evil but as a necessary good. Provided we fight well.

When the American journalist and biographer Louis Fischer met Gandhi at his ashram, he was surprised to find a fit, barrel-chested man, with "long, thin muscular legs" and who appeared much taller than his five feet, five inches. He "looked very male and had a man's steel strength of body and will," wrote Fisher.

Gandhi was obsessed with masculinity. Words like "manliness" and "strength" and "courage" appear frequently in his writing. Even his complaints about Indian Railways were couched in terms of emasculation. "That we tamely put up with the hardships of railway traveling is a sign of our unmanliness."

The British, Gandhi believed, had emasculated India. He was determined to "remasculate" it, though he had a different kind of masculinity in mind: one deriving its strength not from violence but its opposite.

Gandhi considered it "unmanly" to obey unjust laws. Those laws must be resisted and with great force. Nonviolent force. This, he said, demands genuine courage. "What do you think? Wherein is courage required—in blowing others to pieces from behind a cannon, or with a smiling face to approach a cannon and be blown to pieces? Believe me, that a man devoid of courage and manhood can never be a passive resister."

Gandhi abhorred violence, but there was something he hated even more: cowardice. Given a choice between the two, he preferred violence. "A coward is less than a man." Thus Gandhi's true objective: reclaiming his nation's lost virility, and on its own terms. Do that, he believed, and freedom would follow.

I am no fighter. I avoid physical confrontations. My one fistfight took place at age seventeen at 2:00 a.m. at a Howard Johnson's parking lot in suburban Baltimore and ended with a broken nose. Mine. I shy away from more quotidian confrontations, too: calling an airline to change a flight, or a restaurant to inform them I'm running a few minutes late for my 8:00 p.m. reservation and could they please if it's not too much trouble hold the table for me?

I realize most people, most *normal* people, don't consider these sorts of everyday interactions confrontational. I do, and avoid them whenever possible. Ditto the confrontations (*anticipated* confrontations) I avoid with editors, family, neighbors, and fellow subway passengers. I'm not sure where and why I acquired this avoidance strategy, but it has not served me well. By avoiding small confrontations today, I set myself up for much larger ones tomorrow. I hoped a world-class confronter like Gandhi could show me another way.

Shortly after I moved to India, I began to read Gandhi, and about Gandhi. A handful of books soon grew into a bookcase's worth. I visited Gandhi museums and Gandhi ashrams. I took college courses on Gandhi. I bought a Gandhi wallet and a Gandhi T-shirt and Gandhi underwear, the least violent pair of boxer briefs I've ever owned. One day, while in Delhi, I had lunch with Gandhi's grandson Rajmohan, an erudite and kind man, now elderly himself. As we nibbled on naan and chutney, I detected traces of the Mahatma: the way Rajmohan's jawline angled a certain way, the way his eyes flashed, slightly askance and mischievous.

We don't admire the gods. We might revere them or fear them, but we don't admire them. We admire mortals, better versions of ourselves. Gandhi was no god. No saint, either. At age twelve, he stole money from his parents and brother to buy cigarettes. He'd sneak off to eat meat (forbidden among his caste), chewing on goat flesh along the river with a friend who, like Gandhi, was convinced it was the Englishman's carnivorous diet that made him strong.

At the young age of thirteen, Gandhi was married. He was not a good husband. He'd lash out in jealous rages against his wife, Kasturba. Once, he threatened to expel her from the house unless she did certain household chores. "Have you no shame?" she sobbed. "Where am I to go?"

The father of the nation was a lousy father to his children. In the political arena, too, he made mistakes. "My Himalayan blunder," he called one such bungled campaign. As for his experiments, some went too far. At age seventy-five, he decided to test his vow of celibacy by sleeping naked with young women, including his grandniece Manu.

Yet here was a man who owned his shortcomings. Here was a man not afraid to change his mind. Here was a man who attracted "cranks, faddists, and madmen" and embraced them all. Here was a man who overcame terrible shyness and self-doubt to lead a nation. Here was a man willing to die, but not kill, for a cause. Here was a man who stared down an empire, and won. Here was a man—not a god or a saint but a flesh-and-blood man—who showed the world what a good fight looks like.

Gandhi was spiritually omnivorous. He sampled many religious delicacies, from Christianity to Islam, but it was the Hindu *Bhagavad Gita* that reliably satisfied his hunger.

Gandhi first encountered the spiritual poem while studying law in London. Two English Theosophists asked Gandhi about the scripture. Embarrassed, he admitted he hadn't read it. So, together, the three of them read Edwin Arnold's English translation. Gandhi traveled west to find the East.

Gandhi grew to love his "Mother Gita," as he called the spiritual poem. It was his inspiration, and his consolation. "When doubts haunt me, when disappointments stare me in the face, and I see not one ray of hope on the horizon, I turn to the *Bhagavad Gita,* and find a verse to comfort me; and I immediately begin to smile in the midst of overwhelming sorrow."

The storyline of the *Gita* is simple. Prince Arjuna, a great warrior, is poised for battle. But he's lost his nerve. Not only is he weary of bloodshed but he's discovered the opposing army includes soldiers from his own clan, as well as beloved friends and revered teachers. How can he fight them? Lord Krishna, disguised as Arjuna's charioteer, counsels him. The story unfolds as a dialogue between them.

The conventional interpretation of the *Gita* is that it's an exhortation to duty, even violence, if necessary. After all (spoiler alert!), Krishna ultimately convinces Arjuna to wage war against his own kin.

Gandhi read it differently. The *Gita,* he said, is an allegory, one that depicts "what takes place in the heart of every human being today." The true battlefield lies within. Arjuna's struggle is not with the enemy but with himself. Does he succumb to his baser instincts or rise to a higher plane? The *Gita*, Gandhi concluded, is a disguised ode to nonviolence.

Another tenet of the *Gita* is nonattachment to results. As Lord Krishna, an incarnation of God, tells Arjuna: "You have the right to work, but never to the fruit of work. You should never engage in action for the sake of reward, nor should you long for inaction." Sever work from outcome, the *Gita* teaches. Invest 100 percent effort into every endeavor and precisely zero percent into the results.

Gandhi summed up this outlook in a single word: "desirelessness." It is not an invitation to indolence. The karma yogi is a person of action. She is doing *a lot,* except worrying about results.

This is not our way. We are results-oriented. Fitness trainers, business consultants, doctors, colleges, dry cleaners, recovery programs, dieticians, financial advisors. They, and many others, promise results. We might question their ability to deliver results, but rarely do we question the underlying assumption that being results-oriented is good.

Gandhi was not results-oriented. He was process-oriented. He aimed not for Indian independence but for an India worthy of independence. Once this occurred, her freedom would arrive naturally, like a ripe mango falling from a tree. Gandhi didn't fight to win. He fought to fight the best fight he was capable of fighting. The irony is that this process-oriented approach produces better results than a results-oriented one.

My heroic efforts to secure a seat on the Yoga Express continue to prove futile. I am still number one on the wait list. Still drowning. I refresh the app on my phone. Nothing. I push it again and again, like one of those rats pulling a lever, hoping for a morsel. Nothing.

What would Gandhi do? He would fight. He *did* fight. Appalled by conditions in third class, he made a "perfect nuisance" of himself. He complained to Indian Railways about the "evil-looking" restrooms and the "dirty looking" refreshments and the so-called tea, "tannin-water with filthy sugar and a whitish looking liquid miscalled milk which gave this water a muddy appearance." He wrote to managers and directors and managing directors. He wrote to newspapers.

So I persist, as Gandhi surely would. I hop in a taxi and crawl across town. Delhi traffic is heavy today, a statement as self-evident as "the air is polluted today" or "the subway is crowded today." A certain unhappy consistency undergirds the apparent randomness of India.

I arrive at the station to the usual controlled anarchy, as reliable as the heavy traffic and the dirty air. Passing through a perfunctory security checkpoint, I set off the metal detector. The guard waves me through. He waves with his eyes, lest he overexert himself.

I swim upstream against a river of humanity, then climb a flight of stairs. A sign outside an office reads: "International Tourist Bureau. Rail Reservation for Foreign Tourists." I take a seat, joining the bedraggled backpackers.

When I'm called to the counter, I flash my wait-list form as if it were a good report card or winning lottery ticket.

"I'm number one," I say.

"I can see that," says the man behind the counter, unimpressed.

Mr. Roy is a compact, no-nonsense man. He tells me it's festival season, failing to add that, in India, home to a handful of major religions and countless minor ones, it is always festival season.

There is, he informs me, one second-class ticket available on another train, the Rajdhani Express. "A very good train," Mr. Roy assures me.

I'm sure it is. It is not, however, the Yoga Express, and it is the Yoga Express I have my heart set on.

"What do you want to do, Mr. Eric?" asks Mr. Roy, gesturing toward the waiting backpackers, as if to say, "You're not the only person in this land of a billion souls."

I am stuck.

"Well?" says Mr. Roy, irritation seeping into his voice. "Do you want the ticket?"

"Please give me a second. I'm thinking."

"Thinking is very good, Mr. Eric, but please be thinking quickly."

When Gandhi said, "I represent no new truths," he wasn't merely being humble. He didn't invent the concept of *ahimsa*, or nonviolence. It is thousands of years old. In the sixth century BC, Mahavira, a spiritual leader of the Jain religion, implored his followers not to "injure, abuse, oppress, enslave, insult, torment, torture, or kill any creature or living being."

Gandhi knew about the Jains. They were regular visitors at his childhood home. One of his spiritual mentors was Jain. Gandhi also read Tolstoy on love and Thoreau on civil disobedience. Nonviolence wasn't new, but Gandhi's application of it was. What had been reduced to a dietary rule in India, vegetarianism, "emerged from Gandhi's hands as a weapon—a universal weapon—to fight oppression," explains his grandson Rajmohan Gandhi.

At first Gandhi called his new technique "passive resistance" but soon he realized he needed another name. There was nothing passive about it, or about him. Gandhi was always doing *something*: walking, praying, planning, holding meetings, answering correspondence, spinning khadi cloth. Even Gandhi's thinking had a kinetic quality, reflected in his alert eyes and expressive face—a "twinkling mirror," said those who met him. When a journalist pressed Gandhi for a précis of his philosophy, he struggled to answer before saying: "I am not built for academic writings. Action is my domain."

Gandhi eventually settled on a new name for his new type of nonviolent resistance: *satyagraha*. *Satya* is Sanskrit for "truth"; *agraha* means "firmness" or "holding firmly." Truth Force (or "Soul Force," as it is sometimes translated). Yes, this was what Gandhi had in mind. There was nothing passive or squishy about it. It was active, "the greatest and most active force in the world." The *satyagrahi*, or nonviolent resister, is even more active than an armed soldier—and more courageous. It takes no great bravery, or intelligence, to pull a trigger, Gandhi said. Only the truly courageous suffer voluntarily, to change a human heart. Gandhi's soldiers, like soldiers everywhere, were willing to die for their cause. Unlike most soldiers, they were not willing to kill for it.

"These things happen in a revolution," Lenin reportedly said in defense of the mass executions he ordered. Not in Gandhi's revolution. He'd rather see India remain shackled to Britain than gain her independence through bloody means. No man, said Gandhi, "takes another down a pit without descending into it himself." When we brutalize others, we brutalize ourselves. This is why most revolutions fail in the end. Confusing means and ends, they devour themselves. For Gandhi, the ends never justified the means. The means *were* the ends. "Impure means result in impure ends. We reap exactly as we sow." Just as you can't grow a rosebush on toxic soil, you can't grow a peaceful nation on bloody ground.

Like Rousseau, Gandhi was a lifelong walker. Unlike Rousseau, his strides were quick and purposeful. The determined walk of protest. One morning in 1930, Gandhi and eighty of his followers set out from his ashram in Ahmedabad, heading south, toward the sea. They covered twelve miles a day, sometimes more. By the time they reached the coast, the eighty followers had swelled to several thousand. They watched as Gandhi bathed in the Arabian Sea, then scooped up a handful of salt from the natural deposits, in blatant violation of British law. The great Salt March marked a turning point on the road to independence. Gandhi had walked into the hearts of sympathetic people everywhere.

Shortly after, Gandhi announced his intention to raid the Dharasana Salt Works, near Bombay. Webb Miller, a correspondent for United Press International, witnessed the confrontation firsthand. He watched as Gandhi's followers approached the stockpile of salt in silence. The police were waiting for them.

> The officers ordered them to retreat but they continued to step forward. Suddenly, at a word of command, scores of native policemen rushed upon the advancing marchers and rained blows on their heads with their steel-shod lathis. Not one of the marchers even raised an arm to fend off the blows. They went down like ten-pins.

> From where I stood I heard the sickening whack of the clubs on unprotected skulls. Those struck down fell sprawling, unconscious or writhing with fractured skulls or broken shoulders. The survivors, without breaking ranks, silently and doggedly marched on until struck down.

As he watched the horrific scene unfold, Miller wrestled with conflicting feelings. “The western mind finds it difficult to grasp the idea of nonresistance. I felt an indefinable sense of helpless rage and loathing, almost as much against the men who were submitting unresistingly to being beaten as against the police wielding the clubs.”

Like Miller, you might wonder: What was wrong with the Gandhians? Why didn’t they fight back?

They did, Gandhi would reply, only nonviolently. They confronted the police with their presence and their peaceful intentions. Had they fought back physically, they would have provoked more anger from the police—anger, in their minds, now justified. Gandhi found such escalation silly. Any victory earned through violent means is illusory; it only postpones the arrival of the next bloody chapter.

It takes time to soften hearts. Progress isn’t always visible to the naked eye. After the raid on the salt works, and the brutal response, nothing appeared to have changed. India was still a British colony. Yet something was different. Britain had lost the moral high ground, as well as her appetite to bloody those who steadfastly refused to answer hate with hate.

Gandhi never saw nonviolence as a tactic, “a garment to be put on and off at will.” It is a principle, a law as inviolable as the law of gravity. If he’s right, then we’d expect nonviolent resistance to succeed everywhere, and at all times, just as gravity works whether you’re living in London or Tokyo, in the eighteenth century or the twenty-first. Does it, or was Gandhi a one-off, a fluke?

In 1959, Martin Luther King Jr. traveled to India and met with Gandhians, including member of the Mahatma’s family. The trip made a deep impression on King and, a few years later, he deployed the “stern love” of nonviolent resistance in the civil rights movement. Nonviolence has succeeded elsewhere, too: in the Philippines in the 1980s, and in Eastern Europe in the early 1990s. In a comprehensive study of some three hundred nonviolent movements, researchers Erica Chenoweth and Maria Stephan found the strategy worked more than half the time (and was partially successful in another quarter of the cases they studied).

One obvious case where nonviolence didn't work, where it *couldn't* work, is with Adolf Hitler. In 1939 and 1940, Gandhi wrote a series of letters to Hitler, urging him to take the path of peace. Shortly afterward, in what is surely one of history's most wrongheaded statements, Gandhi said: "I do not believe Herr Hitler to be as bad as he is portrayed." Even after World War II, when the enormity of the Holocaust became known, Gandhi suggested the Jews "should have offered themselves to the butcher's knife. They should have thrown themselves from the sea into the cliffs. . . . It would have aroused the world and the people of Germany."

What are we to make of such obviously misguided, naïve comments? Was the "half-naked fakir," as Churchill called Gandhi, a fraud?

I don't think so. It would be a mistake to dismiss his ideas because they don't work everywhere and all the time. Maybe Gandhi's law of love is less like gravity and more like a rainbow: a natural phenomenon that only manifests sometimes, under certain circumstance, but when it does, there's nothing more beautiful.

I've learned a lot about the power of nonviolent resistance from my dog, Parker. Part beagle, part basset hound, he is 100 percent Gandhian. Parker possesses the Mahatma's stubborn streak, and his commitment to nonviolence.

Like Gandhi, Parker knows where he wants to walk and when he wants to walk there. Should I suggest an alternative direction, he expresses his displeasure by planting his not-insignificant weight on his rear haunches and refusing to budge. Sometimes he'll lie prone, paws splayed, eyes averted. He performs this maneuver—the "Full Gandhi" I call it—in public: on sidewalks, in pet stores, in the middle of busy streets. It's embarrassing.

Parker doesn't bite. He doesn't swat. He doesn't bark or growl. He just sits there, peacefully yet persistently resisting. He's not going to hurt me, nor is he going to help me.

My reaction, I confess, is straight-up Raj. I get frustrated. I get angry. Parker, like Gandhi, is conducting an experiment, and I am the subject. How will I respond to an infuriating but thoroughly peaceful provocation? With anger? With violence? If I do, when will I realize the folly of my outburst? Maybe today, maybe tomorrow. That's fine. Parker has time.

Had he lashed out, the experiment would prove less useful. Preoccupied with my indignation—*you bit me!*—I'd lose sight of my own culpability and my heart would harden. Parker's steadfast refusal either to retaliate or relent lays bare my capacity for violence and, once exposed, enables me to consciously reject it. We can only rebuff what we can see. Parker, the little bugger, helps me see.

It is not enough to reject violence, Gandhi thought. We must find creative ways to convert our adversaries into friends. Most violence stems not from an immoral impulse but a failure of imagination. A violent person is a lazy person. Unwilling to do the hard work of problem solving, he throws a punch, or reaches for a gun. Clichéd responses all. Gandhi would take one look at my Parker predicament and urge me to think creatively. Experiment.

So I do, and I'm happy to report that, after a few failed experiments, Parker's Full Gandhi episodes have subsided. Yes, he's still prone to bouts of recalcitrance, but these don't last long, for I've discovered that, unlike the Mahatma, Parker can be bribed with bacon-flavored treats.

Is that cheating? Perhaps, but I prefer to think of it as creative fighting. Parker gets what he wants, and I get what I want: to go home. An imperfect solution, perhaps, but a good one. Gandhi once compared his nonviolent movement to Euclid's Line, a line without breadth. No human has ever drawn it, and never will. It is impossible. Yet the idea of the line, like Gandhi's ideals, has value. It inspires.

Kailash and I sit on a bench outside Birla House in silence. It's the comfortable silence of two people with a shared history. Neither of us feels compelled to fill the vacuum with words.

Most Indians don't appreciate Gandhi, Kailash tells me. They appreciate the money his picture graces. That's about it. "People say Gandhi was a coward. They think, 'If the other person is stronger than me, I have to be like Gandhi. But if I am stronger, I can do what I want.'" This is, sadly, a common misperception. Gandhi's nonviolence was a weapon of the strong, not the weak.

What about Kailash? What does he think of Gandhi?

"Gandhi is very wise," he says. "He has a clean brain."

I smile at the word "clean." India, Gandhi once said, must "be the leader in clean action based on clean thought."

When I first read that, it stumped me. What did he mean? How are thought and action "clean"?

By clean thought, Gandhi meant thought free of "veiled violence." We might act peacefully toward someone, but if we harbor violent thoughts, we are not clean. He once prohibited his followers from shouting "shame, shame" at those they disagreed with. Gandhi would not look kindly on those who today disrupt the meals of politicians they don't like. Such protesters may not physically harm anyone, but they have merely "put on the cloak of nonviolence."

My thoughts are about as clean as the Delhi air. Too often I accede to the wishes of others to avoid confrontation. I register my discontent by silently seething. I fight covertly, uncleanly. I appear docile but am belligerent. Gandhi was not passive-aggressive. He was aggressive-passive. His actions appeared aggressive, or at least assertive, yet scratch beneath the surface and you found no animus. Only love.

In his autobiography, Gandhi recalls the time he wrote a note to his father, confessing to stealing and cigarette smoking and meat eating. Hand trembling, Gandhi handed his father the slip of paper. The elder Gandhi sat up to read the note and, as he did, "pearl-drops trickled down his cheeks, wetting the paper," recalls Gandhi. "Those pearl-drops of love cleansed my heart, and washed my sin away. Only he who has experienced such love can know what it is."

Such love is rare, and not often directed inward. As someone who is often brutal to himself, I found it heartening to learn Gandhi also wrestled with bouts of self-loathing. During outbursts of anger, he'd sometimes punch himself on the chest, hard. He outgrew this self-harming and, toward the end of his life, advised a friend, "Do not lose your temper with anybody, not even with yourself."

Most of us don't battle an empire. Our fights are more quotidian but, for us, no less important. Fortunately, Gandhi's philosophy of nonviolent resistance also works for marital spats, office tiffs, and political brouhahas.

Let's examine a simple dispute from a Gandhian perspective. You and your partner are going out to dinner to celebrate a milestone. You want Indian food, she wants Italian. You know for certain Indian is the superior cuisine, while your partner is just as certain Italian is the better food. There is a conflict. What to do?

The quickest solution is a "forced victory." You could compel your partner to dine with you at Bombay Dreams by bundling her into a burlap sack. There are downsides to this approach. Alternatively, you could insist on Indian food, period. No further discussion. Let's say your partner agrees. You've won, right?

You haven't. The uneasy calm over dinner is illusory. No one likes being bludgeoned into submission. "What appears to be the end of the dispute may be just the opening in another chapter in the conflict," says Mark Juergensmeyer, author of *Gandhi's Way: A Handbook of Conflict Resolution*. And by resorting to "veiled violence" you harm not only your partner but yourself, too.

Conversely, you could "appease" your partner by agreeing to Italian, yet spend the entire evening seething. This result is simply another form of violence—worse, it is dishonest, "unclean" violence. Better to fight for your principles than pretend you don't have any.

You could suggest a compromise cuisine. Japanese, for instance.

But that means neither of you gets what you want, and meanwhile, the underlying conflict festers. Gandhi was wary of such compromises. He was all for give-and-take but not when it came to one's principles. To compromise on principles is to surrender—"all give and no take," he said. A better, more creative solution, is one where both sides get what they didn't know they wanted.

Gandhi would suggest taking a step back. Examine your position, keeping in mind you possess only a portion of the truth. Are you sure Indian food is superior? Maybe Italian cuisine has merits you've yet to appreciate. Examine your attitude toward your partner, too. Do you see her as an opponent or enemy? If it's the latter, that's a problem. "An opponent is not always bad simply because he opposes," said Gandhi. He had many opponents, but no enemies. He strived to see not only the best in people but their latent goodness, too. He saw people not as they were but as they could be.

Get creative, Gandhi would advise. You could, for instance, make your case for Indian, emphasizing how it would be good not only for you but for your partner, too. Maybe she hasn't had Indian in a while or maybe there's a new dish at Bombay Dreams she has yet to try. You make your case gently, for your aim, as Gandhi says, is not to condemn but to convert.

It's now midday, and the Delhi sun has grown stronger. I ask Kailash about altercations he's had. I'm sure he's had his share. Elbow room is India's scarcest commodity. Like Schopenhauer's porcupines, India's 1.3 billion souls are constantly calculating the ideal distance from one another. It's an imperfect science. Sometimes you get pricked.

When attending the Franciscan boarding school my wife and I had enrolled him in, Kailash got into occasional fistfights with the other boys over a stolen pair of socks or T-shirt. Now that he's a homeowner and landlord, Kailash needn't worry about stolen socks. Money doesn't liberate us from disputes, though. It shifts them to pricier arenas. And so it is with Kailash.

He tells me about a dispute with a tenant. He asked her to turn off the light outside her shop after she closed for the day, since a neighbor was taking the light as license to park his car there, blocking the entrance to Emma's Stationery Shop.

"I said, 'Please turn off the light,' again and again." She grew angry, but Kailash remained calm. For a while. One day he saw her leaving yet again without switching off the light. When he asked her to, she pointed out she, not Kailash, paid the electricity bill. He yelled at her. She yelled back. It was not a Gandhian fight.

"Did she have a point?" I ask Kailash. "Was she right?"

"She was right, but at the same time she was wrong," he says.

That is, I think, a Gandhian response. Each side in a conflict possesses a slice of the truth, not the whole pie. Rather than trading slices, aim to enlarge the pie.

In the last hour of the last day of his life, Mahatma Gandhi met with a minister in the new Indian government. Afterward, Manu brought him dinner: fourteen ounces goat's milk, four ounces vegetable juice, and three oranges. While he ate, he weaved khadi cloth with his *charkha*, or spinning wheel. He noticed the time—a few minutes past 5:00 p.m.—and sprang to his feet. He was late for his evening prayers. Gandhi hated being late.

With his grandnieces—my "walking sticks," he affectionately called them—on either side, he walked toward the prayer grounds, where several hundred supporters awaited him. Gandhi lifted his hands from his grandnieces' shoulders and folded them into a Namaste, greeting the crowd.

At that moment, a stout man wearing a khaki tunic approached Gandhi. Manu thought the man was going to touch Gandhi's feet in a show of reverence. It happened often. Gandhi hated it. "I am an ordinary human being," he'd say. "Why do you want to pick up the dust of my feet?"

Manu intervened, chiding the man for further delaying Gandhi. "Do you want to embarrass him?" she asked.

The man replied by pushing her—so forcefully she stumbled backward, dropping Gandhi's rosary and eyeglass case. As she reached down to pick them up, three shots rang out in rapid succession. Smoke filled the air and, recalls Manu, "darkness prevailed." Gandhi, still standing, hands still folded in greeting, was heard uttering the words *Hey Ram,* "Oh God," before collapsing.

Gandhi's last steps are memorialized here. A pathway of white stone footprints leads along a grass walkway, ending where the assassin's bullets struck. Kailash and I stand on the last two markers now. Two bare feet: one brown, one white. The stone feels cool against my skin, and not for the first or last time do I wonder what it is about places of death that I find so peaceful.

"Would you do it?" asks Kailash.

"Do what?"

"Live with Gandhi. Would you have joined his ashram if you could?"

Gandhi had millions of admirers, but his closest followers numbered only in the hundreds. Life with Gandhi was demanding. Acolytes adhered to eleven vows, ranging from the easy (not stealing) to the tricky (physical labor) to the onerous (chastity). Gandhi was, as we've seen, not always a nice man. He was demanding and, at times, harsh. "To live with Gandhi is to walk on the blade of a sword," said one follower. Am I capable of such a balancing act? I wonder.

"Yes," I tell Kailash. "I would join Gandhi."

As I hear my own words, as if spoken by someone else, I realize they are true. Sometimes we don't recognize truth until we speak it.

I would join Gandhi—not despite the demands of such a life but because of them. I spend considerable time and money endeavoring to increase my comfort when, I know, that is not what I need. What did Epicurus say? *Nothing is enough for the man to whom enough is too little.* At his death, Gandhi's worldly possessions consisted of a pair of spectacles, a wooden bowl (for taking his meals), his pocket watch, and, from a Japanese friend, three tiny porcelain monkeys, signifying "see no evil, hear no evil, speak no evil."

Inhaling chunks of Delhi air, I glance out the taxi's window at the traffic, heavier than usual today. We're on our way to the train station. Kailash insisted on seeing me off, even though it's late. I didn't resist.

As we wait for the train, I get a good look at Kailash. He is no longer the scrawny kid I first met all those years ago. He has filled out, and grown up. He is a man. A good man. I see traces of Gandhi in Kailash. The persistence. The openness to new ways of thinking. The unwavering honesty. The innate goodness.

I don't mention this observation to Kailash. He'd find it absurd, I'm sure, and more than a little blasphemous. *Gandhiji? Me? There was only one Gandhiji.*

Maybe, maybe not. Gandhi never saw himself as sui generis. He was not a god or a saint. He was simply a man who experimented with new ways of fighting and a powerful force called love. An Einstein of the heart.

A train pulls into the station and the already frenetic activity on the platform accelerates: porters hauling suitcases the size of small boats; *chai wallah*s calling out in singsong tones, hoping to sell a cup or two; families holding hands lest they be swept away by the torrent of humanity. The train slows to a stop. A placard on the side reads: "Rajdhani Express."

I had decided to accept Mr. Roy's offer for the last remaining ticket on the "good train." The not-the-Yoga-Express train. It was a surrender, of sorts, a bow to reality. I lost the battle. I failed. Like Gandhi. His dream of a peaceful transition to a unified India never materialized. In his last days, he felt adrift in "an aching, storm-tossed and hungry world." Despair threatened to drown him.

Yet he never stopped fighting. When Indians celebrated independence at the stroke of midnight on August 15, 1947, Gandhi spent the day fasting, and praying. Soon after, he crisscrossed the young nation, by train and by foot, trying to stanch the bleeding. He achieved his means, if not his ends.

How you fight matters more than what you're fighting about. I fought well. I recognized an injustice and confronted it. I battled creatively and cleanly against a recalcitrant adversary: Indian Railways. I did not resort to violence, however much tempted to do so. True, the results were not what I wanted, but it is the wanting not the results that lies at the root of my suffering. Besides, there will be other fights. There always are.

Kailash helps haul my luggage on board, reminding me to lock my bags during the overnight journey. I promise him I will. We hug goodbye before he jumps from train to platform. I watch him for a few seconds, then he is gone, swallowed up by the warm Delhi night, thick with pollution, and people: countless souls in motion, negotiating tight spaces and complex relationships, loving and fighting, fighting and loving, usually sequentially but, every now and then, at the same time.

Mahatma Gandhi took one last train journey. Thirteen days after his assassination, his ashes were placed on board a train bound for Allahabad, at the confluence of three sacred rivers. Gandhi's final resting place.

All along the route, people scrambled for a glimpse of the train, eyes tearing, hands joined in a final Namaste. At night, villagers lit bonfires and torches and cried, *Mahatma Gandhi, ki-jai!* Victory to Gandhi. The train, outfitted for the journey, consisted entirely of third-class carriages.

9.

How to Be Kind like Confucius

5:34 p.m. Somewhere in lower Manhattan. On board the New York City subway F train, en route to nowhere.

I've been riding the F train for a long time—longer than most commuters, and mental health professionals, would advise. I have taken the train to Jamaica, Queens, and to Coney Island, Brooklyn, and many places in between. For a solid week, the F train has been my home.

I am not insane, I assure you. I am a man on a mission. I am looking for kindness. I concede the New York City subway is an unlikely place to find it. Many consider it a heartless underworld. That's why I'm here. I figure if you can find kindness on the New York subway, you can find it anywhere.

I scan my surroundings with Thoreau eyes and Schopenhauer ears, alert to the slightest inkling of benevolence. Three young people board. Colleagues, clearly. I catch snippets of their conversation. *She needs to quit. . . . No, she needs to get fired.* No kindness there.

I spot a Hispanic man wearing a New York Yankees cap who accidentally jostles another passenger. "Excuse me," he says. Scan. A woman holding a small white dog tight against her chest stumbles, then pinballs into no fewer than three passengers. "Sorry," she says. Both were certainly polite, but were they kind? Politeness is social lubricant, kindness social superglue. Polite cultures are not necessarily kind ones.

The young man sitting next to me is wearing a hoodie and torn jeans. Earphones securely inserted, he is slumped over, asleep. Or so I think. When a teenager approaches, selling candy bars to raise money for his school, the man perks up, fishes a dollar bill from his pocket, and hands it to the teenager. Then, without missing a beat, he returns to his music and his slumping. I remind myself, once again, to always question assumptions.

My companion on the F train is a strange hodgepodge of a book called *The Analects*. It's how we know Confucius. He didn't write it. His disciples did, distilling his wisdom to its essence, and perhaps adding a dash of their own views, as Plato spiced Socrates. *The Analects* is the perfect subway read. Consisting of a series of short dialogues and snappy sayings, it's easily digested piecemeal, between station stops. The book's herky-jerky rhythm mirrors that of the F train. One moment Confucius is expounding on the virtues of filial piety, the next he's advising which color robe to wear.

It's tempting to conclude the book contains no unifying themes or cogent ideas. Yet it does. The F train may move in fits and starts, but it's still heading somewhere, and so is Confucius.

When we pull into the East Broadway station in Manhattan, I disembark and climb the stairs and am greeted by one of those cruel early-spring days that feel like winter. Zipping my jacket and wrapping my scarf tight, I head west, in search of the man.

After a few blocks, I turn a corner and am dwarfed by a housing and commercial complex with an impersonal, Soviet aesthetic. Confucius Plaza has all the charm of a Greyhound bus station.

I walk past the Confucius Social Day Care Center and the Confucius Pharmacy, turn right at the Confucius Florist, and there, sandwiched between Confucius Optical and Confucius Surgical Supplies is . . . Confucius.

He must be ten feet tall, but somehow he doesn't make me feel small.

He is sporting his trademark beard, long and thin, simultaneously neat and unruly. His hands are clasped, his eyes wise. Aimed at Bowery street, Confucius's wise eyes see all. They see the Lin Sister Herb Shop and the Abacus Federal Savings Bank. They see the Ball Room Dance Studio ("Learn to Dance Ballroom/Latin!") and they see the Golden Manna Bakery. They see kindness, too: a gaggle of schoolchildren, five-year-olds, steered by their adult minders, as a cold wind whips through Confucius Plaza.

I pause at the bottom of the statue, where an inscription, in Chinese and English, reads: "The Chapter of Great Harmony." In this passage, Confucius imagines a utopia where rulers are wise, criminals scared, and everyone like family. It was a bold vision, given that, at the time—the fifth century BC—kindness was a newfangled idea.

I stand there for a long while, oblivious to the spring cold, picturing this perfect world and the imperfect man who conceived it a long, long time ago.

Confucius had a difficult life, even for a philosopher. He was born into a fairly affluent family, but when he was only three years old, his father, a military officer, died. Confucius was raised by his mother, who struggled to make ends meet. Confucius helped by holding a number of menial jobs. All the while, he studied Chinese classics such as *I Ching*, or "Book of Changes."

When he looked around he saw a people splintered into warring factions and governed by rulers more interested in personal gain than public good. This wasn't only immoral, he thought, but impractical. Confucius sensed there was a better way, says journalist Michael Schuman in his excellent biography. "Swords and shields would not win an empire; burdensome taxes and military servitude would not woo loyal subjects. Benevolence was the correct and only route to power and prestige." We've strayed from the Way, Confucius proclaimed. We need to get back on course.

His message landed with a deafening silence. If anything, the corruption and misrule grew worse. The final straw for Confucius came in the form of dancing girls. Hundreds of them were dispatched from a neighboring state. The local ruler, clearly distracted, failed to show up at the royal court for three days.

"I have yet to meet a man who loves Virtue as much as he loves sex," Confucius said, before departing on what would be a thirteen-year exile. He traveled from state to state, offering his services as wise counsel to any ruler who would listen. None did.

Confucius returned home, weary but not defeated. He decided to teach, and thank goodness. Had he succeeded in obtaining a position as royal advisor, we might not know him today. He refused no student, regardless of background or ability to pay. Tuition was a small bundle of silk or a bit of cured meat, the beef jerky of its day.

Confucius was an intimidating presence in the classroom. The Master, as he was known, came across as "an uptight fuddy-duddy, a tireless stickler on points of propriety," writes Schuman. He would not sit on a mat that was not straight, and maintained perfect posture, even when alone. When he saw a young man sitting "with his legs spread wide," in an early display of manspreading, Confucius scolded him, calling him a "pest" and rapping him on the shin with his cane.

Yet the Master could also be gentle, lighthearted even. He sang and played the lute. He laughed and joked with friends, and found pleasure in the everyday: using his elbow as a pillow, for instance, while eating coarse rice.

Thousands of miles separated Confucius and Socrates, yet the two philosophers had a lot in common. They were nearly contemporaries. Socrates was born less than a decade after Confucius died, in 479 BC. Both men occupied precarious positions, admired by their disciples, mistrusted by the elites. Both had an informal, conversational teaching style. Both questioned assumptions. Both valued knowledge a lot and ignorance more. Neither cared for metaphysical speculation. (When a student asked Confucius about the afterlife, the Master replied, "If you cannot understand life, how can you understand death?") Both were sticklers for definitions. "If words are not right, judgments are not clear," Confucius said.

Words mattered to Confucius, but no word mattered more than *ren*. It appears 105 times in *The Analects*, far more than any other word. There's no direct translation (Confucius himself never explicitly defines it), but *ren* has been variously rendered as compassion, altruism, love, benevolence, true goodness, consummate action. My favorite is "human-heartedness."

A person of *ren* regularly practices five cardinal virtues: respect, magnanimity, sincerity, earnestness, and kindness. Confucius didn't invent kindness, of course, but he did elevate it: from an indulgence to a philosophical linchpin, and the basis for good governance. He was the first philosopher to place kindness, and love, at the top of the pyramid. "Do not impose on others what you yourself do not desire," said Confucius, articulating the Golden Rule some five hundred years before Jesus. For Confucius, kindness is not squishy. It is not weak. Kindness is practical. Extend kindness to all, says one Confucian, "and you can turn the whole world in the palm of your hand."

The F train isn't only a train. It is a culture and, as with all cultures, certain rules apply. Some are written, others understood. I look around and see the written variety everywhere. Thou shalt not lean on doors or hold doors. Thou shalt not pass between cars. Thou shalt not eat or drink. Thou shalt stand clear of the closing doors.

Confucius could have written these rules. He saw great value in *li*, or "proper ritual conduct," as expressed in classic Chinese texts such as *The Book of Rites*. Here's a small sample, on the subject of proper dining habits.

> Do not roll the rice into a ball; do not bolt down the various dishes; do not swill down the soup. Do not make noise in eating; do not crunch the bones with the teeth; do not put back fish you've been eating; do not throw the bones to the dogs; do not snatch at what you want. Do not spread the rice to cool; do not use chopsticks in eating millet.

I read that and sigh. This is my image of Confucianism: a rules-based philosophy where one honors one's parents, does not question authority, and always, always, stands clear of the closing doors. No wonder it is Lao-Tzu, with his warm and fuzzy *wu wei*, or "non-doing," who is the darling of the New Age crowd, not Confucius. If Lao-Tzu is the surfer dude of Chinese philosophy, Confucius is its substitute teacher.

I confess: the words "proper ritual conduct" do not appeal to me. Not a single one. For me, ritual is something you rebel against, not embrace. Blindly following tradition flies in the face of philosophy's rallying cry, as articulated by Kant: "Dare to think for yourself!" But there is more to Confucianism. Much more. It doesn't advocate mindless allegiance to ritual. Motivation matters. "Ritual performed without reverence—these are things I cannot bear to see!" Confucius said.

And there is a reason for his punctiliousness, one that relates directly to *ren*, to kindness. Kindness is not free floating. It needs a container. For Confucius that container is *li*, proper ritual conduct. You may not see value in these rituals. That's okay, Confucius says. Straighten your mat *as if* you cared, eat your food in the prescribed manner *as if* it mattered. These might seem like mundane matters. But it is on this quotidian foundation that kindness rests.

Confucius's goal was character development: the acquisition of moral skills. And no skill was more important than filial devotion. Each page of *The Analects* is watermarked with a wagging, parental finger. A son is obliged to honor his father, even if it means covering for his misdeeds. And these obligations don't end with a parent's death. The obedient son or daughter must continue to behave as his or her parents had wished.

Confucius demands unswerving but not unthinking devotion. If an elderly parent veers off course, by all means redirect him, but do so judiciously, respectfully. Filial piety is a means, not an end. Just as we go to the gym not to sweat but to get in shape, we practice filial piety not for its own sake (only) but to develop our kindness muscles. Caring for an elderly parent is heavy lifting. Confucius adds a few pounds by insisting we do so cheerfully, with a genuine smile.

The family is our *ren* gym. It is where we learn to love and be loved. Proximity matters. Start by treating those closest to you kindly, and go from there. Like a stone tossed into a pond, kindness ripples outward in ever-widening circles, as we expand our sphere of concern from ourselves to our family to our neighborhood to our nation to all sentient beings. If we can feel compassion for one creature, we can feel it for all of them.

Too often, though, we fail to make the leap from familial kindness to a broader benevolence. Too often parenting remains "an island of kindness in a sea of cruelty," as two contemporary authors put it. We need to escape the island or, better yet, enlarge it and invite others to join us.

"Stand clear of the closing doors." I stand clear, following proper ritual conduct. Nearby, a woman cradles an enormous Dunkin' Donuts cup, in clear violation of the no-eating-or-drinking rule. A man not more than five feet away outdoes her by retrieving an entire pizza from his backpack and chowing down.

A recorded announcement startles me with its directness: "Attention passengers: Do not carry your wallet or phone in your back pocket." It's a reminder that others can't be trusted, that kindness has no home here, in the big city. If you want kindness, go to a small town, or so we think.

As we pull into the Fifty-Third Street station, the doors slide open and the car fills with the sound of a busker singing John Lennon's "Imagine." He's a bit off key but it is touching despite that fact, or perhaps because of it.

The song, I realize, is Confucius's utopian "Great Harmony" set to music. Callousness is the result not of cruel intentions but of a failure of imagination. The unkind person can't imagine the suffering of another, cannot put himself in her shoes. And yet *it's easy if you try*, says John Lennon, and Confucius, too. "Since you desire status, then help others achieve it, since you desire success then help others attain it."

Did the brief burst of John Lennon affect the mood on the train? Did it make us more prone to human-heartedness? It's impossible to quantify, of course, but I'd like to think so. I'd like to think kindness begets kindness.

I exit at Canal Street and decide to stop at a Chinese restaurant for lunch. It is crowded, like the F train, though less rickety and with a more pleasant aroma.

"How many?" barks the host, accusingly, as if I've interrupted an important meeting.

"One," I say, sheepishly holding up an index finger.

"You sit with other customers, okay?"

It is not okay, but I don't say so. I don't want to disappoint the barking man. He sits me with a group of German tourists.

A New York City Chinese restaurant is not an obviously kind place any more than the F train is. The service is brusque at best. The waitstaff not only barks at you but expects you to order, and eat, quickly.

Yet a current of subterranean benevolence runs through the place, infuses the dim sum and the bok choy, steeps in the metal teapots. It is a kindness that honors the common good. If you're willing to share a table, everyone benefits. If you eat quickly, others waiting can enjoy the shrimp shumai also. These rules are not written but understood. They constitute the *li*, the proper ritual conduct, of a Chinese restaurant. They are the container that holds the kindness.

My Chinese restaurant ticks off many of Confucius's five boxes of *ren*: respect, magnanimity, sincerity, earnestness, and kindness. The staff treats me with respect, up to a point, and they are certainly sincere, something that can't be said of haughtier establishments. They are earnest and, in their own way, kind. Magnanimous? Not so much, but four out of five isn't bad.

Back on the F train, snaking through Queens, I scan my fellow passengers and wonder: Are they good people? Kind? Do we all possess *ren*, human-heartedness, or do only a few exceptional beings, what Confucius calls a *junzi*, a "superior person"?

The question of human nature is one of the thorniest in philosophy. Some philosophers, such as Thomas Hobbes, believed humans are naturally selfish; society tempers this brutish disposition. Thinkers like Rousseau believed man is born good; society corrupts. Still others, such as the French existentialist Simone de Beauvoir, doubted human nature exists at all; it is our nature not to have a nature.

Confucius fell on the people-are-good side, a notion expanded a century later by a philosopher named Mencius. "All people have a heart that cannot bear the suffering of others," he said, and suggested a thought experiment to make his point. Imagine you're passing through a village, minding your own business, when you spot a child teetering on the edge of a well, about to fall in. How do you react?

Most likely, says Mencius, you feel "alarm and compassion." Instinctively, you want to help—not to win favor from the child's parents, or praise from neighbors and friends, but because you are human and "the feeling of commiseration is essential to man." Merely hearing this tale, we experience a "stirring of our hearts." If you don't, he says, you are not fully human. (Nowhere does Mencius predict people would actually help the child. A sizable gap separates compassion and action, and many a good intention has fallen into it, never to be heard from again.)

We each possess the same latent goodness, Mencius says. Just as a denuded mountain still sprouts tiny shoots, even the cruelest person retains a dormant kindness. "Given the right nourishment, there is nothing that will not grow, and deprived of it, there is nothing that will not wither away."

Our capacity for kindness is like our capacity for language. We're all born with an innate ability to speak a language. But it must be activated, either by our parents or Rosetta Stone. Likewise, our inherent kindness must be mobilized, and the way to do that, Confucians believe, is through study. The opening line of *The Analects* sings the praises of studying. "Isn't it a pleasure to study and practice what you have learned?"

By "study" Confucius doesn't mean rote memorization or even learning, per se. He has something deeper in mind: moral self-cultivation. What we are taught, we learn. What we cultivate, we absorb. There are no small acts of kindness. Each compassionate deed is like watering a redwood seed. You never know what heights it might reach.

I have a question for Confucius: If human nature is inherently good, why does the world seem so cruel? From Genghis Khan to Hitler, the story of humanity is written in blood. Flip on your TV or fire up your laptop, Master, and you'll see this is still the case. The news is all bad: terrorist attacks and natural disasters and political brawls. Kindness is truant. Or so it seems.

Kindness is always there, whether we notice it or not. "The Great Asymmetry," the late Harvard paleontologist Stephen Jay Gould called this phenomenon. "Every spectacular incident of evil will be balanced by 10,000 acts of kindness," he said. We witness these acts every day on our streets and in our homes and, yes, on the New York subway. An elderly woman braves a cold November day to feed the neighborhood squirrels; a businessman, late for a meeting, stops to help a single mom carry the groceries to her car; a teenager, skateboard in hand, notices an expired parking meter and drops a quarter in. That these ordinary acts of kindness rarely make the news renders them no less real, or heroic.

It is our duty, almost a holy responsibility, says Gould, "to record and honor the victorious weight of these innumerable little kindnesses." Gould, a hard-nosed scientist, saw a practical reason for registering goodness. Kindness honored is kindness multiplied. Kindness is contagious. Witnessing acts of moral beauty triggers a flood of physical and emotional responses. Observing acts of kindness encourages us to act more kindly ourselves, a phenomenon confirmed in several recent studies.

I experience the kindness contagion firsthand. After my week riding the F train, hyperalert to acts of kindness, I become kinder myself. I hold doors for people. I pick up litter. I thank my barista—and leave a tip when she isn't looking. These small acts won't snare me the Nobel Peace Prize or sainthood, I realize. But it's a start. A few more drops on the redwood seed.

Ride the F train long enough and you start to notice patterns. I do. Acts of kindness are not constant. They ebb and flow. During off-peak hours, I observe relatively few. Yet during rush hour, I notice many: a muscular young man offering his seat to an older woman; an "excuse me" here, a "sorry" there. People have no less kindness in their heart at noon than at 5:00 p.m. of course. There are simply fewer kindness opportunities. Kindness expands to fit the need demanded.

During rush hour, that need swells to galactic proportions. As we inch toward Brooklyn, more and more people board at each stop. By Union Square, the train is full. We can't possibly hold one more passenger, I think. Yet we do.

Everything happens more quickly: people rush for a seat more quickly, scan more quickly. Even the conductor's announcements accelerate. *ConeyIslandboundFtrainstandclearoftheclosingdoors.*

"New Yorkers aren't rude," my friend Abby, a native New Yorker, said when I told her of my plan to seek kindness on the F train. "They're fast."

She might be onto something. Is it possible, I wonder, to act kindly quickly, or does kindness demand slowness? Slow cooking tastes better than fast food and, as we've seen, good philosophy takes time, too. As the F train trundles under the East River, I contemplate the relationship between velocity and kindness. Does kindness decrease as you accelerate? Confucius seems to think so. He describes the benevolent person as "simple in manner and slow of speech."

I'm not so sure. Yes, people moving quickly are less likely to notice a person in distress, but sometimes speediness is kinder. If your house were on fire, would you prefer a slowpoke firefighter or a fleet-footed one? If you were sick, would you want an ER doctor who dawdles or one who moves quickly? If I were to collapse right here on the F train, suffering from a medical crisis triggered by excessive thinking, I'd want my fellow passengers to help swiftly, not slowly.

A friend recently told me about the time he witnessed just such an emergency on the New York subway. A woman collapsed on the floor of a train as it pulled into a station. Reflexively, her fellow passengers sprang into action. One held the door so the train remained in the station, another alerted the conductor, a third administered first aid. Mencius would recognize this display of reflexive compassion. Kindness comes naturally. Cruelty is learned.

Am I kind? I wonder. Yes, I did display Confucian *ren*, human-heartedness, when I helped Kailash in India. But I didn't seek out Kailash. He found me. He was the child in the well. I deserve no more credit for my reflexive reaction than I would for sneezing in a dusty room. The world, now more than ever, demands not only reflexive kindness but a more assertive variety, too.

I hear her before I see her. A plaintive, wounded voice that cuts through me like a rusty knife. "I had a young face," she says, addressing none of us and all of us. "What happened? I had a young face? Why?"

She is dressed in clothes that are little more than rags. She is unsteady, her large frame swaying, as if buffeted by a gale.

I look down and see the source of her unsteadiness (one source anyway). At first, I assume she's wearing old shoes but she is not. She is barefoot. Her feet, swollen and deformed, are grotesque. They do not look like human feet.

For a long time, she stands there, swaying, not soliciting money or help of any kind. This is the worst part: the ambiguity of the situation. I feel alarm and compassion, but don't know what to do.

Kindness is hard. Even if we want to help, we don't know how. Better to do nothing, we tell ourselves. My fellow passengers are uneasy, too, in that subtle New York way. Some move aside to let her pass. Others double down on their straight-ahead stare. I bury my head in Confucius.

The woman moves to the far end of the car. I can't see her anymore, but I can still hear her. "I used to have a young face."

Then she's gone. Everyone exhales, or so I imagine. I lift my head and reflect on what transpired. What to do when faced with such suffering? Yes, I *could* have helped the woman but, as I said, I didn't know where to begin. Nobody did. How, then, can the kindness contagion take hold? Someone has to go first.

Kindness is hard. It includes empathy, but that is not enough. Confucian ritual is needed. There's a reason we turn to rituals during life's weightiest moments—a wedding, a graduation, a death. These events evoke such strong feelings we risk coming unglued. Ritual holds us together. Ritual provides the container for our emotional content. We F train riders needed such a container when this sad woman swayed into our car. There was none, alas, so we did nothing.

"The burden is heavy and the road is long," Confucius said. Kindness is hard. Everything worthwhile is.

10.

How to Appreciate the Small Things like Sei Shōnagon

11:47 a.m. On board Japan Rail East Train No. 318. En route from Tokyo to Kyoto. Speed: 185 miles per hour.

Speed, I've learned, is the enemy of attention. Swiftness fragments our awareness, splinters it into a million tiny pieces, none large enough to grasp.

What about beauty? Does it, too, decrease as we accelerate? Or does speed possess its own blurred beauty? A hummingbird's wings, flapping eighty times per second. A flash of lightning, arcing across the sky. The quiet whoosh of a Japanese *shinkansen*, or bullet train, rocketing from city to city.

When I boarded the one I'm on now, at Tokyo's shiny Shinagawa station, I didn't know whether to gasp or laugh. With a flat platypus nose attached to a toned swimmer's body, the train looks ridiculous. And beautiful. The *shinkansen* is the Robin Williams of trains: an absurdity blatantly flouting the laws of physics but doing so at such mind-boggling speed that all is forgiven.

Just as Robin Williams didn't compete with other comedians, the *shinkansen* doesn't compete with other trains. It competes with the airlines. Japan Rail has done its best to mimic the feel of an airline cabin. I could be on board an Airbus, with the notable absence of seat belts and canned announcements about what to do in the unlikely event of a water landing.

As we departed Shinagawa station, precisely on time, the echoes of air travel grew louder: the high-pitched whoosh, the G forces gently pressing me against my seat—smoothly, without even a hint of Amtrak shake-and-rattle.

If all goes according to plan, and in Japan it almost always does, we will cover the 227 miles from Tokyo to Kyoto in a brisk two hours and eight minutes. We are flying. We are not flying. Only when I glance out the window—not at the horizon but at a nearby house or railroad crossing—do I experience an inkling of our exceptional velocity. Speed is relative. Without reference points, it is meaningless.

A conductor walks by and scoops up a chopstick shard that somebody (okay, me) had dropped. In my mind, it was too small to qualify as litter. Clearly he felt otherwise. My stray speck of wood had upset the aesthetic harmony of the train. In Japan, something is either just right or it is not right at all.

I retrieve my little black notebook, not the gem I lost in England (it is irreplaceable), but a more pedestrian model. I unfurl the elastic band that contains my thoughts. I turn to a fresh page, blank with possibility, and start a list. I like lists. List making is, I believe, a profoundly philosophical activity. Don't take my word for it. Ask Plato. He made lists. He listed the attributes of a philosopher-king, and of the good life. His student Aristotle outdid him. Aristotle was philosophy's great list maker. Keen to superimpose order upon messy reality, he created layers of categories and subcategories.

Some two thousand years later, Susan Sontag offered this eloquent and characteristically cerebral defense of her chronic list making: "I perceive value, I confer value, I create value, I even create—or guarantee—existence. Hence, my compulsion to make 'lists.'" Umberto Eco put it more succinctly: "The list is the origin of culture."

My list making is considerably less grand. My lists do not guarantee existence or establish cultures. My lists do not, as far as I know, perceive value, but they do help me corral my thoughts. They help me make sense of the world, of myself, and what is more philosophical than that?

The key to good list making is getting the category right. It must be large enough to encompass a variety of entries yet small enough to wrap your mind around. "The Greatest Music Ever" is too broad while "The Greatest Polkas Composed by Polish-Americans of 1930s Chicago" is too narrow.

I glance at the list I've just created in my notebook. "Foreign Countries Where I Have Lived." It is not a long list, only three entries, but it has, more than any other list, shaped how I think, and who I am.

Each country on the list taught me something important, even if inadvertently. India taught me how to find stillness in chaos. Israel taught me the importance of *savlanut*, patience. Valuable lessons all, but nothing compared to Japan. Japan taught me, a person of the book, a head-heavy aficionado of words and the people who use words, how to shut the fuck up for five minutes and experience a different way of being. Japan opened my eyes to a philosophy of things. Beautiful small things.

The Pillow Book. What a strange title, I thought, when I first learned of its existence, nearly two decades ago. I was living in Tokyo, working as a correspondent for NPR. It tickled my interest. What *is* this peculiar book named after a nocturnal accessory and penned a millennium ago by a little-known courtier from Kyoto? And how does it attract readers ten centuries later?

My investigations started and ended there. I was busy filing reports about the Japanese economy or the country's aging population or jetting off to cover some simmering conflict in Indonesia or Pakistan. I didn't have the time—or, to be honest, the inclination—to read a thousand-year-old book about nothing in particular. The book, though, the idea of the book, stayed with me, relegated to the exurbia of my brain, waiting patiently for space to open up downtown.

I snuggle with *The Pillow Book* while, appropriately, resting my head on a pillow. I am in a hotel room in Tokyo's Shibuya neighborhood, though in Japan, "room" is a matter of opinion.

Both in style and scale, the alleged room reminds me of a ship's cabin. A masterpiece of spatial efficiency, it supposedly sleeps three, but there's a catch. These three bodies must remain at rest. Any motion requires the sort of advance coordination typically demanded of presidential visits and premarital sex. It is less room than nook.

Nooks don't get their fair due. Not with adults at least. Children appreciate a good nook. They instinctively seek them out, and if none is available create one. I recall, as a melancholic five-year-old, transforming our Baltimore living room into a labyrinth of nooks by stringing together dozens of blankets and sheets, then anchoring them to anything within reach: chairs, couches, the dog. I was too young to articulate my motives, but I now realize what it was I craved: the sublime combination of coziness and wonder, confinement and expansiveness, security and adventure, that only a nook provides.

I still like nooks. I suffer (if that is the right word) from claustrophobia's opposite. I am drawn to confined spaces, thrive in them. Maybe this is why I am so fond of Japan. No one confines like the Japanese. People of the Nook. They shoehorn themselves into subway cars and bars and alleged hotel rooms. Remarkably, they do all this without killing one another.

I turn to the first page. *The Pillow Book* reads like a private diary, and for good reason: it's a private diary. "I merely wrote for my personal amusement things that I myself have thought and felt," writes the author, Sei Shōnagon. She never expected her words to be read by others, which explains why others find them such a joy to read. *The Pillow Book* is written with the naked honesty typically reserved for the anonymous and the dying.

As I turn the pages, adjusting my pillow, I am drawn into Shōnagon's world, seduced by her boldness, her love of details—and how she finds beauty in the most unexpected places.

The title, like so much of *The Pillow Book,* is a mystery. Why a pillow? Perhaps Shōnagon kept the manuscript by her bedside, like a pillow. Perhaps she found comfort in the words it contained the way we find comfort in our favorite pillow. No one knows.

The Pillow Book is not a book, at least not in the conventional sense. It contains no narrative thread, no recurring characters, no overarching theme. *The Pillow Book* is a jambalaya of observations large and (mostly) small, "a crazy quilt of vignettes and opinions and anecdotes," notes Meredith McKinney, who translated *Makura no Sōshi, The Pillow Book* into English.

The book that is not a book is arranged in 297 numbered entries, ranging in length from a single sentence to several pages. Some entries relay anecdotes from the Imperial Palace in Kyoto, while others are simply opinionated lists. The lists are my favorite. In Shōnagon, I have found a kindred spirit, a list-making ally.

Shōnagon refuses to stay in a single lane. She swerves from "Refined and elegant things" to "Worthless things" then back to "Things that are truly splendid." It's tempting to conclude she is lost. She is not. She is engaging in *zuihitsu,* or "following the brush." It's a Japanese literary technique that is not a technique, which strikes me as the perfect way to write a book that is not a book. A writer practicing *zuihitsu* isn't afraid to follow a hunch, scratch an intellectual itch, then circle back, or not. The writer doesn't impose structure but, rather, allows one to emerge.

All of us, I think, could use a bit more *zuihitsu,* and not only when it comes to writing. *Set clear goals and channel all your energies into reaching them,* the self-help books advise. This approach assumes we've identified our destination before beginning our journey. Life doesn't work that way. Sometimes you don't know where you're going until you start moving. So move. Start where you are. Make a single brushstroke and see where it leads.

Shōnagon doesn't describe the world. She describes *her* world. No observation is neutral. She knows what she likes and what she doesn't. She subscribes to perspectivism, the philosophical theory advanced by

Nietzsche centuries later. There is not one truth but many. Choose one, says Shōnagon. Make it your own.

You might object that it is a surplus, not a dearth, of opinions that bedevils us. Thanks to social media, anyone can opine about anything anytime. These opinions, though, are heavily mediated—by friends and "experts" and, most insidiously, algorithms. The result: we see the world through a cloudy lens; our convictions are paper thin. Do you like that new sushi joint or do you only think you do because people give it five stars? Is the Taj Mahal really beautiful or have all of those swooning Instagram posts merely convinced you it is? Sei Shōnagon strived to ensure her lens was clean and clear, her opinions wholly her own.

For every one thing Shōnagon likes there are three she finds unpleasant or disturbing or repulsive or, her ultimate smackdown, infuriating. Among these, she says: "A guest who arrives when you have something urgent to do. A very ordinary person who beams insanely as she prattles on and on. A dog that discovers a clandestine lover as he comes creeping in, and barks. Fleas. Someone who butts in when you're talking and smugly provides the ending herself. (Indeed anyone who butts in, be they child or adult, is most infuriating.) Flies. A mosquito that announces itself with that thin little wail just as you've settled sleepily into bed. Rain all day on New Year's Eve."

Shōnagon is opinionated, but flexibly so. Consider the blossoms of a pear tree. The Japanese considered them ugly, and deployed them in insults, such as "he had a face like a pear blossom." Yet the Chinese adored them, she notes, so "there must be something to it after all." Sure enough, upon further reflection, she concludes they do possess a certain beauty. If you take a "careful and sympathetic look at it, you may notice that just at the tips of the petals there is the barest hint of a rather lovely luster."

Like Gandhi, Shōnagon was fussy. Consider this observation: "I cannot bear people who wear a white shirt that is slightly yellowed." Normally this sort of fastidiousness irritates me no end, but I grow to appreciate Shōnagon. She's not so much picky as she is sensitive.

Like Epicurus, Shōnagon invents a taxonomy of pleasure. She distinguishes the merely pleasurable from the truly *okashii*, or delightful.

Delight, unlike pleasure, contains an element of surprise, an unexpected frisson. And delight, unlike pleasure, leaves no bitter aftertaste. You never saw the delight coming so you don't miss it when it's gone.

For Shōnagon, the smallest detail can tip the balance. She approves of a three-layer fan, but not a five-layer one ("too thick, and the base looks ugly"). It is delightful when there's a feeling of snow in the air but "it ruins the mood of the occasion if the skies are instead heavy with the threat of rain." Hers is the philosophy of just-so-ism. Something is either *just right* or it is not right at all. Miss by an inch and you might as well have missed by a mile. An ox should have a tiny splash of white on its forehead, while cats should be completely black, "except for its belly, which should be very white." Musical performances are delightful but only at night, "when you can't see people's faces."

Something need not be perfect for Shōnagon to declare it delightful, but it must be appropriate. It must fit the mood, or the season. It must align with its essence. Thus "summer is best when it is extremely hot, winter when it is excruciatingly cold."

Shōnagon engages all her senses but especially the olfactory. She delights in the "sudden unfamiliar smell of the ox's leather crupper" and "taking a midday nap snuggled up under a lightly padded kimono that gives off a faint whiff of perspiration." She adored "scenting frames," wooden contraptions designed to infuse an article of clothing with the smell of a certain incense, and she enjoyed a good "scent-off," fierce competitions to see who could mix the most aromatic incense.

Most philosophers dismiss smell. Tomes have been written about the aesthetics of vision and the philosophy of music, yet hardly a word on scent. (Kant denied the sense any aesthetic status at all.) Yet smell is the most deeply rooted of senses. An infant as young as six weeks shows a strong preference for his mother's scent over that of another woman. Smell triggers memory in ways the other senses do not. Sadly, smell is now the bastard sense. To say something "smells" is to imply it smells badly. If something is suspect, we say it "smells fishy."

As Thoreau taught me, we only see what we're prepared to see. Most of us are ill-prepared to see the small. Not Shōnagon. She knew our lives are nothing more, or less, than the sum of a million tiny joys. "Shaved ice with a sweet syrup, served in a shiny new metal bowl. A crystal rosary. Wisteria flowers. Snow on plum blossoms. An adorable little child eating strawberries. A tiny lotus leaf that's been picked from a pond."

Like many Japanese, then and now, Shōnagon was fond of *sakura*, cherry blossoms. The trees are famously fleeting. They bloom for two or three days, and then are gone. Other flowers—plum blossoms, for instance—last considerably longer. Why go to such great lengths to cultivate something so fragile?

The Buddhist concept of *mujo*, or impermanence, holds clues. Life is ephemeral. Everything we know and love will one day cease to exist, ourselves included. Most cultures fear this fact. A few tolerate it. The Japanese celebrate it.

"The most precious thing in life is its uncertainty," wrote Yoshida Kenkō, a fourteenth-century Buddhist monk. He suggests we pay more attention to branches about to blossom or a garden strewn with faded flowers rather than blossoms in full bloom. The cherry blossom is lovely not despite its short life span but because of it. "Beauty lies in its own vanishing," says Japan scholar Donald Richie.

Appreciating life's small, fleeting pleasures demands a loose grip. Hold them too tightly and they break. What has been said of Thoreau applies equally to Shōnagon. "He is paying attention to things, but he is not grasping them, manipulating them, trying to figure them out."

This skill does not come naturally to me. My grip is too tight. I am always trying to figure things out, unearthing hidden meanings that may or may not exist. As for impermanence, it terrifies me.

Shōnagon loves many objects but none more than paper. Writing like a wine connoisseur in Burgundy, she recalls the time she laid her hands "on some Michinoku paper." Paper and wood were thought to possess a divine *kami*, or spirit. Craftsmen made the most cherished objects from wood: gold-lacquered boxes containing sutra scrolls, sandalwood boxes inlaid with mother-of-pearl, painted screens, mirrors, writing brushes, inkstands, musical instruments, *go* sets. Even today in Japan, everyday materials such as paper, wood, and straw receive as much attention and celebration—and sometimes more—as luxurious materials, such as gold or precious stones.

I feel Shōnagon's paper love. Whenever I'm in Tokyo, I make a point to visit Itoya in the Ginza district. Itoya is a stationery store, but that's like saying Yo-Yo Ma is a cellist: technically correct but woefully inadequate. Spread across two buildings and eighteen floors, it is a vertical ode to the analog: Italian-leather planners, sublime notebooks, exquisite pens. Everyone, shoppers and staff alike, shares this love of the tactile. No one rushes you. Fondling is encouraged. I could spend hours—days!—in Itoya, and I'm sure Shōnagon could, too.

Something need not be in pristine condition for her to find it delightful. Many of the objects she celebrates are old, worn—even dirty. She prefers not carefully tended ponds but "the sort that have been left neglected to the rampant water weed, where patches of reflected moonlight gleam whitely on the water here and there between the swathes of green."

The Japanese call this fondness for the imperfect *wabi. Wabi* is a frayed kimono or a cherry blossom lying forlorn on the ground or a "complete" collection of Shakespeare missing a play or two. If you've ever bought torn jeans or a distressed-leather bag, you have bowed to *wabi.*

For someone so quick to expose others, to shine a bright light on their charms and flaws, Sei Shōnagon reveals little of herself on the page. We know only the basics. She was born about AD 966 and was appointed to the court of Empress Teishi. She did whatever Empress Teishi wanted or needed or might conceivably want or need in the future. In exchange, Shōnagon was given room and board in the Imperial Palace in Kyoto and access to a world of beauty. Not a bad arrangement.

Shōnagon's world was highly circumscribed, geographically bounded by the walls of the Imperial Palace and the adjoining gardens, socially demarcated by the invisible but no less formidable wall that separated the aristocracy from everyone else. You'd think such a confined world would dull the senses of its inhabitants, yet it had the opposite effect: it heightened people's perceptions. Shōnagon lived in a nook. A beautiful nook.

I am in a taxi, heading to the Imperial Palace. I decide to walk the last few blocks. I'd like to say I walk mindfully, like Rousseau, but that would be a lie. I walk mindlessly, my head and feet not on speaking terms.

I step inside the walls of the palace and the adjoining gardens, as appealing today as they were in the tenth century. It's an enormous compound; rows of cherry blossoms and orange trees lead to a collection of cedar buildings that blend naturally into their surroundings.

As I walk, the summer sun hot on my neck, sweat soaking my shirt, I imagine Sei Shōnagon's world. She came of age during the Heian period. Heian means "peace." Warring factions sheathed their swords and reached for the calligrapher's brush. Historian Ivan Morris calls the period, which lasted from AD 794 to 1185, "the cult of beauty."

I love that. If I ever join a cult (always a possibility, given my utopian leanings and well-documented naïveté), this is the one for me. No other civilization, with the possible exception of Renaissance Italy, held beauty in such high regard and went to such lengths to cultivate it as Heian Japan. They wrote poetry. They played music. They created exquisite gardens. They mixed incenses with a fierce single-mindedness today reserved for Kona coffee and fantasy football.

The Heian Japanese internalized the artistic impulse, rendering it invisible the way rafters and beams and other supporting structures of a well-designed building are rendered invisible. Life was art and art was life, so closely linked as to be inseparable. The Japanese of the time prized the aesthetic experience more than abstract speculation. More important than what you knew was how you saw, how you listened, and, yes, how you smelled.

Heian Japan valued all the arts but none more so than poetry. Poetry punctuated every milestone of life: birth, courtship, and even death. A respectable Heian gentleman left this world with a parting poem. The good poet could win a lover's heart, or earn a promotion. A bad poet was mercilessly mocked.

It wasn't enough to write a beautiful poem. You had to package it beautifully, too. Imagine you're living in Kyoto of AD 970 and you want to send a message to someone. What do you do?

First, you must choose the paper. Not any paper will do. It must be the "proper thickness, size, design and color to suit the emotional mood that one wished to suggest, as well as the season of the year and even the weather of the particular day." Then you produce several drafts, experimenting with different compositions and brushes. Once satisfied with the words and the calligraphy, you fold the paper in one of several accepted styles, then attach an appropriate branch or spray of blossom. Finally, you summon "a smart, good-looking messenger," dispatch him to the proper address, and wait for a reply. Your poem might be met with approval or derision or, worst of all, silence. Ghosting is not a twenty-first-century invention.

When I learn of these elaborate poetry rituals, I can't help but compare them with our email rituals, such as they are. Sure, I choose the font, and perhaps an emoji or two, but no one has ever questioned the scent of my emails or the aroma of my text messages. Email is convenient, but convenience is never free. It always carries a hidden cost, a "convenience tax," one exacted in intimacy lost and beauty forfeited. Consciously or not, we gladly pay this tax. The people of Heian Japan did not.

They would find our soulless, scent-free missives not only aesthetically wanting but ethically suspect. Immoral. In Japan beauty was—and to an extent still is—considered a moral virtue. A morally upstanding person is an aesthetically attuned one. Beauty is an essential ingredient not only for the good life but the good person, too. Making the world a bit more beautiful is a generous, selfless act. It is ethical behavior, no different from the courage of a brave soldier or the compassion of a wise judge or, as Simone Weil believed, the loving heart of an attentive person.

Sei Shōnagon was clearly a witty, insightful writer, but was she a philosopher? Consult any compendium of history's great philosophers and you will not find her name. That's understandable. She developed no philosophical system, no theories about the universe and our place in it. She expressed little interest in ideas per se. It was people and things, beautiful things, that enthralled her.

Yet if the task of the philosopher is, as one scholar says, "to demonstrate that things can be otherwise," Shōnagon is clearly a philosopher. She shows us the world, her world, and says, in so many words: *Look at this. Isn't it marvelous? So tiny yet so beautiful.* If the task of philosophy is, as Nietzsche said, "to enhance our taste for life," then Shōnagon is a philosopher. After reading her for a few hours, colors appear more vivid, food tastes better.

Implicit in Shōnagon's philosophy is this: Who we are is largely shaped by what we choose to surround ourselves with. And it *is* a choice. Philosophy reveals the hidden choices we make. Realizing something is a choice is the first step toward making better choices. As the German writer Hermann Hesse said: "The man who for the first time picks a small flower so that he can have it near him while he works has taken a step toward joy in life."

I am sitting at a desk in Vermont, writing. I come here every summer. Always the same house, surrounded by the same objects. There's my laptop, with the soft, almost ethereal glow of its backlit keys, and the satisfying click they make as I type. There's my cup of coffee. I savor the pleasant weightiness of the mug, and the way it warms my hands on this, an unseasonably chilly summer day. I sense the gentle swoosh of liquid as I raise cup to mouth, touching its lip to mine and tasting the coffee, warm and pleasantly bitter.

Then there is the desk itself, solid and serious. Embedded in the wood is the intention of the designer, his or her guiding hand suggesting the desk be used for a certain purpose and in a certain way. There is the history of the desk, its biography, for objects have stories to tell, too. There is the lingering presence of the craftsman who made it, the people who owned it before, the movers who lugged it here, the nice woman who cleans it on Sundays. It's only a desk, yes, but it contains multitudes.

I read *The Pillow Book* and, across the centuries, Shōnagon and I lock eyes. Hers is a steely stare. She is sizing me up. She sees the bald head, the endemic keratoses, the mismatched clothes. I can imagine the lists I'd appear in. *Things That You Wish Weren't. Things that are oh-my-God-I-can't-even.* Sure, she also sees a mind that enjoys wrestling with big ideas but, still, she's not impressed, for here is a man who lacks the aesthetic impulse.

She's right. I am not a detail person. Grooming is for lesser mortals. I, a Man of Ideas, have no time for such trifles. I take perverse pride in my slovenliness, believing that intellectual depth is inversely proportional to neatness. My mind favors the big, like a camera stuck in wide angle. It overlooks details and seeks out the grand and the universal.

My size-ism extends to nearly every corner of my life. I excel at opening food containers (big) but forget to close them (small). I remember to feed the dog (big) but not the cat (small). I write books (big) but have awful handwriting (small). I never gave my size-ism much thought—who has time for such trivialities?—until now. My inattention to details, I realize, comes at a cost. It's hobbled me, constrained me. Once, it nearly killed me.

While still a teenager, I took flying lessons. I was doing well. Up to a point.

"You get the big things right but not the small ones," my flight instructor told me after one lesson. I wasn't sure whether this was a compliment or an insult. It all depends, I suppose, on how much you value the small. He did. I didn't.

One day, after our scheduled lesson ended, I taxied the plane back to the ramp and shut down the engine. I was unbuckling my shoulder harness when he said, nonchalantly, "I'm getting out here. Why don't you take it up yourself?"

"Say what?"

"You're ready."

"I am?"

"Yes, you are."

My first solo flight. I was sixteen years old and had not yet driven a car by myself. I gulped audibly.

"You can do this, Eric," said a voice that sounded remarkably familiar, for it was my own.

"Yes, I can do this," I replied to myself.

"I have no doubt," said my instructor, "but let me get out first."

"Oh yeah, of course."

He exited the plane, leaving the right seat eerily empty. I radioed ground control and requested permission to taxi for takeoff.

"Roger. Taxi to Runway 14," came the crisp reply.

I steered the plane until just short of the runway, then ran through my preflight checklist.

Flaps? Set.

Gas? Full.

Altimeter? Set.

Everything looked good. I radioed the control tower. Cleared for takeoff, I eased the throttle forward. Airspeed climbing nicely. Engine power on track. Wait—what's that rattling noise?

Something was wrong. I had seconds to decide whether to continue down the runway or abort the takeoff. As I gained speed, the rattling grew louder. I glanced up and saw the door handle was in the open position.

Damn. I had forgotten to—what's the technical term?—close the door. With one hand on the control yoke, I reached up with the other and latched the door shut. Seconds later, I was airborne. The rest of the flight went the way all flights should go: uneventfully. I nailed the landing.

As I taxied back to the ramp, the air traffic controller broke the usual clinical remove and transmitted a quick "Congratulations, Eric."

"Thank you," I said, all the while thinking, *If you only knew. If you only knew.*

Back home that evening, I replayed the incident in my mind. It was a small oversight, a mere door handle, but one that was potentially disastrous. My instructor was right. I was not good at the small things. Small things can kill you. They can also save you.

No one knew this better than Sei Shōnagon. One day, Empress Teishi, watching the joy Shōnagon derived from a finely woven tatami mat, remarked, “The simplest trifles console you, don’t they?” Shōnagon doesn’t record her reply, but I can imagine what she was thinking. *Yes, they do, Your Majesty, only they are not so trifling as you think.*

Sadness feels like a great weight, but maybe that is an illusion. Maybe it is lighter than we think. Maybe no heroic maneuvers are necessary. Maybe life’s so-called trifles—the great beauty of small things—can save us. Maybe salvation is closer than it appears. All we need to do is reach out—and close the door.

Does any of Japan’s “cult of beauty” remain today? Take one look at the bleak high-rises and concrete-lined rivers and you’d conclude no, it doesn’t. And, from that vantage point, you’d be right. Big Japan is ugly.

Go small, though, and everything looks different. I feel like a ten-year-old peering through a microscope for the first time, marveling at this hidden world that was there all along. I see micro-beauty everywhere: the soft glow of the vending machines; the *onigiri,* small triangles of rice and fish, wrapped so the seaweed remains crisp and crunchy until it’s time to bite into it; a glass of sake served in a perfect wooden box.

Back on the *shinkansen,* bulleting toward Tokyo, I retrieve my bento box from the shopping bag the clerk at the station had packed it in. The bag is made of paper, and it is beautiful. Solid handles. An attractive design on front. I remove the box carefully, grateful for the clerk’s kindness.

After lunch, I reach for my notebook and write, in all caps: “JAPANESE BULLET TRAIN: LISTS.” A good start. Too broad, though. I need to get specific. I need to go small. *Delightful things about a Japanese bullet train.* Better.

1. The way the conductor glides down the aisle then pivots and, facing the passengers, bows. 2. The way a passenger, a young woman in high

heels, teeters ever so slightly while walking down the aisle but steadies herself with the grace of a ballerina. 3. The feel of the Styrofoam coffee cup, one of those solid, thick ones that radiate a pleasant, not painful, warmth. 4. The way the cup says, in English, "Aroma Express Café" and the way the "o" in "Aroma" is shaped like a coffee bean. 5. The way, as you approach Tokyo, the view grows increasingly urban but gradually, so that the city doesn't appear so much as materialize. 6. The spotless toilets. 7. The unexpected glimpse of the sea. 8. The whooshing sound made by a train passing in the opposite direction, moving so fast there is no time to worry about a head-on collision. 9. The way the rain droplets bead across my window, forming rivulets and tributaries, moving with alacrity and seeming agency.

Dispiriting Things about Riding a Japanese Bullet Train. 1. That momentary thrill of spotting Mount Fuji only to be followed by the sharp stab of disappointment when you realize that, no, it is not Mount Fuji but just another mountain, nothing special. 2. Reveling in the sight of an empty seat next to you only to have it occupied at the last minute by a man who looks like an off-duty sumo wrestler. 3. The dated aqua-blue seats. 4. The fact that everyone on board is quiet, not a peep, even though you are not in the Quiet Car.

I've written my lists on quality paper—not Michinoku but, still, good stuff. Acid-free, it will last a long time. A few centuries, maybe longer. Not forever, though. Eventually, my lists will disintegrate, and join the other casualties of impermanence. This fact saddens but does not devastate me. It is the sadness of the moving van, of high school graduation, of the retirement party. It is the sadness of a late autumn day, when a wind gust stirs a pile of fallen leaves, and they dance.

We arrive in Tokyo on time. Good. I am meeting my friend Junko at a bar and don't want to be late. It is not just any bar. It is an *otaku* bar. An *otaku* is a geek, only in Japan, a nation of geeks, the word carries less opprobrium than it does elsewhere. *Otaku* is, in certain circles, a badge of honor.

The bar is a train *otaku* bar. A bar for train geeks. In the middle of the room, a model train runs with *shinkansen* punctuality. Such an arrangement could easily slide into gimmickry, but not here. The train—and the miniature town it passes through—seem natural, and thoroughly *okashii*, delightful. No detail was too small, too insignificant, for the person who designed this little railroad town. Not the tiny signboards fronting the tiny store or the tiny cars in the tiny parking lot or the tiny shrubbery lining the tiny road. The bar itself is small, too: six or seven chairs arranged in a circle with the train in the middle. A nook.

Junko orders a beer, and I order a Suntory. My whiskey arrives in a sturdy, serious glass that oozes quiet elegance. The bartender, a smiley man, had chiseled a single ice cube, as if it were *David* and he Michelangelo.

As he works, I ask him about—what else?—trains. He explains how as a child he could see trains rolling past his bedroom window, a reassuring presence during the bumpy years of his youth. Most children outgrow trains. Not him. As an unhappy salaryman, he spent his free time taking train rides to nowhere. "Riding a train makes me feel calm and happy," he explains. "On a train, I can think more clearly about life."

I nod and sip my whiskey, delighting in the solidity of the serious glass and the oaky taste and the slightly sweet aroma, all the while gazing at the tiny, beautiful world that lay before me.

PART THREE

DUSK

11.

How to Have No Regrets like Nietzsche

2:48 p.m. Somewhere in the Swiss Alps. On board Swiss Federal Railways, Train No. 921, en route from Zurich to St. Moritz.

My tray table locks into place with a solid and satisfying click. Nice. My window reveals a *Heidi* vista of soaring peaks and emerald fields. Nice. A few minutes later, a strange thought gate-crashes my reverie: all of this is nice but too nice.

Too nice? Is that possible? Everyone likes nice. Americans in particular. We sprinkle "nice" in our conversations like paprika. Sometimes we elongate it: *niiiiiice*. We can't get enough nice. When we say, reflexively, "Have a nice day," we don't add, "but not too nice." Too much niceness is like too much Rocky Road or too much love: theoretically possible but no one has experienced it.

Until now. After several hours of unrelenting nice, I crave grit, roughness. Grime.

Maybe I've been traveling too long and have gone a bit "coco-nuts," as a friend calls this road-induced loopiness. Maybe, I wonder, as the train noses into a nice tunnel (I didn't know tunnels could be nice), I've roused my latent masochism and will soon go full Rousseau, exposing my backside and inviting a good spanking.

There's another possibility, though, one that occurs to me as the cabin attendant, perfectly coiffed, pushing a perfect cart brimming with perfect pastries and perfectly brewed coffee, asks me if there's anything she can do to make my journey nicer. Maybe, I think, as I consider her question, suffering is essential to the good life. Maybe suffering is, in its own twisted way, nice.

"Sir? Can I offer you something?"

Yes, you can, I think. You can rough me up a bit, smear me with dirt and muck. Hurt me. Make me suffer, please.

More than a century ago, another traveler riding a Swiss train had similar thoughts. A failed composer and poet, an academic wunderkind who walked away from early success to live in the mountains, an "aeronaut of the spirit" who celebrated laughter and dance and whose motto was "Live dangerously!," he, too, craved suffering.

Groundhog Day is my favorite movie. By a mile. I must have watched it dozens of times. *Groundhog Day* is my favorite movie. By a mile. I must have watched it dozens of times. *Groundhog Day* is my favorite movie. By a . . .

I haven't merely watched the movie, I've communed with it, imbibed its ethos. I loved it when it first came out in 1993. I loved it before it became a cultural meme, before people used the word "meme" in conversation. I still love it. More than ever.

The protagonist is a curmudgeonly TV weatherman named Phil Connors. He is in Punxsutawney, Pennsylvania, to cover the annual Groundhog Day festival. Again. Phil isn't happy with this assignment and takes every opportunity to share his unhappiness with his earnest crew. Phil files his report, then goes to sleep. The next morning he wakes to find it is Groundhog Day again. And again and again. Phil is stuck in plebeian Punxsutawney, fated to relive the same day and cover the same insipid story, over and over. He responds to his plight with incredulity, indulgence, anger, deceit, despair, and, ultimately, acceptance.

The movie is classified as a romantic comedy, but *Groundhog Day* is, I believe, the most philosophical movie ever made. As Phil Connors wrestles with the blessing and the curse that are his eternally recurring day, he also wrestles with philosophy's major themes: What constitutes moral action? Do we possess free will or are our lives fated? How many blueberry pancakes can a grown man eat without exploding?

I am pleased though not surprised when I learn how closely the movie parallels an enthralling, mind-boggling theory posited more than a century ago by the German philosopher Friedrich Nietzsche. Nietzsche is the bad boy of Western philosophy. The delinquent too smart and prescient to ignore. Much as we'd like to dismiss him as crazy or anti-Semitic or misguided, Nietzsche was none of these. He was, and is, the most seductive, the most inevitable, of philosophers.

I arrive in Sils-Maria 124 years after Nietzsche. I see why he liked it. The gingerbread houses, authentic as they are adorable; the air, sharp and clear; and, everywhere I look, the Alps, stretching skyward. If there is such a thing as Swiss dirt, I see no evidence of it. Even the trash cans are spotless.

I walk the few yards from my hotel to the small house where Nietzsche lived. At the time, a shop selling tea and spices and other staples occupied the ground floor. Nietzsche rented a room on the second floor. It's been faithfully preserved, furnished simply, as it was in Nietzsche's day, with a narrow bed, a small writing desk, an Oriental rug, a kerosene lamp.

Simple, as I learned in Japan, need not mean lacking. Simple can be beautiful, and there's an elegant, aesthetically pleasing quality to the room. Nietzsche chose the wallpaper himself. Like Sei Shōnagon, he found beauty in the small. "We want to be the poets of our life—first of all in the smallest, most everyday matters," he wrote.

Nietzsche craved routine. He woke early, took a cold bath, and then sat down for a monkish breakfast: raw eggs, tea, an aniseed biscuit. During the day, he wrote and walked. In the evening, between seven and nine, he sat still in the dark. An admirably rigid routine, but hardly heroic. Where, I wonder, is the philosophical daredevil, the aeronaut of the spirit?

Physically, Nietzsche was no superhero, as the black-and-white photos on display here attest. They portray a wisp of a person, more mustache than man. He had large, dark eyes that made an impression on people—none more so than Lou Salomé, the alluring Russian writer and iconoclast who broke Nietzsche's heart. His eyes, she recalled, "had none of the searching, blinking quality which make so many short-sighted persons look unconsciously intrusive." Instead, she says, his defective eyesight "lent his features a very special kind of magic, for instead of reflecting changing impressions from outside, all they rendered was what was going on deep down within him." The mustache, bushy and Bismarckian, enhanced the opacity Nietzsche cultivated. It tricked people into thinking he was someone he was not.

One of the few philosophers to celebrate health as a virtue, Nietzsche enjoyed precious little himself. From age thirteen, Nietzsche suffered from migraine headaches that, along with a panoply of other ailments, plagued him throughout life. His terrible eyesight worsened over the years. He suffered fits of vomiting that lasted hours. Some days he couldn't get out of bed at all.

He tried many medical interventions and, for someone otherwise so skeptical, was remarkably susceptible to quackery. One doctor prescribed a regiment of nothingness: "no water, no soup, no vegetables, no bread." Nothing, that is, except the leeches he applied to Nietzsche's earlobes.

Nietzsche felt death's shadow keenly. His father died at age thirty-six. "Softening of the brain," the doctors said. (Cancer, most likely.) Nietzsche feared a similar fate awaited him. References to impending doom pepper his correspondence. His books are written in the urgent prose of a man who knew his days were numbered.

He was almost superhumanly prolific, publishing fourteen books from 1872 to 1889. Without exception, the books sold poorly. Nietzsche paid the printing costs of some himself. The world was not ready to hear what the "hermit of Sils" had to say.

Personally, I would have quit after the third flop. Not Nietzsche. He persisted, not even slowing down, despite the rejection and the physical ailments. How did he do it? What did he know?

The house contains a small library, books by and about Nietzsche, and a few scores, testimony to his aborted musical ambitions. What intrigues me most are the letters. He wrote a lot about the weather and was extremely sensitive to meteorological nuances. Wherever he went, he noted temperature and barometric pressure, recorded rainfall and dew points. Cloudy days depressed him. He craved "a sky that is eternally cheerful."

He found it in Sils-Maria. If it's possible for a place to save a life, Sils-Maria saved Nietzsche's. Yes, he still experienced headaches and stomach upset but these bouts were far milder. The Alpine air calmed his nerves, too. He could breathe again.

He birthed his biggest ideas here. It was in Sils-Maria that he pronounced, "God is dead," one of philosophy's most brazen assertions. It was in Sils-Maria that he conjured his dancing prophet and alter ego, Zarathustra, a fictionalized version of the Persian prophet who descends from the mountain to share wisdom with humanity. And it was in Sils-Maria that his greatest thought—"the thought of thoughts"—struck him with a ferocity he did not think possible.

It was August 1881. Nietzsche was on one of his usual walks along the shores of Lake Silvaplana, high above sea level, "6,000 feet beyond man and time." He had just come across "a mighty pyramidal block of stone" when the thought of thoughts arrived unbidden—an earthquake of an idea that led to a rethinking of the universe and our place in it, as well as a major motion picture starring Bill Murray and Andie MacDowell. The idea hit him hard and fast, heated and expanded to unimaginable size. Only later did it cool and congeal into these words.

> Imagine you are visited in the dead of night by a demon, who says to you: "This life, as you live it now and have lived it, you will have to live again and again, times without number; and there will be nothing new in it, but every pain and every joy and every thought and sigh and all the unspeakably small and great in your life must return to you, and everything in the same series and sequence—and in the same way this spider and this moonlight among the trees, and in the same way

> this moment and I myself. The eternal hour-glass of existence will be turned again and again—and you with it, you dust of dust!

Nietzsche is not speaking of reincarnation. You do not return as the same soul in a different body. It is the "self-same you" that returns, again and again. You do not, like Phil Connors of *Groundhog Day*, recall your previous iterations. You cannot, like Phil, edit your recurring life. Everything has happened before, and it will happen again, exactly the same way, forever. All of it. Even seventh grade.

How would you respond to the demon? asks Nietzsche. Would you "gnash your teeth and curse the demon who thus spoke? Or would you bow down before the demon and say, 'You are a god and never did I hear anything more divine!'"

Nietzsche called his idea Eternal Recurrence of the Same. It enthralled him. It terrified him. He walked, practically ran, back to his simple room in Sils-Maria, and for the next few months, despite excruciating head and eye pain, he could think of little else.

I wake to another day in Sils-Maria. I brush my teeth, just like yesterday, and splash cold water on my face. I shave, nicking my cheek, again, and tumble downstairs to the breakfast room—the same room where Nietzsche dined regularly. I see the same hostess as yesterday and the day before and who, once again, tolerates my garbled *guten morgen* and seats me at the same table by the same window.

At the buffet station, I find the same choices: the same hunks of Jarlsberg, the same flaky croissants, and the same fruit salad arranged in the same perfect semicircle. I order a coffee just as I did yesterday and the day before and pour precisely the same amount of milk. As I stand to leave, the hostess says, "Have a nice day," just as she did yesterday and the day before and, once again, I think but do not say, *Yes, but not* too *nice.*

I walk past the front desk, again, and say hello to Laura, who today like yesterday and the day before is wearing lederhosen. I step outside to a perfect Swiss day, a day like yesterday and the day before, and I set out on one of the nearby hiking trails. It is a different hiking trail from yesterday and, as Bill Murray's exasperated character in *Groundhog Day* says, different is good. I am on a mission. Not from God (we killed Him, Nietzsche reminds me) but from Zarathustra, Nietzsche's dancing prophet. I am determined to find the mighty stone, the place where the philosopher first imagined Eternal Recurrence. By seeing it, touching it, I hope to think what he thought that day—better yet, to feel what he felt.

I walk like Rousseau, as if I had all the time in the world. It feels good, not only the melodic cadence of my steps but the way sun and shade alternate as I step in and out of the pine trees that line Lake Silvaplana. The ground feels soft and spongy underfoot, as if it were conversing with me.

I walk and walk some more. My legs ache. Still I walk. I walk despite the pain, *because* of the pain. Nietzsche would approve, noting that I'm exercising my "will-to-power," overcoming an obstacle, on my way to becoming an *Übermensch* (literally "overman"), one step at a time.

I'm tempted to stop and read Nietzsche, but the philosopher dissuades me: "How can anyone become a thinker if he does not spend at least a third of the day without passions, people and books?"

His poor eyesight was a secret blessing. It liberated him from the tyranny of the book. When he couldn't read, he walked. He walked hours at a stretch, covering great distances. "Do not believe any idea that was not born in the open air and of free movement," he said. We write with our hands. We write well with our feet.

"All truth is crooked," Nietzsche said. All lives, too. Only in retrospect do we straighten the narrative, assign patterns and meaning. At the time, it's all zigs and zags. And white space: breaks in the text that cleave our former selves from some incipient future self. These white spaces look like omissions. They are not. They are wordless transitions, points where the currents of our life shift course.

One such bifurcation occurred early in Nietzsche's life. He was studying theology at Leipzig University when one day he popped into a secondhand bookshop. He felt drawn, he recalled, to one book in particular: Schopenhauer's masterpiece, *The World as Will and Representation.* He usually dithered before purchasing a book. Not this time.

Once home, Nietzsche threw himself on the sofa and "let that energetic and gloomy genius operate upon me." Nietzsche was delighted—and horrified. "Here I saw sickness and health, exile and refuge, Hell and Heaven." Shortly afterward, he switched his study from theology to philology, the study of language and literature. That may not seem momentous, but for the son and grandson of Lutheran pastors, it represented an act of rebellion.

Nietzsche excelled. At the age of twenty-four, he was appointed professor of classical philology at Switzerland's Basel University. The honeymoon proved brief.

His first book, *The Birth of Tragedy*, flouted academic norms. No footnotes, no dry, measured prose. An old mentor called it "a piece of pseudo-aesthetic, unscholarly religious mystification produced by a man suffering from paranoia." The wunderkind's shine had dulled. The academy likes nothing less than a smart rebel.

The second bifurcation came in 1879. His health had deteriorated. At times he could barely see and asked students to read to him. His attempt to gain a professorship in philosophy, his new passion, had failed. Most people, I imagine, would muddle along, seek better doctors, mend fences with department heads, make peace with the cushioned cage that is academia. No one walks away from a tenured position at one of Europe's most prestigious universities.

But Nietzsche walked. He set his affairs in order and fired off a brief letter to his publisher. "I am on the verge of desperation and have scarcely any hope left," he said, signing the letter, in all caps: "A HALF-BLIND MAN."

And so with that dramatic gesture he traded the settled life of a professor for that of a feral philosopher, answerable to no one but himself, unaffiliated and unbound. It was an incredibly courageous, or knuckleheaded, move. "Perhaps no one," says the writer Stefan Zweig, "has hurled a former life so far from himself as Nietzsche."

Like Rousseau, Nietzsche wandered. Unlike Rousseau, his wandering had a pattern, a cadence: Switzerland in the summer, Italy or southern France in the winter. His only property was the clothes he wore, the paper he wrote on, and the large trunk where he kept them.

He traveled by train. He hated trains. He hated the unheated carriages. He hated the rocking motion. He vomited a lot and paid for a single day's journey with three days of recovery.

Changing trains befuddled him. Sometimes he'd end up heading in the wrong direction. Once, while visiting the composer Richard Wagner, Nietzsche left a bag at a railway station. Inside were a precious volume of Ralph Waldo Emerson's essays and an autographed copy of Wagner's *Ring des Nibelungen* operas. Nietzsche, like Hemingway and T. E. Lawrence, could point to nothing redeeming about the incident. Sometimes a loss is just a loss.

I've yet to find Nietzsche's "mighty pyramidal block of stone" and decide to stop walking and read, an act of rebellion I'm sure he'd understand. I spot a bench. I sit down and crack open Nietzsche's book *The Gay Science* or, as it's sometimes translated, *The Joyful Wisdom*. After only a few sentences I realize Nietzsche doesn't speak to me. He shouts at me! If Socrates was the philosopher of the question mark, Nietzsche is the philosopher of the exclamation mark. He loves them! Sometimes he'll string two or three together!!!

Nietzsche is both a delight and a burden to read. It's a delight because his prose rivals that of Schopenhauer for its clarity and refreshing simplicity. He writes with the unabashed exuberance of a teenager with something important to say. He writes as if his life depended on it.

Nietzsche thought philosophy should be fun. He is playful, and funny in a biting way. Every truth, he said, should be accompanied by at least one laugh. He toys with ideas, and with literary devices. He writes in aphorisms, nursery rhymes, songs—and in the faux-biblical voice of his most famous invention, Zarathustra. His short, snappy sentences feel right at home on Twitter.

Nietzsche is a burden because, like Socrates, he demands we question entrenched beliefs, and that's never pleasant. I've always assumed philosophy was powered by hard reason and cold logic. If Rousseau put a dent in that belief, Nietzsche demolishes it. Infusing the pages is a quiet (and often not so quiet) celebration of the impulsive and the irrational. For Nietzsche, emotions are not a distraction, or a detour on the road to logic. They are the destination. The virtuous are irrational, and the most noble of all "succumbs to his impulses, and in his best moments his reason *lapses* altogether."

Rousseau embraced the heart. Nietzsche aims lower. He is the philosopher of the viscera—that place, says scholar Robert Solomon, "where doubts and rebellion grow, the parts of the body not easily tamed by merely valid arguments or the authority of professors."

Nietzsche was no fan of purely abstract thought. Such fuzzy ruminations never inspired anyone to do anything, he argued. "We have to learn to think differently . . . to feel differently," he said. He suffered from a kind of affective synesthesia. He thought the way most of us feel: instinctively, and with a ferocity not entirely under his control. Nietzsche didn't formulate ideas. He birthed them.

I'm immersed in his taut words, possibly on the verge of "flow," when I sense a presence. I look up and see a butterfly. It has alighted on Nietzsche, its golden-brown wings fluttering atop page 207. I'm not sure what to do. I'm tempted to snap a photo but fear that might spook the butterfly. Besides, recording the moment seems a poor substitute for experiencing it.

The butterfly has landed on a passage called "At the Sight of a Learned Book." A fine selection. Classic Nietzsche. "Our first question concerning the value of a book, a man, or a piece of music is: Can it walk? Or still better: Can it dance?"

Some philosophers shock. Many argue. A few inspire. Only Nietzsche danced. For him, there was no finer expression of exuberance and *amor fati*: love of fate. "I would only believe in a God who knows how to dance," he wrote. Nietzsche's Zarathustra dances wildly, fervently, with not even a trace of self-consciousness.

The spirit of every good philosopher, Nietzsche said, is that of a dancer. Not necessarily a good dancer. "Better to dance ponderously than to walk lamely," he said, and did. He couldn't muster even a few decent steps on the dance floor. So be it. The good philosopher, like the good dancer, is willing to make a fool of himself.

Nietzsche's philosophy dances superbly. It has rhythm. It skips and sashays across the page, and occasionally moonwalks. Just as dancing has no purpose—the dance *is* the purpose—so, too, with Nietzsche's philosophy. For Nietzsche, dancing and thinking move toward similar ends: a celebration of life. He's not trying to *prove* anything. He simply wants you to see the world, and yourself, differently.

Like an artist, a philosopher like Nietzsche hands us a pair of glasses and says, "Look at the world through these. Do you see what I see? Isn't it miraculous?" What we see may or may not be true in a scientific sense, but that is not the point. The philosopher conveys the truth not of the scientist but of the artist or novelist. It is an "as if" approach. View the world *as if* another level of reality, the noumenon, lies beneath the surface. Live your life *as if* it repeats endlessly. See what happens. Does looking at the world this way illuminate yours? Good. Then it has value. Viewing the world in a different way—even an "incorrect," different way, like Thoreau peering between his legs—enriches our lives.

The butterfly departs, its golden-brown wings lifting it skyward, and I resume my walk along the lakeshore. The air is thin and crisp. I see why Nietzsche craved it. Warm air dulls the mind. Cold air sharpens. I've covered several miles but, still, no sign of Nietzsche's mighty stone. I look everywhere. I look where it should be and where it shouldn't. Nothing. I backtrack, twice, and I hate backtracking. Still nothing. I'm exhausted and consider quitting but, no, I must persevere. Nietzsche's will to power demands it. He didn't quit when rejected by lovers and ignored by readers. Neither will I.

Nietzsche wasn't the first to suggest the universe repeats itself. The Greek philosopher Pythagoras posited a similar idea some 2,500 years ago, and the Indian Vedas even earlier. Nietzsche surely knew of these theories. Like Marcus Aurelius, he was a wisdom scavenger, casting his mind far and wide.

Nietzsche wanted to take the idea further. He wanted to convert Eternal Recurrence from myth to science. For days, weeks, he scribbled possible "proofs" on notepads. In one, he likens the universe to a pair of dice. There are only so many combinations possible. Eventually you'll roll them all. In tic-tac-toe, there are many more combinations: 26,830 possible games. That's a big number, but finite. Eventually, every possible game repeats, move for move. In chess, considerably more games are possible: 10 to the 120th power (one followed by 120 zeros). That's a mind-boggling number but, still, finite. It may take a very long time, but eventually two chess players will exhaust every possible combination of moves, play every possible game. The universe is, in a way, a large and complex game. Eventually everything repeats.

Nietzsche's belief, though, was just that: supposition propped up by ancient myths and fascinating but dubious statistical probabilities. Nietzsche never felt confident enough to publish his notes. Today most physicists dismiss Eternal Recurrence as more fiction than science.

There's another possibility, says Nietzsche. Maybe the question of proof doesn't matter. The lack of scientific evidence renders Eternal Recurrence—the "impossible hypothesis"—no less arresting. "Even the thought of a possibility can shatter and transform us," he says, pointing to the Christian concept of eternal damnation. Hell may not be real but the idea of it motivates. We need not prove Eternal Recurrence in order to act as if it were true, then see what happens.

Consider the case of Robert Solomon. In the 1960s, he was an "unhappy first-year medical student" at the University of Michigan. On a whim, he decided to take a course called Philosophy in Literature. When the professor introduced Nietzsche's Eternal Recurrence, Solomon was floored. It stirred a "whirlwind" of emotions and thoughts. Doubts, too. Did he really want to live this unhappy life over and over again, forever? That struck him as an especially fiery hell.

After the class, Solomon dropped out of medical school and pursued a life of philosophy, eventually becoming one of the world's top Nietzsche scholars. It's a decision he has not once regretted.

Eternal Recurrence is a thought experiment. An existential stress test. When it comes to life's pleasurable moments, we pass the test easily. We'd gladly relive eating that ice cream sundae, or sinking that game-winning three-pointer at the buzzer. Despairing over his Punxsutawney plight, Phil Connors, Bill Murray's character in *Groundhog Day*, muses: "I was in the Virgin Islands once. I met a girl. We ate lobster, drank Piña Coladas. At sunset, we made love like sea otters. *That* was a pretty good day. Why couldn't I get *that* day over and over and over?"

Eternal Recurrence doesn't work that way. It is all or nothing. A package deal. Your life repeats *exactly* the same way, "nothing to be different, not forward, not backward, not in all eternity," says Nietzsche. No editing allowed. You must relive *this* life, with all its flaws and lengthy dialogue. The director's cut. Nietzsche knows this scenario makes you squirm. He knows you'd love to revise your life, delete some scenes, add others, airbrush a few more, hire a body double.

I'd love to go back to that day of my first solo flight, only this time close the door *before* taking off. And I'd give anything to return to one warm Chicago evening. I was traveling with my daughter, six years old at the time. It was late. She was sleepy, and sometimes when children are sleepy, buried fears surface. As we walked, she looked at me and asked: "Are you my real daddy?"

I had a chance, as an adoptive parent, to supply a loving and reassuring answer. Instead, for reasons I still don't understand, I replied briskly, coldly. "Of course I am," I snapped. "Why would you even ask such a thing?" Her eyes swelled with tears and hurt. I had blown it. If only I could relive that moment but, this time, answer her question with love.

No, says Nietzsche. *No editing. Were you not paying attention? Affirm the entirety of your life, in every detail, or not at all. No exceptions.*

No wonder Nietzsche calls Eternal Recurrence "the heaviest burden." Nothing is weightier than eternity. If everything recurs infinitely, then there are no light moments, no trivial ones. Every moment, no matter how inconsequential, possesses the same weight and mass as others. "All actions are equally great and small."

Think of Eternal Recurrence as a daily check-in with yourself: Are you living the life you want to live? Are you sure you want to drink that bottle of tequila and endure an infinite hangover? Eternal Recurrence demands we ruthlessly audit our lives and ask: What is worthy of eternity?

One way of wrapping your mind around Eternal Recurrence is by taking what one scholar calls the "Marriage Test." Imagine you're recently divorced after a long marriage. Knowing what you know now, would you say "yes" again?

That's not a bad test, but I've devised another: The Teenager Test. Back home, I was having dinner with my daughter. Between talk of science projects and soccer schedules, I explained Nietzsche's Eternal Recurrence. What did she think? Would she sign up?

Sonya knows what she likes and what she doesn't and she does not like Nietzsche's Eternal Recurrence. She promptly declared it "the idea of a sociopath." No way would she want her life to recur forever. "Think of how miserable that would be. You're stuck in an infinite loop. Everyone has made one huge mistake in their life—I haven't yet, but I know it's going to happen—so imagine reliving that over and over again. Like imagine, you're murdered by an ax murderer. Do you want to relive that over and over? What if you had cancer? Would you want to relive that?"

"Fair point," I said, before rallying to Nietzsche's defense. "But what about the good things in life: concerts and friends and chicken nuggets? Don't they compensate for the bad?"

"No," she said without hesitation. "No one's life is that good. Nothing in my life could make me want to relive any bad things I potentially do."

I found myself in an unaccustomed state: silence. I had no rejoinder. Life's bad moments do seem to outweigh the good. The pleasure of Rocky Road dims when compared to the agony of chemo. Or does Nietzsche know something that Sonya—and the rest of us—do not?

If anyone had reason to go full Schopenhauer and conclude we are living in "the worst of all possible worlds," it was Friedrich Nietzsche. Instead, toward the end of his troubled, too-short life, he declares himself grateful for it all and adds a hearty *Da capo!* Again.

Suffering is inevitable—you don't need a philosopher to tell you that—but how we suffer, and about what, matters more than we think. Do we experience "essential suffering," as Nietzsche called it, or something else, something less? Do we merely tolerate suffering or do we value it for its own sake?

Nietzsche was no masochist. He saw suffering as an ingredient in the good life, a means of learning. "Only suffering leads to knowledge," he said. Suffering is the call we didn't solicit but must answer anyway. Do we reply by numbing ourselves or, as Schopenhauer suggests, retreating to art and asceticism? Or do we answer suffering by engaging with the world more deeply? Recklessly, even? Nietzsche called this option the Dionysian way, after the Greek god who loved wine and theater and life. "I want to learn more and more to see as beautiful what is necessary in things; then I shall be one of those who make things beautiful," he said. Don't love life despite the suffering, he says, but because of it.

Writing to his sister in 1883, Nietzsche offers what I think is his most honest account of the role suffering played in his life. "The whole meaning of the terrible physical suffering to which I was exposed lies in the fact that, thanks to it alone, I was torn away from an estimate of my life-task which was not only false but a hundred times too low. Some violent means were necessary in order to recall me to myself . . . an act of self-overcoming of the highest order."

I love that one phrase in particular: "recall me to myself." You need not look outside yourself for meaning, says Nietzsche. You needn't look inside yourself, either. Look up. "Your true being does not lie deeply concealed within you, but immeasurably high above you, or at any rate above what you usually regard as your 'I.' "

Eternal Recurrence strips our illusions bare and gives the lie to our accomplishments. You've closed the big deal, finished the book, earned the promotion? Congratulations—except now it's evaporated and you must start over. Again and again. Forever. We're all Sisyphus, the poor slob from Greek mythology condemned by the gods to push a boulder up a hill, only to watch it roll down again, for all eternity. I think back to that deck in Montclair, New Jersey, and my friend Jennifer's question. "What does success look like?" I know how Nietzsche would answer: It looks like radical acceptance of your fate. It looks like Sisyphus happy.

Like many philosophers, Nietzsche was better at dispensing wisdom than acting on it. "Die at the right time," he said, but didn't. He died too early—and too late.

He was in Turin, Italy, in 1889, when he saw a man whipping a horse. Nietzsche rushed toward the animal, hugged it—and collapsed. Nietzsche's last cognizant action was an attempt to ease the suffering of another being. When he gained consciousness, he was insane. He began signing his letters "Dionysus," and suggested he was God.

Concerned friends intervened and brought Nietzsche home to Germany. Incapacitated, possibly due to syphilis, and only forty-four years old, he would never write another word. For the next decade, family members cared for him—first his mother, then, after she died, his sister. Though now mute, his fame grew with each passing year.

It is this Nietzsche, broken and gone, that, sadly, is the one immortalized in photographs and exploited by his ambitious and anti-Semitic sister. Her misuse of his legacy led to Hitler's mercenary embrace of Nietzsche.

At the time of his collapse, Nietzsche was working on a book he called *The Revaluation of All Values.* A clunky title but a profound idea, one that, had he finished, might have offered important insights into Eternal Recurrence. If our life—indeed the entire universe—does repeat, what do we control? Not our actions, Nietzsche thought, but our attitude. His philosophy was, at its heart, "an experiment in reorienting oneself within a world of total uncertainty." Typically, we run from uncertainty and toward certainty. But that, says Nietzsche, is not an immutable fact. It is a value, and anything we value we can revalue.

We can *choose* to find joy not in certainty but in its opposite. Once we do that, life—the same life from an outsider's perspective—feels quite different to us. Find joy in uncertainty and the tumult at the office becomes cause for celebration, not teeth gnashing and an extra glass of wine at the end of the day. Find joy in uncertainty, and even illness, while still physically painful, no longer terrifies. This shift in perspective is subtle but profound. The world looks different. A reorientation like this is not easy, Nietzsche acknowledges, but it is possible—and what is philosophy but an exploration of heretofore undreamt-of possibilities?

My walk ends in failure. Despite much searching, and even more backtracking, I do not find the pyramid-shaped boulder. Oh well, there's always tomorrow. Then I recall the words of *Groundhog Day*'s Phil Connors: "What if there is no tomorrow? There wasn't one today."

In Eternal Recurrence, every tomorrow is today and every today tomorrow. I will walk this same path an infinite number of times. In the Hollywood version, I'm able to make course corrections, adjustments large and small, until I find the boulder and get the girl and all is well. Roll credits.

Nietzsche's version of Eternal Recurrence supplies no such happy ending. Yes, I will walk the same path, again and again, but without deviation. I will choose the same bench, encounter the same butterfly, and I will seek but not find Nietzsche's boulder. *Every time. Forever.*

Can you accept that endless failure? asks Nietzsche. More than that, can you embrace it? Can you *love* it?

About a missed rock—sure, Friedrich. About life's larger disappointments—botched job interviews, bungled parenting, fickle friends—I'm less certain. I can resign myself to their existence, accept them even. But love them? That is asking an awful lot. I'm not there yet. Maybe I never will be, no matter how many times the universe and I repeat.

There's a reason *Groundhog Day* is a comedy. If we do live the selfsame life over and over again in the selfsame way, forever and ever, then what can we do but laugh?

Better yet: dance. Don't wait for a reason to dance. Just dance. Dance feverishly and with abandon, as if no one is watching. When life is good, dance. When it hurts, dance. And when your time is up and the dance is over, say—no, shout—*Da capo!* Again, again.

12.

How to Cope like Epictetus

4:58 p.m. Somewhere in Maryland. On board Amtrak's Capitol Limited, en route from Washington, D.C., to Denver, via Chicago.

Not more than thirty minutes into our journey, we stop. We wait. And wait. I do so impatiently, knowing I am disappointing Simone Weil but unable to stop myself.

It's not the waiting that irks me so much as the not knowing why. A downed tree on the tracks? A freight train with the right of way? An imminent nuclear strike? I look at my phone as if it has the answers. (It does not.) I fidget. I look at my watch. I fidget some more.

We will sit here for hours, I fear. I will miss my connection in Chicago. That is not good, not good at all. The situation, I decide, calls for fretting. So I fret.

I am aware of the beauty that lies just outside my window: rows of chestnut oaks and flowering dogwoods lining the C&O Canal, and up there, a rich, blue sky. I do not enjoy this view, though, for that would interfere with my fretting. I need help. I need Stoic Camp.

I knew this the moment I spotted the ad. Nothing flashy. Black-and-white, no fancy graphics. "Gain a sense of 'stoic calm' by escaping to camp at the foot of the Snowy Range mountains," it said.

We're moving again. Perhaps my worrying was pointless, or perhaps its not insignificant energy propelled us forward. I've always believed my fretting holds the world together and, should I stop, even for a second, the universe would cease to exist.

I make my connection in Chicago and, before long, am heading west, toward Denver and, eventually, Wyoming's Snowy Range. Amtrak goes many places. It does not go to Laramie, Wyoming. I must travel the last leg of the journey by bus. Except when we arrive at Denver's Union Station there's no sign of the bus. Reflexively, I catastrophize, and fret. The bus has left without me, or it doesn't exist, never did and never will.

After what seems like hours but may have been twelve minutes, the bus arrives. I clamber on board and find a seat in the back. We're moving, traversing space, just like a train. Only, it's not the same.

A common Stoic exhortation is to "live in accord with nature." The organizers of Stoic Camp take this advice literally. The grounds are snuggled in thick Wyoming forest, miles from the nearest town, which isn't much of a town—just a gas station and three bars.

We Stoic campers gather in the main lodge for orientation. It's a vast room, with high ceilings and, at one end, a serious fireplace, much needed even though it is late May. There's talk of snow. From one wall, a giant stuffed elk looks down on us. The lodge's so-called furniture consists of a hodgepodge of mismatched couches and stiff, plastic chairs—a jarring aesthetic that would displease Sei Shōnagon. If a ski lodge mated with a minimum-security prison, this would be the result.

We're an odd bunch, we Stoic campers. There's Greg, a thirty-something digital entrepreneur from New York, and Alexander, a cheery German consultant, and a smattering of grad students from the University of Wyoming: serious young men and women who look pained by existence, by the *thought* of existence, and who, during breaks, rush outdoors, no matter the weather, and smoke. Then there are us "graybeards," as we've been dubbed: those drawn to Stoicism just in the nick of time.

We gather in a circle, the universal geometry of philosophical jam sessions and group therapy, sipping coffee from Styrofoam cups. A stout, cherubic man calls the meeting to order. Rob Colter is middle-aged, with an impressive paunch, a gray goatee, and quick, probing eyes. He looks like an aging, hipster Santa. When he is conveying something profound, which is often, he gently strokes his goatee.

"Welcome," says Rob, in a tone that gives nothing away. "If you've seen the weather forecast, you know our Stoic abilities will be challenged." It is late May, yet there is snow in the forecast. Lots of snow. I am concerned. I have packed for spring, not winter, and I have a flight to catch after Stoic Camp.

Rob is as paradoxical as the philosophy he loves. He reads ancient Greek *and* fly-fishes. He leads a healthy, outdoorsy life, yet also confesses to a "Panda Express problem." He possesses a deep understanding of philosophy, yet isn't afraid to confess ignorance, too. "I don't know," he says when asked a particularly sticky question. "I'll have to think about that." I like Rob.

A few years ago, he detected a surge of interest in Stoicism. "And I thought, well, the Stoic motto is 'live in accord with nature' and, hey, we've got plenty of nature around here." He floated the idea of a Wyoming Stoic Camp to his fellow philosophers at the university, who replied, philosophically, "That's fucking crazy. It will never work, but go ahead and try." So he did. And here we are.

Rob tells us how he came to love Stoicism. It was the 1990s. He was studying philosophy in Chicago, home to "a real Plato scene." Rob studied Plato, and his protégé Aristotle, not because he loved their ideas but because that was what serious students of philosophy did. "They were *real* philosophers, *damn it*," he says, pounding his fist for emphasis. Sure, he was aware of others: Epicurus, the Cynics, and, yes, the Stoics, but these were not "real" philosophers, or so he thought.

Different philosophers appeal to different people at different times. Thoreau's rebellious spirit attracts teens. Nietzsche's flame-throwing aphorisms draw young adults. Existentialism's emphasis on freedom appeals to the middle-aged. Stoicism is an older person's philosophy.

It is a philosophy for those who have weathered a few battles, suffered a few setbacks, known a few losses. It is a philosophy for life's rough patches, large and small: pain, illness, rejection, annoying bosses, dry skin, traffic jams, credit card debt, public humiliation, delayed trains, death. Asked what he learned from philosophy, Diogenes, a proto-Stoic, replied: "To be prepared for every fortune."

Stoicism, the unlikely progeny of a shipwreck, came of age during a time of great upheaval in ancient Greece and thrived during the rough-and-tumble world of the Roman Empire. Its most famous practitioners were variously exiled, executed, maimed, and ridiculed. Yet as Marcus Aurelius, himself a Stoic, demonstrates, they were also wildly successful.

More recent adherents include American war heroes and presidents. A Stoic thread runs throughout U.S. history: from the Founding Fathers, including George Washington and John Adams; to Franklin Roosevelt, who, when he famously said, "The only thing we have to fear is fear itself," expressed a quintessentially Stoic idea; to Bill Clinton, who considers Marcus's *Meditations* a marvelous piece of wisdom writing and his favorite book.

"Wisdom" is one of those words everyone knows but nobody defines. Psychologists have struggled for decades to nail down a working definition. In the 1980s, a group of researchers at the Max Planck Institute for Human Development in Berlin sat down to hammer one out once and for all. The Berlin Wisdom Project identified five criteria that define wisdom: factual knowledge, procedural knowledge, life-span contextualism, relativism of values, and management of uncertainty.

The last criterion, I think, is the most important. We live in the age of the algorithm and artificial intelligence, with their tacit promise to manage the uncertainty, the messiness, of life. They have not. If anything, life feels less predictable, and messier, than ever.

This is where Stoicism shines. The philosophy's core teaching—change what you can; accept what you can't—is appealing in our tumultuous times. Stoicism offers a handrail, a way forward. I knew this, having read Marcus. What I didn't know was how demanding the philosophy is, and how much fun.

Stoicism, the philosophy of tough times, was born of catastrophe. In about 300 BC, a Phoenician merchant named Zeno was sailing to the Athenian port of Piraeus when his ship capsized, his precious cargo of purple dye lost. Zeno survived the shipwreck and wound up in Athens, broke. One day, he stumbled upon a biography of Socrates, who was by then long dead.

"Where can I find a man like that?" Zeno asked the bookseller.

"Follow yonder man," he replied, pointing to a shabbily dressed Athenian who happened to be walking by.

It was Crates, a Cynic. The Cynics were the hippies of the ancient world. They lived on little, owned nothing, and questioned authority. Zeno found the Cynics' contrariness admirable, up to a point. Lacking, he thought, was a comprehensive philosophy, so he founded his own school.

Zeno set up shop under the *stoa poikile* (literally, "painted porch"), a long colonnade where people came to shop, conduct business, and talk. There, amid murals depicting battles real and mythological, Zeno delivered his lectures while pacing vigorously. Since they gathered at the *stoa*, these philosophers became known as Stoics.

Unlike the Epicureans, ensconced behind their garden wall, the Stoics practiced their philosophy publicly, in view of merchants and priests and prostitutes and anyone else passing by. For the Stoics, philosophy was a public act. They never shied from politics.

Toward the end of his life, Zeno liked to joke, "I had a good voyage when I was shipwrecked." This would become a major theme of Stoicism: in adversity lies strength, and growth. As the Roman senator and Stoic philosopher Seneca said: "No tree becomes rooted and sturdy unless many a wind assails it. For by its very tossing it tightens its grip and plants its roots more securely . . . disaster is virtue's opportunity."

On day one of Stoic Camp, I discover that everything I thought about Stoicism is wrong. The stereotype of the stony, heartless Stoic is as erroneous as is the one about the gourmand Epicurean. The Stoic is no cold fish. He does not suppress strong feelings, putting on a brave face as he trembles inside. Stoics do not jettison all emotions, only the negative ones: anxiety, fear, jealousy, anger, or any of the other "passions" (or *pathe*, the closest ancient Greek word to "emotion").

Stoics are not joyless automatons. They are not Mr. Spock. They do not endure life's bad bits with a stiff upper lip, or any other body part. "It's not bad and there's nothing to endure," says Rob.

Stoics are not pessimists. They believe everything happens for a reason, the result of a thoroughly rational order. Unlike grumpy Schopenhauer, they believe we are living in the best of all possible worlds, the *only* possible world. Not only does the Stoic consider the glass half full; he finds it a miracle he has a glass at all—and isn't it beautiful? He contemplates the demise of the glass, shattered into a hundred pieces, and appreciates it even more. He imagines life had he never owned the glass. He imagines a friend's glass breaking and the consolation he'd offer. He shares his beautiful glass with others, for they, too, are part of the *logos*, or rational order.

"Joyful Stoic" is not an oxymoron, says William Irvine, a professor of philosophy at Wright State University and a practicing Stoic. He explains: "Our practice of Stoicism has made us susceptible to little outbursts of joy. We will, out of the blue, feel delighted to be the person we are, living the life we are living, in the universe we happen to inhabit." I confess: that sounds appealing.

Stoics are not selfish. They help others—not out of sentimentality or pity but because it is rational to do so, the way fingers help the hand; and they are happy to endure discomfort and even pain while helping others.

Stoic altruism sometimes appears clinical, but it is exceptionally effective. I have a friend, Karen, who is a Stoic, though she doesn't know it. I first met her in Jerusalem, where we were both working as journalists. There are a lot of stray cats in Jerusalem, more than in most places. It broke my heart to see these scruffy felines, with matted fur and open sores. I felt bad for them. That was the extent of my "helping."

I responded to their suffering by suffering myself, as if that somehow constituted a form of aid.

Not Karen. She sprang into action, scooping up a stray tabby here, a gimpy Oriental shorthair there. She fed them, and took them to a veterinary clinic. She found them homes. She did more than just emote.

Rob hands each of us a Stoic Camp workbook and a slim ancient text. More of a pamphlet, actually. Only eighteen pages. The *Enchiridion*, or *Handbook*. The teachings of the former Roman slave turned philosopher Epictetus. Stoicism distilled to its essence.

We turn to the first line on the first page, which Rob reads aloud: "Some things are up to us and some are not up to us." This strikes me as both extremely true and extremely obvious. *Of course* some things are up to us and some aren't. I traveled two thousand miles for this?

But that single sentence expresses the essence of Stoicism. We live in an age where we're told everything is up to us. If you're not smarter or richer or thinner it's because you're not trying hard enough. If you get sick, it's because of something you ate, or didn't eat, or a medical test you failed to get, or did get, or an exercise you didn't do, or overdid, or a vitamin you did or did not take. The message is clear: you are in control of your destiny. Are you, though? Where exactly does your sovereignty reside?

Not where you think, the Stoics reply. Most of what we consider under our control is not. Not wealth or fame or health. Not your success or the success of your children. Yes, you can exercise regularly, but you can also get hit by a bus on the way to the gym. You can eat only the healthiest foods, but that is no guarantee of longevity, either. You can put in fourteen-hour days at the office, but maybe your boss doesn't like you and sabotages your career.

The Stoics have a word for these circumstances and achievements that lie beyond our control: "indifferents." Their presence doesn't add one iota to our character or our happiness. They are neither good nor bad. The Stoic, therefore, is "indifferent" to them. As Epictetus says:

"Show me a man who though sick is happy, who though in danger is happy, who though dying is happy, and who though in disrepute is happy. Show him to me! By the gods, I would then see a Stoic!"

An enemy can harm your body but not you. As Gandhi, who had read the Stoics, said, "Nobody can hurt me without my permission." Even the threat of torture at the hands of a tyrant needn't rob you of tranquility and nobility, adds Epictetus. His teachings helped James Stockdale, an American pilot shot down over North Vietnam, endure seven long years of imprisonment and torture.

They helped Rob Colter, too. He was in New Zealand, looking forward to delivering a lecture, when he began to experience stomach pains. At first he dismissed the pain as a touch of tummy upset from the long journey. Soon, though, it grew worse, much worse. "The kind of pain that morphine doesn't put a dent in," Rob recalls. At the hospital, doctors diagnosed an obstructed bowel, a potentially life-threatening condition.

Amid the waves of pain, Rob managed to recall the words of Epictetus: "You are nothing to me." He repeated that, over and over, addressing the waves of pain crashing into him. *You are nothing to me.* He felt better—not a lot better, but better. "My body is not under my control—any illusions of that were stripped away."

Rob's world shrank: the hospital room, the doctors and nurses. And his pain. Five tubes protruded from his body. He hadn't bathed in six days. He faced a difficult surgery, one that might leave him dependent on a colostomy bag for the rest of his life. He made his choice the Stoic way, rationally. "If I don't do this, I'm going to die, so let's do it."

The surgery was a success. No bag. His recovery was slow but steady. His insurance company sprang for a first-class seat for the flight home. The Stoics call this sort of bonbon a "preferred indifferent," something nice to enjoy occasionally but not central to our happiness.

Looking back at the episode, Rob knows his Stoic attitude didn't change the outcome, but it did change how he endured it. He suffered but he did not compound his suffering by wishing life were otherwise.

Epictetus was born a slave in AD 55 in what is today Turkey. His master, an advisor to Emperor Nero, beat him. Epictetus bore the mistreatment stoically. One day, the story goes, Epictetus's owner began to torture him by twisting his leg. "If you keep that up, you're going to break it," said Epictetus calmly. The owner continued twisting Epictetus's leg until it broke. "Didn't I tell you it would break?" said Epictetus matter-of-factly. He was lame for the rest of his life.

Eventually freed from slavery, he moved to Rome, where he studied philosophy and soon gained a reputation as a dedicated and effective teacher. When, in AD 93, Emperor Domitian banished all philosophers from Rome, Epictetus moved to Nicopolis, a thriving coastal city in western Greece. There he attracted even more students, famous ones, like Hadrian, a future emperor, but mostly ordinary young men who traveled far to reach Nicopolis. Many were homesick. All were eager to learn.

Epictetus admired Socrates, and in many ways emulated him. Like Socrates, he lived simply, in a hut, with only a mattress as furniture. Like Socrates, Epictetus had no interest in metaphysics; his was a rigorously practical philosophy. Like Socrates, Epictetus valued ignorance as a necessary step on the road to true wisdom. Philosophy begins with "consciousness of our own weakness," he said.

Much of life lies beyond our control, but we command what matters most: our opinions, impulses, desires, and aversions. Our mental and emotional life. We all possess Herculean strength, superhero powers, but it is the power to master our interior world. Do this, the Stoics say, and you will be "invincible."

Too often we place our happiness in the hands of others: a tyrannical boss, a mercurial friend, our Instagram followers. Epictetus, the former slave, likens our predicament to self-imposed bondage. Only the man or woman who wants nothing is free.

Imagine, says Epictetus, you handed over your body to a stranger on the street. Absurd, right? Yet that's what we do with our mind every day. We cede our sovereignty to others, allowing them to colonize our mind. We need to evict them. Now. It's not so difficult. It is far easier to change ourselves than to change the world. This is one problem with trigger warnings, so prevalent on college campuses. They reinforce the presumption that college students are unable to control their reactions to potentially disturbing content. It disempowers them. It is not the Stoic way.

Think of an archer, says Cicero. He pulls the bow, as expertly as his abilities allow, but once released, exhales, knowing the arrow's trajectory is no longer in his hands. As the Stoics say: "Do what you must; let happen what may." We can inoculate ourselves against the bite of disappointment by switching from external to internal goals: not winning the tennis match but playing our best game; not seeing our novel published but writing the best, most honest one we are capable of writing. Nothing more, nothing less.

The fire has dwindled to hot ash, the coffee grown cold, but no one notices. We're knee-deep into Stoicism and ready to dive deeper. One by one, we read the crisp entries from Epictetus's *Handbook*. Some merit lengthy discussion, others a simple nod. Then we come across this line: "What upsets people is not things themselves but their judgments about things." We sit there in silence, absorbing this two-thousand-year-old nugget, as obvious as it is profound.

The Stoics believe our emotions are the product of rational thought, but it is flawed thought. We can change the way we feel by changing the way we think. The Stoic aims not to feel nothing but to feel correctly. I realize that sounds odd. We don't think of our emotions as either correct or incorrect. They just are. We have no control over them.

Not true, say the Stoics. Emotions don't wash over us like waves on the beach. They happen for a reason. As the classicist A. A. Long explains, "We don't typically get angry or jealous *for no reason*, but precisely because we think that someone is treating us badly or someone is achieving success that we, rather than he, deserves." We are as responsible for our emotions as we are for our thoughts and actions. They are the result of judgments we make, and these judgments are often faulty. They are not misguided, or muddled, the Stoics say, but empirically wrong.

Imagine a traffic jam. Two drivers sit bumper-to-bumper. One is frazzled and angry, banging on the steering wheel and cursing. The other sits calmly, listening to NPR and recalling a meal of lobster ravioli he enjoyed recently. Clearly, the Stoics say, both drivers can't be "right." And they aren't. The frazzled driver is incorrect, as incorrect as if he had concluded that two plus two equals three. To wish life is otherwise represents an egregious failure of reason.

Let's examine how a faulty emotion is born. It starts with a reflexive reaction (called "pre-emotions" or "proto-passions") to an external event (an "impression" in Stoic-speak). We stub our toe, then scream. We get stuck in traffic, then curse. This is natural. We are human after all. That initial shock is not an emotion but a reflex, like blushing when you're embarrassed. It *becomes* an emotion when you "assent" to it, the Stoics say. When you assent, you elevate its status from reflex to passion.

All of this happens quickly, in a flash, but none of it happens without our permission. Every time we choose to honor, and amplify, these negative proto-passions we are *choosing* unhappiness. Why in the world, ask the Stoics, would you want to do that?

We must sever the link between impression and assent. This is where the Socratic pause—the "Mighty Pause," I call it—comes in handy. Says Epictetus: "Be not swept off your feet by the vividness of the impression, but say, 'Impression, wait for me a little. Let me see what you are and what you represent. Let me try you.'" Only when we realize our reaction to hardship is not automatic but a choice can we begin to make better choices.

But doesn't everyone get upset when they're stuck in traffic or stub their toe? No, they don't, and, besides, says Rob, "Just because lots of people get upset when they stub their toes doesn't mean you should, too." We are always free to withhold assent. *That* is fully up to us.

If you must assent to these proto-passions, assent in a different direction, suggests Epictetus. Relabel them. If you're alone, relabel your solitude as tranquility. If you are stuck in a crowd, relabel it a festival, "and so accept all contentedly." Another mind trick? Sure, but a helpful one. Your mind is always playing tricks with reality anyway. Why not put those tricks to good use?

There's a scene in the movie *Lawrence of Arabia* where Lawrence, played by Peter O'Toole, calmly extinguishes a match between his thumb and forefinger.

A fellow officer tries it himself, and squeals in pain. "Ouch, it damn well hurts," he says.

"Certainly it hurts," replies Lawrence.

"Well, what's the trick, then?"

"The trick," says Lawrence, "is not minding that it hurts."

Lawrence's response was Stoic. Sure, he felt the pain, yet it remained a raw sensory sensation, a reflex. It never metastasized into a full-blown emotion. Lawrence didn't *mind* the pain, in the literal sense of the word: he didn't allow his mind to experience, and amplify, what his body had.

Stoic Camp is not merely a philosophy salon set in the Wyoming woods. It is a laboratory. We campers are the guinea pigs. A number of experiments are under way. Like this one: Take a middle-aged man, accustomed to certain creature comforts—including but not limited to pillows, blankets, single malt—and immerse him in a rustic cabin with fifteen malodorous grad students. Withhold bedding and single malt. Add continuous noise; season with bright fluorescent lights. Stir frequently. Freeze overnight.

It is in my nature to whine. It is in my name, too. I *want* to moan and groan and carp and kvetch and bellyache. I restrain myself, recalling an old Stoic maxim: "No good man laments, nor sighs, nor groans." Complaining, Marcus reminds me, won't lessen the pain and may exacerbate it. "Either way," he says, "it is best not to complain."

I look for a suggestion box—a suggestion, I decide, is technically not a complaint—but there is none. Of course. This is Stoic Camp. So I stop. I pause. Not a Mighty Pause, more a micro-pause, but I'll take it. I slow down and ask: What aspects of this situation are up to me? Not the lack of heat or blankets. These are beyond my control. If I want a single malt, I could walk three miles into town. It's my choice. The Scotch, as well as heat and blankets, are indifferents, even if they are ones I prefer. They are not under my control. Only my attitude, my assent or lack thereof, is. Epictetus uses the analogy of a dog tied to a cart. The cart is moving, and will continue to move no matter what. The dog has a choice: be dragged on the ground or trot alongside it. I need to start trotting.

Besides, I am engaging in what the Stoics call Voluntary Deprivation. (All right, not so voluntary in my case.) Seneca, among the wealthiest of Romans, recommended practicing poverty for a few days each month. Eat the “scantiest and cheapest fare” and wear “coarse and rough dress,” he advised. When Stoics practice Voluntary Deprivation they are, on one level, adhering to their maxim: “live in accord with nature.” Sweat when it’s hot, shiver when it’s cold, feel hunger pangs when famished. The goal of Voluntary Deprivation, though, is not pain but pleasure. By occasionally denying ourselves certain comforts, we appreciate them more, and lessen their hold on us.

Voluntary Deprivation teaches self-control, which has all sorts of benefits. Refrain from eating that piece of chocolate cake and you will feel good about yourself. Forgoing pleasure is one of life’s greatest pleasures.

Voluntary Deprivation cultivates courage. It also inoculates us against future deprivation, which might not be voluntary. We experience a prick of pain now but much less later.

I realize I’ve been practicing a version of Voluntary Deprivation for years, though I’ve called it by another, cheerier, name: Intermittent Luxury. The habit began when I was a foreign correspondent for NPR. I made several reporting trips to Iraq during the reign of Saddam Hussein. Due to UN sanctions, flights were banned. That meant a long overland journey from Amman, Jordan, to Baghdad.

I had a routine. I’d spend a few days in Amman, applying for an Iraqi visa and stocking up on provisions (chocolate, chemical suits, single malt). The Jordanian hotel was nice. Not the world’s best but nice. Good enough, as Epicurus would say. Once credentialed and supplied, I’d hire a driver for the twelve-hour journey across the Badia desert. My hotel in Baghdad, a creepy place called the Al-Rashid, was less nice. The rooms smelled of mildew and I suspect were bugged by Saddam’s agents.

When I returned to Amman several weeks later, the "nice enough" hotel felt like a palace. The bed was plusher, the food tastier—even the water pressure felt stronger. The hotel hadn't changed. I had.

Years later, while living in Miami, I'd periodically switch off my car's air conditioner, even during summer. Within seconds, the interior grew hot, my sweaty skin sticking to the leather seats of my VW. Yet I enjoyed it, for I had reminded myself what hot feels like and thus renewed my deep and abiding gratitude for Willis Carrier, inventor of the modern air conditioner. Voluntary Deprivation? I suppose, but I prefer to think of it as Intermittent Luxury—the unexpected upgrade to first class, the splurge at that restaurant everyone's talking about, the hot shower after a weeklong camping trip.

So I decide to stop whining (internal whining is still whining) about the rough conditions. What had I expected from a place that contained the words "Stoic" and "Camp," and in such proximity? Know what you're getting into, Epictetus advised. If you're going to the public bath, remember "there are people who splash, people who jostle, people who are insulting, people who steal." Don't be surprised if you get wet, or robbed. He's right. Why should I be surprised that the accommodations at Stoic Camp are on par with a Baghdad hotel? It is not the lodging that must change but my attitude. Besides, the Stoics remind me, it can always get worse.

This brings us to another vaccine in the Stoic dispensary: *premeditatio malorum*, or "premeditation of adversity." Anticipate the arrows of Fortune, says Seneca. Imagine the worst scenarios and "rehearse them in your mind: exile, torture, war, shipwreck."

Imagining adversity is not the same as worrying about it, the Stoics say. Worrying is vague, inchoate. Premeditated adversity is specific—the more specific the better. Not "I imagine suffering a financial setback," but "I imagine losing my house, car, my entire bag collection and am forced to move back in with my mother." Oh, suggests Epictetus, helpfully, also imagine you've lost the ability to speak, hear, walk, breathe, and swallow.

By imagining the worst-case scenario we rob future hardships of their bite, and appreciate what we have. When catastrophe strikes, as it inevitably will, the Stoic is no more surprised than when a fig tree produces figs or a helmsman encounters a headwind, says Epictetus. Adversity anticipated is adversity diminished. Fears articulated are fears lessened. That, at least, is the theory.

My daughter isn't so sure. When I tell her about the Stoic notion of premeditated adversity, she declares it "stupid," possibly even stupider than Nietzsche's Eternal Recurrence. Not only is contemplating adversity depressing, she says, but it's unnecessary. "You already worry about bad stuff happening anyway. Why would you force yourself to do it more?" She has a point. Then again, she's only thirteen years old, not exactly the target demographic of Stoicism, the philosophy of hard knocks. Give her time, I tell myself.

By the third day of Stoic Camp, we fall into a routine. We devote mornings to Epictetus and his *Handbook*. In the afternoons, we break into smaller groups and discuss Marcus Aurelius. The grad students struggle with the philosopher-emperor. He's too squishy. There's nothing to grab on to, nothing to dissect. Marcus isn't trying to prove or disprove anything. He is not postulating. He is a man wrestling out loud with endemic self-doubt, working out what it means to be a human being.

We're isolated out here. There are no distractions. No television. No Wi-Fi. A weak and irregular cell phone signal. Yet a quiet joy prevails. Partly it is the joy of kindred spirits, joining forces against the elements, but it is also the rare joy of humans grappling aloud with weighty, urgent questions. This, I imagine, is how Epictetus's students must have felt, far from home, with only each other and their philosophy.

We Stoics bond. We roast marshmallows over a fire, braving the cold stoically. We make goofy Stoic jokes. A typical exchange goes like this:

"Hey, I'm going into town to buy a six-pack of preferred indifferents. Anyone want anything?"

"No thanks. I'm practicing Voluntary Deprivation."

"Okay. I'll be back soon. Fate permitting."

That last phrase, "fate permitting," expresses something called the "Stoic reserve clause." When Rob first mentioned it, I worried it was some legal mumbo jumbo—a disclaimer to sign, perhaps—but my fears were misplaced. The reserve clause is not legal but therapeutic. Another Stoic technique for coping with life's uncertainty.

At the heart of Stoicism lies a deep fatalism. The universe follows a script not written by you. And as much as you aspire to one day direct, forget about it. You are an actor. Embrace your role. "Were I a nightingale, I would act the part of a nightingale; were I a swan, the part of a swan," says Epictetus.

Pining for a different role is futile and will only cause you to suffer needlessly, like the dog dragged by the cart. We must learn, say the Stoics, "to desire what we have." That sounds odd, I realize. Isn't desire, by definition, a yearning for something we lack? How can we desire what we already have? Nietzsche, I think, answers the question best. Don't resign yourself to your fate. Don't accept your fate. Love it. *Desire* it.

The "reserve clause" serves as a reminder that we are following a script we haven't written. Events unfold, "fate permitting." If a Stoic is about to board a train for Chicago, she says to herself, "I'll be in Chicago tomorrow morning, fate permitting." If she is up for a promotion, she tells herself she will get it, fate permitting. The reserve clause is similar to the Muslim *inshallah* (God willing) or the Jewish *b'ezrat hashem*, only stripped of theology.

Not everyone at camp is buying Stoic determinism. The grad students, rigorous logic-choppers, are particularly skeptical. If everything is fated, where does that leave human agency? Why bother doing anything? Why get out of bed in the morning? I share these concerns and notice Rob is busy stroking his goatee. I'm eager to hear his rebuttal.

It comes in the form of an analogy. (The Stoics love analogies.) People are like cylinders rolling down a hill, he says, eyes twinkling. All of the cylinders are going to reach the bottom of the hill. That is a given. Whether they have a rough or smooth journey, though, is up to them. Are they polished, perfectly shaped cylinders or rough and uneven ones? In other words, are they virtuous cylinders? We don't control the hill or the force of gravity, but we do control the kind of cylinder we are, and that matters.

My bunk is shaking. Violently. In my half sleep, I think, *Earthquake!*—an adversity I had not premeditated and now wish I had. No, not an earthquake. The shaking is too methodical, possibly human induced.

"Time to live in accord with nature," a voice says. I open my eyes and glance at my watch: 5:00 a.m. What is going on?

Oh yeah, good old Marcus. He had waxed poetic about waking at dawn to watch the stars and greet the sun. "Dwell on the beauty of life. Watch the stars, see yourself running with them." Marcus, I'm fairly certain, never woke at dawn, never ran with a single star, yet Rob has taken the philosopher-emperor at his word and decided that waking before sunrise is just the bracing tonic we aspiring Stoics need.

I stumble to the bathroom, splash cold water on my face, then join my fellow campers. I scramble up a hill, nearly tripping several times, all the while shivering. I had packed for spring in Maryland, not Wyoming.

Our predawn maneuver does have some rational basis. There was a physicality to Stoic philosophy. The school's founder, Zeno, was famously fit, no doubt a result of all that vigorous pacing in the colonnade. His successor, Cleanthes, was an ex-boxer and his successor, Chrysippus, a long-distance runner. The goal of all this athleticism wasn't to win medals or even gain fitness. It was, like everything else with the Stoics, a way to practice virtue—specifically the virtues of self-discipline, courage, and endurance.

The wind cuts through me. I am whining. Externally. There are only three of us climbing the hill. Where are the others? I wonder.

Then I spot them, already positioned on the ridge. "Hey," I say to Rob, "what happened to 'No Stoic Left Behind'?"

"There's nothing in the *Handbook* about that," he deadpans.

I switch tack and ask him what Marcus would say about this biting cold.

"He'd say, 'Man up,'" Rob replies.

Stoicism is demanding. It's not easy and they don't pretend it is. It contains little of that Greek moderation. It is an all-or-nothing philosophy. One is either virtuous or one is not. One either lives in accord with nature or one does not.

Like the Epicureans, Stoics saw philosophy as medicine for the soul. Tough medicine. At one point, Epictetus compares the philosopher's school to the physician's office, adding that "you shouldn't leave it in pleasure but in pain." The goal, he adds, is not dependency on the physician but to heal yourself, to become your own physician.

This emphasis on self-reliance helps explain why Stoicism appealed to America's Founding Fathers, and to soldiers everywhere today. It locates responsibility for your happiness squarely on your own shoulders. When a young student complains of a runny nose, Epictetus replies: "Have you no hands? Wipe your own nose, then, and don't blame God."

We each possess a bit of the *logos*, a divine intelligence that infuses the universe, the Stoics say. Reason is our greatest blessing, the only true source of happiness. The cosmos is infused with a divine but wholly rational intelligence. Every time we act rationally, we shake hands with this intelligence. For the Stoics, acting "rationally" doesn't mean acting like a cold fish. To act rationally is to act in harmony with the cosmos, and there is nothing cold about that. "We are agents of divine providence," says Rob, and I can tell he means it.

So, to live in accord with nature is to align yourself with the kingdom of reason, and you can do that anywhere. "You can just as easily be in accord with nature in Manhattan," says Rob, making me wonder what I'm doing in the wilds of Wyoming, underdressed, in pitch-darkness.

Then the sky lightens, as the sun peeks above the horizon, and it is beautiful and I forget about the cold and the rough lodging and no longer wonder why I am here. As I gaze at the brightening sky, something Rob had said earlier comes to mind: "The world's a pretty big place and I'm not."

He was articulating the Stoic notion of "the View from Above." Imagine yourself hovering high above the earth, looking down at your puny world: the inconsequential traffic and dirty dishes and petty arguments and lost notebooks. Indifferents, all of them. You are nothing. You are everything.

Another word for adversity is loss, and here the Stoics have much to say. I'm glad. I could use some help in that department. Epictetus suggests coping with small losses and moving to bigger ones. Have you lost your coat? Well, yes, that's because you had a coat.

Only, in the Stoic worldview you haven't actually lost the coat. You've returned it. You should no more be traumatized than when you return a library book or check out of a hotel. My beloved notebook I took to England? Not lost. Returned. As Epictetus says, "And when something is removed, to give it up easily and immediately, grateful for the times you had the use of it—unless you would rather cry for your nurse and your mummy!" Man up.

Too often we confuse what is ours and what is not. There's no need for this confusion, say the Stoics. It's simple. Nothing is ours, not even our bodies. We always rent, never own. This is liberating. If there is nothing to lose there is nothing to *fear* losing.

I lost a hat recently. I had just purchased it a few days earlier, and took the loss hard. When I mentioned this to my daughter, I decided to fully articulate my reaction: "That hat made me happy, so when I lost it I lost my happiness." Spoken aloud it sounded childish and absurd. I didn't lose the hat, I returned it, and, besides, it was a mere indifferent.

Like the Japanese, the Stoics know "all things everywhere are perishable." They see this fact as cause for neither sadness, like many of us, nor celebration, like the Japanese, but merely a fact of life. Rationally there is nothing we can do about it, so best not to worry. Marcus reminds us that all we cherish will one day disappear like leaves on a tree so we must "beware lest delight in them leads you to cherish them so dearly that their loss would destroy your peace of mind."

What about bigger losses? Surely there is none greater than the death of a loved one. Grief is natural and the Stoics encourage it, right? Wrong. The Stoics acknowledge the need for some grieving, but not much. "Let your tears flow, but let them also cease," wrote Seneca to a friend who had lost a loved one. Another time, he admonished a woman for letting grief for her dead son rob her of time better spent with grandchildren. When greeted with the news of the death of a child, the proper response, Stoics say, is: "I was already aware that I had begotten a mortal."

Here the Stoics lose me. By suppressing our grief, aren't we suppressing our joy, too? Shouldn't we open ourselves to the full spectrum of our humanity, including grief?

I suspect Rob struggles with this aspect of Stoicism, too, a suspicion confirmed when, toward the end of Stoic Camp, he tells us a story. The fireplace is going full tilt. Outside, it has turned cold and cloudy. Snow is coming.

Rob's daughter had her ears pierced at a young age, and added several piercings later. One time, though, when she was thirteen years old, the bleeding wouldn't stop. They took her to the family doctor and discovered "the blood counts were all wrong." More tests. Then the bad news. Rob's daughter had a rare disease called aplastic anemia. Her bone marrow had stopped producing platelets, cells that clump together to help blood clot.

It is an extremely difficult disease to treat. "Cancer is easy compared to this," one doctor told Rob. They watched a friend who had the disease die. Rob googled life expectancy for those with the disease: sixteen years.

"So," Rob continues, his voice calm and steady, "for me this is the value of Stoicism, where the rubber hits the road. I'll be honest. It's hard. It's hard to say of my daughter, 'You are only an appearance,' but I have to do this." Rob asked himself the Stoic question: What part of this situation is up to me? His answer: Be the best father you can. "All of the analyses and proofs don't matter for shit if I can't be a better father. What does that mean? It means I get to be the one who drives her to the hospital and I get to be the one who gets her meds. It means I get to be the one who does *not* freak out." Being a Stoic makes Rob a more useful father, a better father, and, though the Stoics seldom use this word, a more loving father.

On the last day of Stoic Camp, I wake to driving snow. Several inches have fallen, and more is on the way. Snow. In late May. Nature doesn't seem to be in accord with Herself, but what do I know?

I do know the road to Denver is closed, and I have a flight to Paris to catch. People are worried, and by people I mean me. Rob suggests calm.

"I wish there was an app for that," I say.

"There is," he replies. "It's in your hand."

"My iPhone?"

"No, your other hand. The *Handbook*. Epictetus."

Of course. Haven't I learned anything at Stoic Camp? All these grand ideas about withholding assent and reserve clauses and premeditated adversity evaporate when I confront actual adversity. Not much adversity, either. My disrupted travel is nothing compared to Rob's health scare in New Zealand, or his daughter's illness.

I take a deep breath, close my eyes, and imagine the View from Above. This vantage helps a bit, but not much: in my mind's eye I see the airliner flying to Paris without me.

I turn to Seneca, who promptly pisses all over my immediate predicament—as well as my life's work: therapeutic travel. "Do you suppose that wisdom, the greatest of all skills, can be assembled on a journey? Believe me, there is no journey that could deposit you beyond outbursts of temper, beyond your fears." Roman bastard.

I turn to Epictetus, who is more encouraging. He sees the traveler as an "intelligent cosmic spectator." Much better. He offers no direct advice about snowstorms in May, so I improvise. What in this situation is under my control? Not the snow or the closed roads or, for that matter, my philosophical journey. I am too attached to all of it. I am, Epictetus says, like those travelers who find a nice hotel and never want to leave. "Have you forgotten your intention, man? You were not traveling to this place, but only through it."

My anxiety, I realize, is a reaction to perceived loss. I will lose my flight and therefore lose time and therefore lose . . . what?

I'm not sure. I had not thought through the ramifications. Now that I have, I realize how little is actually at stake. My flight is an indifferent. My happiness does not depend on it. Not one iota. I have no claim to it. It is not mine to lose. I am a temporary tenant here, just passing through. Besides, whether I make it to Paris or not is beyond my control. If the road is closed, it is closed.

Some relabeling is in order, I decide. I relabel my predicament a mini-vacation, a chance to spend more time with my fellow Stoics. Paris has been there for many centuries. It can wait a while longer. The snow won't last forever; nothing does. Soon it will stop and I'll be driving south, past the Snowy Range, under the big Wyoming sky, on my way to Denver International and eventually the bright lights of Paris. Yes, I will be there soon enough. Fate permitting.

13.

How to Grow Old like Beauvoir

1:42 p.m. On board the high-speed TGV, Train No. 8534, en route from Bordeaux to Paris.

A blur of green—farmland, presumably—streaks past my window. On the horizon giant white windmills circle lazily in the hot, still air. Sitting across from me is a teenage girl wearing a sweatshirt that reads "Reality Sucks." Ah, but what is reality? I'm tempted to say, if I could muster the French.

I look around and discover I am the oldest person within sight. This has been happening a lot lately. I find this sudden abundance of adjacent youth disconcerting. I can't explain it. I'm certain it has nothing to do with me, though. I am not old.

A few weeks ago, I decided to write at a coffee shop near a university. Big mistake. I was awash in a shiny sea of youth: perfect specimens with perfect teeth, perfect hair and perfect, wide-open futures. They wore studied sweatpants and expensive headphones and greeted one another with explosive fist bumps.

Fuck them, I almost thought, but caught myself, for that is exactly the sort of thought a bitter old man would have, and I am not old. When the chirpy young barista announced my Earl Grey was ready and I didn't reply because I was thinking about existentialism or Plato maybe and she had to repeat herself, I worried she concluded I was old, and I am not old. Not like that geezer who requested a copy of the *New York Times*—the paper version!—which the barista retrieved from underneath the counter, like pornography; or like that sad shrub of a man with a calculator—a calculator!—propped on his table like some ancient artifact. No, that is not me. I am not old.

Our train is late arriving in Paris. The conductor announces a twenty-minute delay, then an hour, then two. The young people on board grow restless, compulsively checking their watches, as if that will hasten our arrival. The older passengers do not check their watches. When the conductor announces, regrettably, a further delay, I twist my wrist and stare purposively at my watch, for, you see, I am not old.

Old age is a large, immovable object, and closer than it appears. Encounters with it are never gentle. You do not brush up against old age. You do not sideswipe old age. You collide with it head-on.

One morning Simone de Beauvoir looked in the mirror, as she did every morning, and saw a stranger staring back. Who was this person? This woman with "the eyebrows slipping down toward the eyes, the bags underneath, excessive fullness of the cheeks, and that air of sadness around the mouth that wrinkles always bring." It couldn't be her. Yet it was. "Can I have become a different being while I still remain myself?" she wondered.

Beauvoir was fifty-one years old at the time and beautiful, but age, as she'd argue in her book on the subject, is in the eyes of those who behold us. She worried those eyes didn't approve of what they saw or, worse, saw nothing at all. For the twenty-year-olds, she surmised, she was "already dead and mummified." The final, piercing blow came when, not long after her mirror episode, a young woman stopped her on the street and said, "You remind me of my mother."

Beauvoir felt confused, and betrayed. Time, once her friend, now schemed against her. She had always lived prospectively, "stretched toward the future," planning her next great project or expedition, but now she was doubling back, looking over her shoulder at the past. Beauvoir had collided with her age.

You'd think she'd have seen the collision coming. She had obsessed about growing old since she was a young girl. She feared old age even more than death. Death is "absolute nothingness" and therefore oddly comforting, she reasoned. But old age? Old age is "life's parody."

Old age is what her longtime partner, the philosopher Jean-Paul Sartre, called an "unrealizable." An unrealizable is a state of being we inhabit but never fully internalize; only others do. We may look old, act old, and, by any objective measure, be old, but we never *feel* old. We never realize our elderliness. Thus, a dozen years after she collided with her age, Beauvoir notes: "I am sixty-three: and this truth remains foreign to me."

There are few road maps for old age, and even fewer role models. Sure, there are plenty of old people impersonating young people, but they are role models for old people impersonating young people. They are not role models for growing old.

Simone de Beauvoir, novelist, philosopher, and feminist hero, is an unlikely candidate, I concede. Her writings on old age make for grim reading. She did not age gracefully. She aged reluctantly, combatively. She raged, raged against the dying of the light, and against those who denied her this rage, too. Yet in the end she made her peace with old age, came to accept it, and, though she'd probably deny this, came to love it.

I could use a role model, for I sense my collision coming. The warning signs are there. Just this morning a small brown spot materialized on my left cheek, joining its twin on the other cheek, its siblings on my head, and its distant cousins on my neck. It wasn't there yesterday. I don't think it was there. To be honest, I don't look at myself in the mirror very often. When I do, it is more of a squinty glance than an actual look. Just enough visual data is imported from mirror to brain to confirm my continued existence in the physical universe but not enough data to register inconvenient truths, like this newborn spot. Now that I think about it, I haven't actually seen myself in years.

Can you blame me? I am not a man of a certain age but an uncertain one. Older yet not old. What to call this awkward interval? "Late middle age" is not ideal, owing to the word "late," but is far preferable to "early old age," owing to the word "old." And I am not old.

When I see an actual old person, I see what Beauvoir calls the Other: someone so alien we view him as an "object; the inessential." He is old, I tell myself. I am not. Implicit in that statement is *and I never will be.* It is a lie, I know, but a useful one, for it allows me to get out of bed each morning, like Marcus, and continue the fight.

It is a losing battle, I know. Already my retreat has begun. When my beard first turned gray, I dyed it brown every week, lest I become a graybeard. Now one week slides into two, then three. I can envision the day when I surrender to the gray. I can see my collision coming. But not now. Not yet. I am not old.

My capacity for self-deception didn't begin with the first wisps of gray. As the Roman philosopher Cicero noted, many of the deficiencies we blame on old age are really failings of character. Old age does not produce new personality traits so much as it amplifies existing ones. As we age, we become more intensely ourselves. Usually, not in a good way. The fiscally cautious young man grows into a miserly old grouch. The admirably determined young woman grows into an infuriatingly stubborn old lady. Must this character amplification always trend negative? Can we reverse the trajectory as we age? Can we become older, *better* versions of ourselves?

Most philosophers are curiously silent about old age. I say curiously not only because aging is such an important part of life but also because so many philosophers lived long, productive lives. Plato was still hard at work when he died at eighty. Isocrates lived until ninety-nine and wrote his most famous work at ninety-four. Gorgias made them all look like young bucks; he lived until 107, and worked up until the end.

Good for them, you say, but do we really need a philosophy of aging? After all, there's no shortage of scientific research about "successful aging." (Such a ridiculous term. *Oh, now I have to age successfully, too? Great. Something else to feel inadequate about.*) There is no shortage of books on diet, exercise, preventative medicine, and no shortage of glossy brochures touting the good life at "senior living communities." What can philosophy contribute to the conversation?

Quite a lot. Philosophy doesn't teach us what to think but *how* to think, and we need a new way of thinking about old age. The truth is we don't really think about growing old. We think about staying young. We don't have a culture of aging. We have a youth culture to which an aging cohort desperately clings.

Old age is not a disease. It is not a pathology. It is not abnormal. It is not a problem. Old age is a continuum, and everyone is on it. We're all aging all the time. You are aging right now as you read these words—and not any faster or slower than an infant or a grandfather.

Philosophy helps us define our terms, à la Socrates. What do we mean by "old"? Chronological age misses the mark. It is meaningless. It tells us nothing about a person, says the philosopher of aging, Jan Baars. "Chronological age is not the cause of anything."

The ancient Greeks had two words for time: *chronos* and *kairos. Chronos* is chronological time: the minutes on your watch, the months on your calendar. *Kairos* signifies opportune or appropriate time. Ripe time. When you say "it's now or never" or "now's not the time," you're speaking of *kairos*.

This seemed like the right time for a father-daughter journey. My daughter no longer finds my jokes funny (she insists she never did) and no longer hugs me, but we're still on speaking terms. In an uncertain universe, who knows how much longer that will last?

Our children are like those rings arborists use to date trees. Empirical evidence of years passing. They grow, and change, and we know we are changing, too, even if it's less obvious. As an older father, the rings matter more. I sense their concentric accumulation more acutely than most. I resist the temptation to postpone joy. Why not Paris? Why not now—before the rapids of adolescence sweep her away? The cincher was that Sonya, unlike me, speaks French. If this wasn't *kairos*, I didn't know what was.

I had it all figured out beforehand and, as Socrates warned, that's always dangerous. In my mind, it would be a touching father-daughter journey to Paris. I pictured us exploring Beauvoir's haunts. I pictured us discussing the precepts of existentialism while sipping chardonnay and Sprite at a Left Bank café. I pictured me and my thirteen-year-old daughter getting to know each other better.

This trip was my "project," a favorite existentialist term. Projects enable us to transcend the circumstances of our lives and go beyond ourselves. But, Beauvoir warns, our projects are forever bumping into other people's. Our freedom is intertwined with theirs. We are only as free as they are. My project—tender father-daughter trip to France—collided head-on with Sonya's project: eat at McDonald's and text friends back home.

I'm having trouble operating the ticket machine at the subway station. It's not a linguistic issue but a digital one. I can't seem to press the right buttons in the right sequence.

"Let me do it, Old Man," she says. Sonya has begun calling me Old Man. As in, "Let's get some nugs, Old Man." She's joking. I'm not old. Her fingers fly across the keypad and, boom-boom, our tickets are dispensed and we're through the turnstiles in a flash.

We arrive at our destination: the Sorbonne. Existentialism is a fuzzy philosophy, more than most. I need something solid to grab on to, so I, a creature of place, zeroed in on the elite university where Simone de Beauvoir studied.

Sonya takes one look and declares herself unimpressed with "the big beige building." Worse, we discover casual visitors are not allowed. We stand for a few minutes in the cold drizzle, gazing inside like children waiting for a candy store to open. At least I am gazing. Sonya is eye-rolling.

I reach into my satchel and retrieve a sheath of paper. A guide to Simone de Beauvoir's Paris. It is a slim sheath. Beauvoir receives far less attention than Sartre, France's philosopher-hero. There is, though, a pedestrian bridge across the Seine named after her. This sounds promising. Bridges, in my experience, refresh the body and stir the intellect. Also, they make excellent metaphors.

"We are going to the Simone de Beauvoir Bridge!" I announce, as if I were de Gaulle declaring Paris liberated. Sonya's reply is nonverbal, a roll of the eyes as cutting as it is subtle.

We walk along the Seine, bundling ourselves against the unseasonable chill in the spring air.

"Dad," says Sonya. "I have a question."

A question! The seed of all philosophy. The root of wonder. Perhaps she's wondering whether the world is an illusion, or how we can lead authentic lives in an inauthentic age. Or maybe it's Kant's Categorical Imperative—the notion that the upstanding person acts ethically regardless of circumstances or motive—that intrigues her. In any event, I am delighted, and poised to impart parental wisdom.

"Yes, Sonya. What is your question?"

"When did your hairline start to recede?"

"Uh, when I was about twenty-four years old, I think."

"Why didn't you just shave it off entirely?"

"I guess I was holding out hope."

"That's not how it works, you know."

"Yes, I know."

Okay, not exactly a Platonic dialogue. But a start, I suppose.

As we walk, I take the initiative and dadsplain about existentialism. I dadsplain how it is a philosophy, as the name implies, focused on existence, and thus represents a return to the original, therapeutic mission of philosophy. Not a what but a how. How can we lead more authentic, meaningful lives?

The good news, existentialists say, is that the answer is entirely up to us. Not God or human nature. There is no human nature, only possible *natures.* Or, as Beauvoir said: "Man's nature is to have no nature."

This is incredibly empowering—and terrifying. We are, in the famous words of Sartre, "condemned to be free." We yearn for freedom but also fear it, for if we are truly free we have no one but ourselves to blame for our unhappiness.

For the existentialists, we are what we do. Period. We are no more and no less than our projects fully realized. There is no such thing as love in the abstract, only acts of love; no genius, only acts of genius. In our deeds, we draw our self-portrait, one brushstroke at a time. We are that portrait "and nothing but that portrait," Sartre said. Stop trying to find yourself. Start painting yourself.

We can become anything we want, I dadsplain. Just because you're a waiter in a café, to use one of Sartre's best-known examples, doesn't mean you must remain a waiter. You have choices, and it is through these choices, consciously made and rigorously pursued, that we create our essence.

When I finish dadsplaining, I turn to Sonya. She had been listening quietly. I take this as a good sign—dadsplaining works!—but the look in her eye tells me she's not buying it.

"So I can be anything, just by choosing?"

"That's right."

"What if I want to be a chicken? I can't be a chicken just because I choose to be one. I can sit on eggs all day and I can cluck like a chicken, but I can't be a chicken. Do you see me growing feathers?"

"Ah, no, but that's because it's not in your facticity to be a chicken."

"Facticity?"

Facticity is another existentialist term. It refers to elements of our life we did not choose. You didn't choose to be born in this country at this time to these parents. You have no control over your facticity. The good news, I dadsplain, is you can transcend it and go beyond your facticity, and beyond yourself, too.

"Facticity? Really, man? This Simone de Beauvoir is overrated. What about Shakespeare?"

"What about him?"

"He invented a crap-ton of words. Like 'eyeball' and 'awesome.' You couldn't say, 'Awesome eyeball, dude,' if it wasn't for Shakespeare. Think about it."

"You have a point."

"See, I could be the next Simone de Beauvoir."

"You could. You'll need some philosophical terms, though. All real philosophers have them. Let's see. How about 'awesome-icity'?"

"What does it mean?"

"Well, uh, it is the state of being awesome. It is the notion that everyone has a little awesomeness in them."

"Do some people have more awesomeness than others?"

"No. Some people, though, are more attuned to their awesomeness than others. When you tap into your reservoir of awesomeness, it's known as awesome-icity."

Sonya says nothing, nor does she roll her eyes. High praise.

As we walk, sunlight breaking through the clouds, it dawns on me that we were just doing philosophy. Not reading philosophy or studying philosophy but *doing* it. We wrestled aloud with an important aspect of our shared humanity—experiencing awesomeness—and invented a terminology designed to illuminate it. I realize awesome-icity isn't on par with Plato's Theory of Forms or Kant's Categorical Imperative, but it's a start. Who knows where it might lead?

At last, we reach the Simone de Beauvoir Bridge. It is, I think, an extremely philosophical bridge. You enter the bridge from one of three ramps, then, after crossing the Seine, exit the bridge from one of three additional ramps. You needn't enter and exit on the same level; you can switch levels at any time.

I dadsplain how life, like the bridge, consists of a series of endless choices. We select one direction but are always free to change course. We never stop choosing our ramps, our essence, and to pretend otherwise is an abdication of our agency. The bridge is existentialism rendered in steel.

"Dad?"

"Yes."

"Do you know what a hysterical pregnancy is?"

"Um, no," I reply, not sure where she is going with this.

"It's when you have all the physical symptoms of pregnancy, only you're not pregnant. You've just convinced yourself you are."

"That's interesting, Sonya, but I'm not sure what it has to do with—"

"You're having a hysterical thought. You think this cool-looking bridge is a metaphor for some big idea, but I'm pretty sure it's just a cool-looking bridge."

Philosophers are prone to overreach. Eager for profundity, they run the risk of intellectual hallucination; sometimes the shimmering light is not an oasis but your mind's eye playing tricks on you, and sometimes the simplest explanation is the best. This is why Socrates believed philosophy is best practiced in pairs. The buddy system. You need someone else, another mind, to keep you on track. Sonya is my Socrates. She questions my assumptions. She sows doubt.

Simone de Beauvoir, lover of cafés, was born above one. The family's flat had a balcony overlooking the Café de la Rotonde on the Left Bank. One day, when their parents were away, Beauvoir convinced her younger sister they should sneak downstairs for a *café crème*. "The utter daring! The audacity!" recalls her sister, Helene.

Beauvoir was, by her own account, a "bossy little girl." Curious, too. She devoured books—all kinds, but especially tales of voyages, sparking a wanderlust that would stay with her. Then one day a teacher suggested she study philosophy, and that was that. She was hooked.

At a young age, before she was an existentialist, before the term existed, Beauvoir said, "My life would be a beautiful story come true, a story I would make up as I went along." This is existentialism. There is no script to follow, no stage directions. We are author, director, and actor of our own life story.

Beauvoir passed the demanding *agrégation* exam in philosophy at the age of twenty-one, the youngest ever to do so, finishing second, behind Sartre. Beauvoir was so industrious, and humorless, one classmate dubbed her *Castor*, the Beaver. The nickname stuck. She wore it as a badge of honor. The word "work," say her French biographers, "seems to have some magic in it, it rings out with a special brilliance, a special tone. It has been her password to life."

Beauvoir was always working on something, often several somethings simultaneously. When she was in a serious car accident, she worked while recuperating in the hospital. During Sartre's long illness, she worked on her book about aging. "My defense is work," she said. "Almost nothing can prevent me from working."

Philosophy, as I said, has mostly ignored the subject of old age, but with one notable exception: Cicero. He was sixty-two years old and in terrible pain when he wrote his taut and optimistic essay "On Old Age."

"Everyone hopes to reach old age, but when it comes, most of us complain about it," he says. Why? Old age isn't so bad. Advancing years makes our voice more melodious, our conversations more pleasurable. "There is no greater satisfaction to be had in life than a leisurely old age devoted to knowledge and learning," he concludes.

Bollocks, says Beauvoir. She had no patience for Cicero's cheery assessment. She was determined to stare down old age, and not blink. The result: *The Coming of Age,* a 585-page tome that is tough slogging. Here is a sample:

> A limited future and a frozen past: such is the situation that the elderly have to face up to. In many instances, it paralyzes them. All their plans have been carried out or abandoned, and their life has closed about itself; nothing requires their presence; they no longer have anything whatsoever to do.

It gets worse. The elderly, she says, are "walking corpses . . . condemned to poverty, decrepitude, wretchedness, and despair." Beauvoir enlists anthropology in her bleak cause, noting that the Nambikwara people have a single word for "young and beautiful" and another for "old and ugly." She's got history on her side, too. Old people have been mocked for as long as there have been old people and younger ones to mock them.

A thought experiment: Imagine a woman growing up on a desert island entirely alone. Does she age? She will develop wrinkles, and inevitably health problems. She will slow down. But is this aging? Beauvoir didn't think so. For her, aging was cultural, a social verdict rendered by others. If there is no jury, there is no verdict. The girl on the island will experience senescence, biological deterioration, but she will not age.

Beauvoir's grim treatise on aging was surely influenced by her own circumstances. She wrote the book at age sixty, when her health, until then "embarrassingly excellent," began to flag. Her step slowed. She was often out of breath. She sneered when anyone mentioned "life's golden years." She was determined to write about old age "without glossing it over."

Beauvoir fell into a cognitive trap, I think, a version of Hume's Guillotine. Not an "is-ought" problem, but what I call a might-must problem. Just because I *might* expose my rear end in public like Rousseau doesn't mean I *must*. Just because older people *might* slip into despair doesn't mean they *must*. They have choices, something you'd think an existentialist like Beauvoir would recognize.

No wonder people like contemporary philosopher Martha Nussbaum reject Beauvoir's grim fatalism. "I don't recognize my own experience at all, nor that of my friends of similar age," Nussbaum writes in her own book on aging.

Beauvoir, I think, overcompensated for Cicero's sunniness. She traded the Roman's rose-colored lenses for dark sunglasses. They protected her from harmful rays but also blocked the light. And there is light. Old age need not be the dismal slow-motion death Beauvoir makes it out to be. It can be a time of great joy and creative output. And the best person to make this case? Simone de Beauvoir.

One evening, over a meal of Le Nuggets, I broach the subject with Sonya. Talking to a thirteen-year-old about growing old is like talking to a mermaid about mountain climbing.

"It's just not my thing," she says, as if growing old were optional, like playing pachinko or attending the ballet. Something she might do if the mood strikes, but she just can't see it striking.

I remind Sonya she's getting old, too, just like me.

"Yeah, but you're getting bad old and I'm getting good old."

"Good old?"

"Yeah, soon I'll be able to go to high school, and drive."

"So what exactly is the difference between good old and bad old?"

"Good old is getting closer to liberty. Bad old is getting closer to death."

I pursue a different line of questioning. I explain how I'm trying to find an upside to aging. Surely there's an upside, right?

"No, actually, there isn't," she says.

"What about knowledge? Old people know stuff."

"Not necessarily. Actually, young people know more because they have the old people's knowledge along with the new knowledge."

I change tack, again. "What about memories? Old people have more memories than young people. It's like having a bigger selection of Netflix movies to choose from. Surely that's good."

"Not everything is worth watching, Old Man."

Then, sensing my despair, she throws me a bone.

"It's a bit of a struggle, I can see. You're writing about how to grow old gracefully but you don't know how. Why don't you just do a fliparoo and write a different chapter: How *not* to grow old? Not physically but mentally."

It's not easy, she concedes. When young people wear checkered pants or listen to vinyl records, it's called "retro," but if an old person dresses like a teenager it's called "pathetic."

So, I ask, if growing old is a bummer and society won't allow me to act young, at least not without being brutally mocked, where does that leave me?

"That leaves you at acceptance."

"Acceptance?"

"Yeah, you should write 'How to Accept Being Old,' or some crap like that."

The kid might be onto something.

"So how does one accept being old? What would you advise?"

"You just go with the flow, don't disrupt the brain waves."

"Brain waves?"

"Figurative brain waves, Old Man, figurative. If your brain is telling you, 'Hey bro, we're old. Let's chill out,' you should chill out."

What Sonya is suggesting is very Stoic. If the heart of wisdom is, as the Stoics believe, distinguishing what's under our control from what is not, changing the former and accepting the latter, then old age makes an excellent training ground for Stoic wisdom. As we age, the balance shifts, from control to acceptance. Acceptance is not the same as resignation. Resignation is resistance masquerading as acceptance. Pretending to accept something is like pretending to love someone.

"Acceptance" appears infrequently in Beauvoir's work. The Beaver was so busy choosing and becoming and working her projects she rarely had time to simply *be*. Projects can take many forms, though. Sometimes they demand beaverlike industriousness, but not always. Learning acceptance—not resignation but genuine openhearted acceptance—is itself a project, perhaps the most important one of all.

I am at the Café de Flore, on the Left Bank. Two compelling reasons bring me here. One: I've had my fill of Le McDonald's. I can't take it anymore. (I've left Sonya to her devices and her nugs back at the hotel.) Two: This was one of Beauvoir's and Sartre's favorite cafés. They conversed here, drank here, thought here.

They wrote their books here, too—at first because the café, unlike their postwar apartments, was heated, and later because, well, they liked writing in cafés. Existentialism is a philosophy grounded in lived experience and nowhere is experience more lived than in a Parisian café. You couldn't ask for a better laboratory of human failings and possibilities. That was true in Beauvoir's time, and is true today. One glance at the café's inhabitants reveals life in all its manifestations. The young couple swooning over their espresso; the older men embroiled in intellectual fisticuffs; the elegantly dressed woman, alone with her chardonnay and her thoughts.

Inevitably, café life seeped into Beauvoir's and Sartre's philosophy. Consider the waiter, says Sartre, in a passage about the importance of authenticity.

A waiter is not a waiter the way a glass is a glass or a pen is a pen. There is nothing in his nature that makes him a waiter. He didn't simply wake one day and say, "I am a waiter in a café." He chose this life, and voluntarily succumbs to its customs. He doesn't *have* to wake at 5:00 a.m. each day. He could stay in bed, even if it means getting fired. To view his job as anything other than a choice is to deceive himself—to act in "bad faith."

Sartre observes the waiter more closely. He is a good waiter, a little too good, a little "extra," my daughter would say. "His movement is quick and forward, a little too precise, a little too rapid," says Sartre. "He bends forward a little too eagerly; his voice, his eyes express an interest a little too solicitous for the order of the customer." He is not a waiter in a café, concludes Sartre. He is *playing at* being a waiter in a café.

A lot of us sleepwalk through life like this. We confuse our social roles with our essence. We get "taken hold of by others," says Sartre, and see ourselves only as they do. We forfeit our freedom, and lack authenticity (a word derived from the Greek *authentes*, meaning someone who acts independently).

This abdication is particularly true, I think, of the elderly. Others see them as helpless and inconsequential, and soon they begin to see themselves this way, too. They play at being an old person. They order the early-bird special and take Caribbean cruises and drive for three miles with their left-turn-signal indicator on because, well, that's what old people are *supposed* to do. Hold on, says Sartre. Do you genuinely like the early-bird special? Is it a choice you made consciously, purposively, or one you simply slid into?

It doesn't have to be this way. Consider retirement. After a lifetime playing a certain role—banker, journalist, waiter—we're suddenly stripped of this identity. Who are we then? Maybe, like Ivan Ilyich in

Tolstoy's novella, we come to the realization our life has been a lie—and, worse, one we told ourselves. Confronted with finitude, we're more willing to discard our roles, like an actor stepping out of character as soon as the show is over. We might, like Ivan, experience a moment of liberation, even if it comes too late.

I decide to reread Beauvoir's *The Coming of Age*. Maybe it's not so dark after all. This time I mark passages with either a "B," for bummer, or a "G," for glimmer, as in glimmer of hope. Afterward, I review my markings. The "B"s outnumber the "G"s by a wide margin. Case closed, right?

Not so fast. I am a free and authentic being, acting in good faith. I can choose what to focus on. I cannot *not* choose. So I choose to focus on the "G"s.

Taken together, they form a much shorter but considerably cheerier book. I also read Beauvoir's memoirs, all four of them, as well as several biographies.

What I discover is a story within a story, like one of those messages written in invisible ink, only visible when you hold it up to a certain kind of light. When I hold Beauvoir up to the light, I see someone who aged extremely well. Her fear of old age faded, replaced by quiet acceptance and even joy.

Beauvoir, proud French intellectual that she was, would never deign to compile a list of the "Top Ten Ways to Grow Old." I, neither proud nor French, have no such qualms.

1: Own Your Past

What to do with our past? That is a knotty question for people of any age but especially the elderly. They have more past than the rest of us. Everywhere they turn, they're bumping into their past, tripping over it. It takes up precious closet space. They might be tempted to discard their past, or donate it to charity. That would be a mistake. The past is valuable, and in two distinct ways: one therapeutic, the other creative.

"There is a kind of magic in recollection, a magic that one feels at every age," says Beauvoir. The magic traces its roots to the past but blooms in the present. We always experience our past, no matter how distant, in the now.

Our past animates our present. Beauvoir couldn't imagine a present life without a rich past. "If the world behind us were bare we would hardly be able to see anything but a gloomy desert."

Recall is not replay. Memory is selective. It requires not only retention but forgetfulness, lest we end up like poor Funes, the character in the Borges story who, after being thrown from a horse, recalls everything in great detail, and suffers terribly.

We are, the existentialists remind us, free to choose which memories to activate. Why not recall the good? Why not be more like the ancient Greeks, who had a category for words expressing retrospective joy but none for its negative counterparts: guilt and regret?

There is another kind of recollection, one more creative. I call it the Great Summing Up. The old, standing near life's summit, can see further. They discern hidden contours of their past, narrative arcs that eluded their younger selves, and see their life whole. They also begin to notice benign coincidences—"the meeting-point of many converging lines," says Beauvoir.

As I begin to trace my own narrative arc, I, too, notice serendipities. The new friend who materialized when needed most. The dream job that appeared at precisely the right time, and the subsequent firing from said job, which wasn't so dreamy after all. I'm reminded of what an Icelandic composer named Hilmar once told me: "I met everyone I needed to meet when I needed to meet them." That is a wise observation, one accessible only to someone who has lived awhile.

In the Great Summing Up we don't merely trace our narrative arc. We construct it, one memory at a time. Beauvoir describes it in tactile terms, deploying the language of the craftsman. "At present I am concerned with recovering my life—reviving forgotten memories, re-reading, re-seeing, rounding off incomplete pieces of knowledge, filling gaps, clarifying obscurities, gathering scattered elements together."

Too much recollection isn't good. We risk remaining shackled to our past selves: forever the heroic soldier or beautiful young woman. This kind of past is frozen, and a frozen past is a dead past.

Another hazard of recollection—one that trips up Beauvoir for a while—is the "what-if trap." Looking back, she ruminates on choices not made, paths not taken. What if she were born in a different era, or to a different family? She might have fallen ill and never completed her studies. She might have never met Sartre. Such thoughts, she eventually realizes, lead nowhere. So she lets them go. "I am satisfied with my fate and that I should not want it changed in any way at all," she says, answering Nietzsche's demon with a resounding *Da capo*. Again.

2: Make Friends

The latest research confirms what Epicurus observed two millennia ago: friendship is one of our greatest sources of happiness. The quality of our relationships is the most important variable in the happiness equation. Beauvoir knew this intuitively. "My relations with others—my affections, my friendships—hold the most important place in my life," she writes in her memoir, *All Said and Done.*

Friends matter when you're young. They matter more when you're old. In addition to the usual benefits—shared interests, a shoulder to cry on—friends link your present self with your past self. That's why losing a friend is especially painful when you're older. You're losing not only a friend but a piece of your past, too. A piece of yourself.

Beauvoir's friendship with Sartre, spanning half a century, was her most important, but another, begun much later in life, came a close second.

Beauvoir guarded her time jealously but was a sucker for entreaties from students. So when a letter arrived from one Sylvie Le Bon, a seventeen-year-old philosophy student from Brittany, Beauvoir readily agreed to meet.

They connected instantly and soon were inseparable. They saw each other nearly every day. They read the same books, saw the same shows, and on weekends went for long drives in the French countryside. They had season subscriptions to the opera and took vacations in Europe and beyond.

Beauvoir felt rejuvenated by the friendship with this woman forty years her junior. "There is such an interchange between us that I lose the sense of my age: she draws me forward into her future, and there are times when the present recovers a dimension that it had lost." (Beauvoir bristled at suggestions the two were lovers. "We are *very very very* good friends," she said.)

It was Sylvie who lifted Beauvoir's spirits when she stumbled across a negative review. It was Sylvie who helped her navigate the world of young feminism. And it was Sylvie who rescued Beauvoir from depression after Sartre's death.

She and Sylvie took a cruise through the Norwegian fjords. She began to write again. Says Sylvie: "It was as if she had put it all behind her. She talked about our relationship and said it gave her a taste for life, a reason to live. She said, 'I don't live *for* you, but I live thanks to you, *through* you.' And that was the kind of relationship we had."

3: Stop Caring What Others Think

Something curious and wonderful happens when we age. We no longer care what others think of us. More precisely, we realize they weren't thinking of us in the first place.

And so it was with Simone de Beauvoir. She grew more sure of herself, more accepting of her idiosyncrasies. More humble, too. She had her Copernican Moment, losing "the childish illusion of standing in the very middle of the world."

This came as a tremendous relief. We are planets, each of us, not suns. We absorb the light, reflect it. We do not create it.

This sort of de-caring helps explain why old age can be intellectually liberating. "By a curious paradox," says Beauvoir, "it is often at the very moment that the aged man, having become old, has doubts about the value of his entire work that he carries it to its highest point of perfection." This was true for Rembrandt, Michelangelo, Verdi, Monet, and others. No longer seeking praise, they were free to doubt their own work and thus, as Beauvoir puts it, "go beyond themselves."

Consider the fate of one of Beauvoir's last books. A collection of short stories, *The Woman Destroyed,* was published on her sixtieth birthday and universally panned. Critics dismissed it as "the bitter expression of an old woman who nobody wanted anymore, either in life or literature." Beauvoir, unfazed, continued to write.

4: Stay Curious

The problem with the elderly is not that they act too young but that they don't act young enough. They act like twenty-seven-year-olds when they should be emulating seven-year-olds. Old age is a time to reconnect with curiosity or, better yet, wonder. What is a philosopher, after all, but a seven-year-old with a bigger brain?

"None are so old as those who have outlived enthusiasm," Thoreau said. Beauvoir never outlived enthusiasm. She never stopped wondering. She talked about cinema and opera like a professional critic. She read newspapers regularly and discussed world events with authority and genuine passion. She developed a new interest in the Americas. She despised Ronald Reagan. (Nothing keeps decrepitude at bay like a healthy and vigorous hatred.) She met with scholars and journalists, dispensed favors, and saw friends, usually in her trademark red bathrobe.

Pursuits she had abandoned a decade ago interested her again. At age fifty-two, she claimed no interest in seeing a world "emptied of its marvels," but a decade later was on the road again, confident that "travel is one of the few things that can bring novelty back into our lives." She subscribed to the playwright Eugène Ionesco's formula: two days in a new country are worth thirty in familiar surroundings. Travel enabled her to remain open to the world, receptive to its beauty. On the road, she was at peace. "I live in a moment that embraces eternity," she said. "I forget my own existence."

5: Pursue Projects

Old age, Beauvoir believed, should rouse passion, not passivity, and that passion must be directed outward. Have projects, not pastimes. Projects provide meaning. As she says: "There is only one solution if old age is not to be an absurd parody of our former life and that is to go on pursuing ends that give our existence meaning—devotion to individuals, to groups or to causes, social, political, intellectual or creative work."

Beauvoir was more politically active in her seventies than in her twenties. After decades of hesitancy, she lent her name to many causes. She protested the French wars in Indochina and Algeria, the American one in Vietnam. She intervened on behalf of imprisoned rebels, censored artists, evicted tenants.

She was following a long tradition of elder activism. Voltaire, so bold on the page, only translated that boldness into action late in life. The British philosopher Bertrand Russell, at age eighty-nine, was jailed for seven days for taking part in an antinuclear demonstration. (The magistrate offered to exempt Russell from prison if he promised to behave himself. "No, I won't," he replied.) Benjamin Spock, the renowned American pediatrician, was convicted in 1968 on charges related to his protesting the Vietnam War. He was eighty years old. "At my age, why should I be afraid to make public protests?" he said. This is one of the advantages of old age: you have more to give and less to lose. "A blazing, fearless passion in an old man's frail body is a moving sight," says Beauvoir.

6: Be a Poet of Habit

We think of the aged as creatures of habit, and pity them for it. But should we? Beauvoir didn't think so. Habit isn't necessarily bad, and possesses a beauty of its own.

We need habits. Without them, our lives threaten to splinter into a million meaningless pieces. Habits tether us to this world, to *our* world. Habits are useful, provided we recall why we formed them and continually question their value to us. We must own the habit, and not the other way around.

Beauvoir gives the example of a man who plays cards every afternoon. He freely chooses to play cards at this café at this time. The habit has meaning. But if he grows angry because, say, "his" table is occupied one day, then the habit has eroded into a "lifeless" demand, one that restricts his freedom rather than expands it.

A habit is not a rut. Think of it as a container—or, if you will, a bag. A bag enables us to hold the pieces of our lives. This makes a bag useful. We get into trouble when we confuse a bag with its contents, habits with the meaning they contain.

In her sixties, Beauvoir embraced the poetry of habit. She did what she always did: she wrote, she read, she listened to music. But she did not read the same books, listen to the same music. "In their rhythm, in the way I fill them, and in the people I see, my days resemble one another. Yet my life does not seem at all stagnant to me." Beauvoir owned her habits.

7: Do Nothing

There is a time for activity, and there is a time for idleness. *Kairos.* As a culture, we value the former but not the latter. Beauvoir and Sartre were certainly prolific, but they could occasionally stop doing and just be. Their summers in Rome were a time of expansive nothingness. Beauvoir set aside her projects and her endless striving and "bathed" herself in Rome. The Beaver at rest.

And though "acceptance" is not a word she used often, Beauvoir did achieve something akin to that. On the eve of her seventy-fifth birthday, she said: "There is something to this getting old after all." Like Nietzsche, she had no regrets. "I have enjoyed everything as much as I could and as long as I could."

8: Embrace the Absurdity

When I was growing up, a single cartoon adorned our refrigerator. I don't recall when my mom posted it there. In my mind, it was always there. The cartoon depicted a mad scientist in a room populated by monsters of all shapes and colors. Sitting dejectedly alongside his giant laser machine, the scientist says to his assistant: "Twenty-seven years making monsters and what does it get me? A roomful of monsters."

Albert Camus would chuckle at the cartoon. The French-Algerian writer was a leading proponent of a philosophy called Absurdism. The world is irrational. It makes no sense. All our accomplishments crumble under the unforgiving boot of time. Yet we persist. This is Absurdity. This is life. An elaborate stage production performed enthusiastically and repeatedly to an empty theater. Beauvoir was wrong, the Absurdists would say. Old age isn't life's parody. Life is life's parody. Old age is simply the punch line.

How to respond to such absurdity? We can ignore it, for a while. Our Fitbits and 401(k)s give the illusion of progress, of meaning. We monitor calories burned, interest earned, and assume we're getting somewhere. *My life has meaning. I can see it flashing brightly on this tiny screen.* But Sisyphus wearing a Fitbit is just as absurd as Sisyphus without one. More absurd, in fact, for he is seduced by the illusion of progress while the Fitbit-free Sisyphus is not. Absurdity quantified is more, not less absurd.

Interesting, but what does this have to do with growing old? Isn't life just as absurd when we're twenty-five years old as when we're seventy-five? Yes, but at seventy-five we're more aware of it. We've amassed enough accolades, saved enough money, to know how meaningless they are. Sisyphus at twenty-five still holds out hope that maybe, maybe this time the rock won't roll down the hill. Sisyphus at seventy-five has no such illusions.

Sisyphus's task, and ours, too, is to accept "the certainty of a crushing fate, without the resignation that ought to accompany it," says Camus. We must imagine Sisyphus happy. But how? How can a conscious, intelligent being find happiness in such a monotonous, pointless task?

By throwing himself into his task, despite its futility, *because* of its futility. "His fate belongs to him," says Camus. "His rock is his thing. . . . Each atom of that stone, each mineral flake of that night-filled mountain, in itself forms a world. The struggle itself toward the heights is enough to fill a man's heart."

Beauvoir didn't subscribe fully to Camus's Absurdism, but she did embrace a "passionate heroism," as she called it, delighting in the magic of work for its own sake. Standing in a roomful of monsters, she continued, until the very end, to create more.

9: Disengage Constructively

As we age, we cling more tightly to life. We must learn how to let go. We need to practice what I call Constructive Disengagement. It is not apathy, a turning away from the world. It is a gentle stepping back. You are still a passenger on the train, still care about your fellow passengers, but are less unnerved by each bump and shimmy, less concerned about reaching your destination.

Bertrand Russell, who lived until the age of ninety-seven, suggests expanding the circle of your interests, making them "wider and more impersonal, until bit by bit the walls of the ego recede, and your life becomes increasingly merged in the universal life."

Think of a single life as a river. At first, it's narrowly contained within its banks, rushing past boulders, under bridges, over waterfalls. "Gradually the river grows wider, the banks recede, the waters flow more quietly, and in the end, without any visible break, they become merged in the sea, and painlessly lose their individual being."

This, I think, is the final task of old age: not a narrowing of our waters but a widening. Not raging against the dying of the light but trusting that the light lives in others. The wisdom of *kairos*. Everything has its time. Even this.

10: Pass the Torch

What the French critic Paul Valéry said of poems applies equally to our lives. They're never finished, only abandoned. Unfinished business isn't a sign of failure. The opposite. The person who departs this world with no unfinished business hasn't lived fully.

As our future shrinks, other futures grow. Our unfinished business will be finished by others. This thought, perhaps more than any other, takes the sting out of old age. As Beauvoir said: "I love young people and if in their schemes I recognize my own, then I feel that my life will be prolonged after I am in my grave."

There are no guarantees, of course. The young generation might make a mess of our projects, just as we did the previous generation's. We stake no claim. We are like travelers at an inn, just passing through, observing the "No Smoking" sign, leaving the room the way we found it, and perhaps dropping a note or two in the suggestion box.

I'm not ready to pass the torch. Not yet. I am not old. But if—no, when—I collide with old age, what note would I leave for my daughter?

Traveling with her on yet another train, I glance at this girl on the verge of womanhood. Earbuds firmly inserted, fingers flying across her smartphone, she doesn't notice when I reach for my Old Man notebook and my Old Man pen, and write:

Dear Sonya:

Question everything, especially your questions. Gaze at the world with wonder. Speak to it with reverence. Listen to it with love. Never stop learning. Do everything, but make time for nothing, too. Cross bridges on any damn level you want. Don't curse your Sisyphean rock. Own it. Love it. Oh, and cut back on the McDonald's.

Or not. It is your choice.

14.

How to Die like Montaigne

11:27 a.m. On board TGV train No. 8433, en route from Paris to Bordeaux.

Outside, a gray sky swaddles the French countryside like a down blanket. Inside, uncertainty reigns. We have slipped on board without a reserved seat. We must change seats at every station, as more passengers board. It makes for an unsettled journey. Just as I get acquainted with my seat, I'm evicted and have to start again.

This is the way of unreserved train travel, and of philosophy, too. Just as we become comfortable with a certain position—all knowledge is derived from the senses, for instance—something upends our certainty and we must begin again. It's exhausting, this constant fleeing from comfort and certainty, but necessary.

I glance at Sonya, wired into her digital world, unfazed by our displacements. Why can't I be more like her, I wonder?

I am wrapping my mind around this thought, getting comfortable with it, when my cogitation is jarred by another influx of passengers. I gather my Old Man books and Old Man pens and amble down the aisle, in search of a new home.

Picture an enormous swimming pool: one large enough to hold seven billion people. No one has ever seen the pool, but there's no denying its existence. At some point, everyone is thrown into the pool. Most are tossed when they're older, but some are tossed in middle age and a few while still young. Only the timing is in question. No one escapes being thrown into the pool. No one has ever emerged.

Given all these facts, you'd think there'd be enormous public interest in the pool. Questions. How deep is the pool? Is the water warm or cold? How can I prepare for getting tossed in the pool? Is this tossing something I should fear?

Yet people rarely discuss the pool and, when they do, it is indirectly. Some people won't even utter the words "swimming pool." They'll say "body of water" or, more obliquely, the "big you-know-what." Teachers do not discuss the pool with their students. Parents (with few exceptions) do not discuss it with their children. It is considered impolite to raise the swimming pool at dinner parties or other social occasions. People steadfastly avoid even thinking about the pool. Better, they conclude, to leave it to the pool professionals.

Yet, try as they might to push it away, the giant swimming pool is always there, looming in the back of their minds like an unseen watery monster. As they sip their lattes, file their expense reports, tuck their children into bed, a question, faint but undeniable, bubbles into consciousness: Is today the day I get tossed in the pool?

All the philosophers I've encountered on my journey speak to me. Some more loudly than others. None speaks as loudly and clearly as Michel de Montaigne. The sixteenth-century Frenchman is the philosopher I most want to have a beer with. I see myself in Montaigne, and Montaigne in me. It is not so much his ideas but how he arrives at them—circuitously, tentatively—that attracts me. Montaigne gets me. He is my philosophical soul mate.

Like me, Montaigne is restless in mind and body. Like me, he enjoys traveling but enjoys coming home more. Like me, he is a compulsive underliner and annotator. Like me, he has atrocious handwriting and struggles to unscramble what he's written. Like me, he is terrible with money and extraordinarily incompetent in the world of business. ("I would rather do anything than read through a contract.") Like me, he can't cook. ("If you give me all the equipment of a kitchen, I shall starve.") Like me, he engages with the world but periodically has a strong, almost irresistible need to flee it. Like me, he is moody. Like me, he is uncomfortable writing about himself but does so anyway. Like me, he has two, and only two, speeds: fast and slow. Like me, Montaigne fears death. Unlike me, he faces his fear head-on.

Death makes philosophers of us all. Even the least contemplative person wonders at some point: What happens when we die? Is death really something to fear? How can I come to terms with it? Death is philosophy's true test. If philosophy can't help us deal with life's most momentous and terrifying event, what good is it? As Montaigne puts it: "All the wisdom and reasoning in the world boils down finally to this point: to teach us not to be afraid to die."

Yet most philosophers approach death the way the rest of us do: by ignoring, or dreading, it. Marcus Aurelius sank into a deep funk whenever he thought of death. Schopenhauer worried how historians might mangle his ideas once he was gone.

Best not to think about death, concludes Epicurus. "Death is nothing to us." You don't wake every morning worrying about the time before you were born, so why worry about death? You were absent then and you shall be absent again. "When we exist, death is not present, and when death is present, we do not exist."

I'm not buying it. The nothing that was me before I was born is not the same nothing that will be me after I'm gone. One is a nothing that was always nothing while the other is a nothing that was once something, and that makes all the difference. The void of space and a hole in the earth are not the same. Nothingness is defined by its proximity to what was, and what still is.

Montaigne read Epicurus, and others, on the subject of death and wasn't satisfied, either. They touched the subject superficially, "barely brushing the crust of it," he says. He was determined to dive deeper—and did. No philosopher writes about death and dying more honestly and courageously than Michel de Montaigne.

Just as Beauvoir obsessed about growing old, Montaigne obsessed about death, or, to be more specific, dying. "It is not death; it is dying that alarms me," he said. It occupied his mind when he was ill and when he was well, even "in the most licentious seasons of my life . . . amid ladies and games."

I can't blame him. At the time, the sixteenth century, death was in the air. "Gripping us by the throat," Montaigne says. Catholics and Protestants were killing each other at an alarming rate. War was only one way to die. The plague killed nearly half the residents of Bordeaux. Only one of Montaigne's six children survived infancy. His brother Arnaud was just twenty-three years old when he died in a freak accident involving a tennis ball. Killed by a tennis ball! Death is absurd. If it weren't so final, we'd laugh it off.

The death that stung the most was that of Montaigne's close friend Étienne de La Boétie. When he died of the plague at age thirty-two, Montaigne felt "as if I had been cut in half."

Death may not cast as long of a shadow over our day as it did Montaigne's, but that is small comfort. A shorter shadow is no less dark. Then, as now, the odds of a human being dying are precisely 100 percent, with a margin of error of zero. Everyone gets thrown in the pool.

Grief can crush. Grief can paralyze. Grief can also motivate. It was grief that drove a heartbroken Mughal emperor named Shah Jahan to build the Taj Mahal in memory of his beloved wife. It was grief—over the loss of his wife, daughter, and eyesight—that inspired Milton to pen *Paradise Lost*. And it was grief that propelled Michel de Montaigne up three winding flights of stairs to the top floor of a red-roofed tower, perched high atop a hill and exposed to the winds, and where he would pen his *Essays*. From great suffering great beauty arises.

Sonya and I climb a circular staircase, the same one Montaigne climbed some 450 years ago. This is where he savored his solitude. I suspect Montaigne was, like me, an introvert capable of doing a decent extrovert imitation when circumstances demanded. We can fool the world, we outgoing introverts, but at a personal cost. All this feigned extroverting drains us. Exhausts us.

The tower is largely unchanged from Montaigne's day. The three narrow windows overlooking the Aquitaine countryside are still here. So is Montaigne's writing desk and his saddles. He loved everything about his tower. He loved the way it overlooked the family vineyard. He loved the quiet. He loved how, wherever he looked, his eyes alighted on a book.

His treasured library began with a gift from La Boétie, who insisted Montaigne accept the books as "a remembrance of your friend." Montaigne did, reluctantly at first, hauling the books up the spiral stairs and carefully arranging them on shelves. He grew to love his library, and it grew, too. By the time of his death, Montaigne had amassed one thousand volumes.

He'd spend hours, days, in his tower, alone with his books and his thoughts. Distance mattered for Montaigne. Alone in his tower, he cleaved himself from the world *out there,* and, in a way, from himself, too. He took a step back in order to see himself more clearly, the way one half-steps away from a mirror. We are too close to ourselves to see ourselves. "We are all huddled and concentrated in ourselves, and our vision is reduced to the length of our nose," he writes. So, move your nose. Stick it here, then there. Exterior distance makes interior closeness possible.

It was here, in his beloved tower, that Montaigne ended his conversation with the world and began one with himself. "It is time to turn my back on company," he said, "and retire into my shell like a tortoise."

I look up and see wisdom staring back at me: some fifty quotations carved into the rafters. Among the ancient sayings is one of Montaigne's own: *Que sais-je*: "What do I know?" These four words neatly sum up his philosophy, and his way of life.

Montaigne was a Skeptic, in the word's original meaning: not a naysayer who punctures the ideas of others for sport but a doubter in search of truth. Montaigne doubted so he could be certain. He built his tower of certainty one doubt at a time.

Humans, he thought, can never know absolute truth. The best we can do is snare provisional, contingent truths. Truth nuggets. These truth nuggets are not fixed but fluid. "Flutterings," Montaigne calls them. You can flutter a long way though, and Montaigne did.

Montaigne, like Thoreau, had angular vision. He held up an idea and looked at it from various perspectives. He did this with everything, even his cat. Was he playing with his cat or was his cat playing with him? he wondered. That notion is pure Montaigne. Take something everyone knows—everyone *thinks* they know—and test it. Play with it. You think you know what death is, says Montaigne, but do you? Play with it.

Socrates did. Maybe death isn't so bad, he wondered aloud after his death sentence was handed down. Maybe it is a pleasant "dreamless sleep," or maybe there really is an afterlife. Wouldn't that be great, said the gadfly of Athens, imagining himself happily spending eternity philosophizing and annoying people with his pesky questions.

Like Socrates, Montaigne was, by his own account, "an accidental philosopher." A personal one, too. He amuses himself, irritates himself, and surprises himself. What I admire about Montaigne is how, rather than dismissing these thoughts as mindless fancies, he examines them. He took himself but not his philosophy seriously. "Know thyself," the Greeks implore but don't tell us how. Montaigne does. You know yourself by taking chances, making mistakes, then starting over, Sisyphus-like.

Montaigne needed a literary form for his accidental philosophy. None existed, so he invented one: the essay. From the French *assay*, it means "try." An *assay* is a trial, an attempt. His essays are one giant attempt. At what? At getting to know himself. He couldn't die well until he lived well and he couldn't live until he knew himself.

Montaigne is no more linear on the page than in life. Like Sei Shōnagon, he is practicing *zuihitsu*: following his brush. He writes about cannibals and chastity, idleness and drunkenness, flatulence and thumbs. Salted meats, too. He writes about his itchy ears and his painful kidney stones. He writes about his penis. He writes about sleep and sadness, smells, friendship, children. He writes about sex and he writes about death. But the true subject of Montaigne's book is Montaigne. "I presented myself to myself," he says, calling it "a wild and monstrous plan."

Humans excel at denying inconvenient truths, and no truth is more inconvenient than death. I look at death the way I look at my aging visage in the mirror. Sideways, if at all. A desperate, and futile, attempt to inoculate myself against its bite.

Montaigne thought avoidance comes at too high a price. When we avoid death, "every other pleasure is snuffed out." We can't live fully, he says, without facing death, *our* death, fully. "Let us rid it of its strangeness, come to know it, get used to it. Let us have nothing on our minds as often as death. At every moment, let us picture it in our imagination in all its aspects. At the stumbling of a horse, the fall of a tile, the slightest pinprick. Let us promptly chew on this: well, what if it was death itself?"

Death can come at any time, Montaigne reminds us, noting that the Greek playwright Aeschylus was supposedly killed by a falling tortoise shell dropped by an eagle. "We must always be booted and ready to go."

I toggle between Montaigne's tower and Saint-Émilion, one of those perfect little French towns that make you wonder why everyone isn't French. It is just me and Montaigne. Sonya has retreated into Adolescent World, rarely emerging from the hotel. Each morning, I lug my copy of *The Complete Essays of Montaigne*, stretching to some 850 pages, and order a double espresso at a local café. It is a low-rent place, populated by chain-smokers steadying their morning beers on shaky tables. The café also does a brisk business in cheap wine and lottery tickets. I am drawn to these sorts of slovenly places. They make fewer demands of me. I can think more clearly.

Montaigne, I learn, is a fully embodied philosopher. He walks. He rides his horse. He eats. He fucks. What Henry Miller said of the philosopher Hermann von Keyserling holds true for Montaigne as well. "He is a thinker who attacks with the whole body, who emerges at the end of a book bleeding from every pore."

Montaigne tells me he has a quick, firm walk, and that he is short and stocky. He has chestnut-brown hair, and a face "not fat but full." He is proud of his teeth, straight and white. He loves poetry, hates the summer heat. He can't bear the scent of his own sweat. He never has his hair cut after dinner. He likes to sleep in. He takes his time while defecating and hates to be interrupted. He is a poor athlete, save for horseback riding, in which he excels. He dislikes small talk. He loves chess and checkers but is inept at both. He dreams that he dreams. He has a poor memory. He eats quickly, greedily, occasionally biting his tongue or even a finger. He dilutes his wine with water, like the ancient Greeks.

Montaigne's is a patchwork philosophy, a quilt of borrowed ideas. He puts his stamp on them, makes them his own. Montaigne trusts his own experience in a way we—*I*—do not.

It took him a while. The earlier essays "smelt a little of the property of others," he says, but with each page he grows more confident, bolder. I find myself rooting for him. I do so even when he dings me for snoozing during one of his long digressions. ("It's the inattentive reader who loses my subject, not I.") I applaud as he finds his voice. Though trained to borrow and beg, he says, we are each "richer than we think."

Montaigne isn't afraid to contradict himself. He reverses his stance on matters large and small. Radishes, for instance. First they disagree with him, then agree, then disagree.

Nowhere is he more inconsistent than on the subject of death. In his earlier essays, Montaigne believes study and contemplation can free a man from the horrors of dying. "That to Philosophize Is to Learn to Die" is the title of one essay. By the end, he has fully reversed course. To philosophize, he concludes, is to learn to live. Death is the end, but not the goal, of life.

Montaigne did not have a death wish. He had a life wish. Yet he knew this wish could not be fully realized without coming to terms with death. We might think life and death are strictly sequential: we live, then we die. The truth, says Montaigne, is that "death mingles and fuses with our lives throughout." We don't die because we are sick. We die because we are alive.

Montaigne thinks of death in ways I didn't believe possible. Not only does he contemplate it but he plays with it and even—I realize this sounds odd—befriends it. "I want death to have a share in the ease and comfort of my life. It is a great and important part of it."

I struggle with this idea. I'm not sure I want death to be a part of my life, great or otherwise. How, I wonder, can I come to terms with death while keeping it at a safe distance?

You can't, says Montaigne. You must, if not befriend death, then at least defang it. You think of death as the enemy, something *out there.* Wrong. "Death is the condition of your creation. It is a part of you. You are fleeing from your own selves." We must reorient ourselves toward death. It is not an "it" and you are not its victim.

Montaigne, an experimenter like Gandhi, believed in trying anything once. "We must push against a door to know it is closed to us," he said. No door is more closed than death. Still, we must push. Don't mock death until you've tried it, he says.

What are you talking about, Michel? We can rehearse for many events—weddings, bar mitzvahs, job interviews—but surely not for death. There are experts on death and dying but no expert "diers." (My spellcheck doesn't even recognize the word.) We can't practice dying. Or can we? Montaigne did.

The year is 1569. Montaigne is riding, not far from his house. He has selected a gentle, compliant horse. He's made this journey many times, and thinks he is perfectly safe, when another rider, astride a powerful workhorse, attempts to pass him at full speed. "[He] hit us like a thunderbolt with all his strength and weight, sending us both head over heels," recalls Montaigne.

Montaigne, thrown from his horse, is lying on the ground, bruised and bleeding, with "no more motion or feeling than a log." Passersby were convinced he was dead. But then they detected slight movement.

They lifted Montaigne to his feet, and he promptly "threw up a whole bucketful of clots of pure blood."

"It seemed to me that my life was hanging only by the tips of my lips," he recalls. Oddly, he experienced neither pain nor fear. He closed his eyes and took pleasure in letting himself go, as if sliding gently into sleep. If this is death, Montaigne thought, it's not so bad, not bad at all.

Friends carried him home. He saw his house but did not recognize it. People offered him various remedies. He refused them all, convinced he was mortally wounded. Yet, still, he felt no pain, no fear—only "infinite sweetness." It would have been, he recalled, "a very happy death." He let himself slip away gradually, effortlessly.

Then he began to recover, and with his revival came pain. "It seemed to me that a flash of lightning was striking my soul with a violent shock, and that I was coming back from the other world."

The accident had a profound effect on Montaigne. He questioned his assumption that death is something we can't practice. Maybe we can. Maybe we can give it a try, an assay. We can't see death itself but we can "at least glimpse it and explore the approaches to it."

Death is not something we master, like chess or winemaking. It is not a skill. It is an orientation, one aligned with nature. "There is nothing useless in nature, not even uselessness itself," says Montaigne. Death is not life's failure but its natural outcome.

Slowly, Montaigne begins to approach death "not as a catastrophe but as something beautiful and inevitable," like an autumn leaf falling from a tree. The leaf doesn't worry about how to fall, and nor should we. "If you do not know how to die, don't worry; Nature will tell you what to do on the spot, fully and adequately. She will do the job perfectly for you; don't bother your head about it."

Will she, Michel? I hope so. She is awfully mercurial. One moment she's blooming cherry blossoms, the next she's unleashing a category 5 hurricane. I don't subscribe to the if-it's-natural-it-must-be-good theory. Cockroaches are natural. Earthquakes are natural. Nasal hair is natural.

What does a good death look like? It usually (but not always) comes at the end of a good life. The atmospherics are important, too. The less drama, the better. Too often, in Montaigne's day, a dying person was surrounded by "a number of pale and weeping servants, a darkened room, lighted candles; our bedside besieged by doctors and preachers; in short, everything horror and fright around us." Today, our hospital rooms are lit by fluorescent, not candlelight. But the doctors and preachers are still there, as is the horror and fright.

My most intimate experience with death was watching my father-in-law die. He died two ways: slowly, then quickly. A disease called frontotemporal dementia explained the paranoia, and the anger. A stroke sent him to the hospital, then a nursing home, then, when his kidneys shut down, back to the hospital. We knew it was the end. The doctors knew, too. Yet nobody acknowledged it. A conspiracy of silence enveloped the hospital room, and we were all unindicted co-conspirators. Such is the charade of feigned ignorance that defines dying in our age.

I watched my father-in-law's chest heave up and down, his eyes glazed over by the morphine while a cockpit's worth of machines beeped and pinged. I fixated on one screen, which monitored his oxygenation levels. Forty-five then 75, then down to 40. I watched the number fluctuate, as if the act of watching would somehow keep him alive. Medical technology comforts us by numbing us and numbs us by distracting us. As long as the machines beep and the screens flash, all is well.

Montaigne would not approve. It's not the palliative care that would distress him but the denial. Technology distances us from the reality of death, which is nothing more and nothing less than nature. Since we are part of nature, we are only distancing ourselves from ourselves. Fleeing ourselves. One beep at a time. He'd look at the flashing monitors and the pinging cardiograph and the metered IV drips and see clear as day what was missing from the room: acceptance.

The remedy for death is not more life—any more than the remedy for despair is hope. Both states call for the same medicine: acceptance. That is where Montaigne, like Beauvoir, ends up. Not a half-hearted acceptance but a full and generous one. Acceptance of death, yes, but of life, too, and of himself. Acceptance of his positive traits ("To say less of yourself than is true is stupidity, not modesty") and acceptance of his flaws as well. Like idleness. Montaigne often chastised himself for wasting time. Eventually he realized how silly that was. "We are great fools, 'He has spent his life in idleness,' we say; 'I have done nothing today.' What, have you not lived?"

It's a truism that men make lousy patients. It is a truism that happens to be true. I am a big baby when I'm sick. Montaigne was, too. Unlike me, he suffered from an actual illness: painful kidney stones that tormented him for much of his adult life. Montaigne cursed "the stone," which had killed his father and now threatened to take him, too.

Illness is nature's way of preparing us for death, easing us into it. Just as a tooth falls out, painlessly, so, too, do we slip away from ourselves. To go from healthy to dead is too much for us to bear, but "the leap is not so cruel from a painful life to no life," he says.

Montaigne is suggesting a radically different version of the "good death." We consider a good death one that follows a brief illness, or no illness at all. No, says Montaigne. Too big a leap. Better to slip away gradually than fall suddenly.

On the one hand, Montaigne's slippage theory makes sense. Better a small fall than a large one. But try telling that to someone in mid-fall. For the past few years, I've watched my mother-in-law fall, as Parkinson's disease steals her, piece by piece. First, it took her steady gait, then her ability to walk at all. Not satisfied with this plunder, it went after her mind, robbing her of the ability to read a book or conduct a conversation. When her final fall comes, yes, it will be a small one, but only because she's been plummeting for a long time now. Illness may be nature's way of preparing us for death but, as I know from public speaking, it's possible to overprepare. Sometimes we're better off blustering into a situation, ignorant of the risks. And sometimes a big fall is better than a small one.

Like Montaigne, I, too, am starting to slip away from myself. My hair slipped away several decades ago, along with my washboard abs and unblemished skin. As far as I'm concerned, that's enough slippage. Can we stop now? I don't want to die, nature be damned. I could get used to immortality. Or could I?

Simone de Beauvoir plays with that question in her novel *All Men Are Mortal*. The protagonist is an Italian nobleman named Raymond Fosca. He is immortal, thanks to a potion he drank back in the fourteenth century. At first he considers immortality an incredible blessing, and strives to put it to good use. He wants to improve the lives of his people. Yet he comes to view his immortality as a curse. Everyone he loves dies. He is bored. (Even his dreams are boring.) He lacks generosity since, as an immortal, he has nothing to sacrifice. His life lacks urgency, and vitality. We may fear death, but the alternative, immortality, is far worse.

An awareness of death enables us to live more fully. The ancient Egyptians knew this. In the midst of feasts, they carted in skeletons to remind guests of their fate. The ancient Greeks and Romans knew this. "Persuade yourself that each new day that dawns will be your last," says the poet Horace, "then you will receive each unexpected hour with gratitude."

Montaigne died in his chateau on September 13, 1592, at age fifty-nine. He was not old. The cause of death was quinsy, a painful abscess in the throat caused by an infected tonsil. In his final days, he was unable to speak, an especially cruel affliction for a man who considered conversation "sweeter than any other action in life."

In his final hours, he summoned his household staff and paid them their inheritance. A friend reports that he "tasted and took death with sweetness." We don't know much more. Was that sweetness of the "infinite" variety he reported after his riding accident—or something else? Did Montaigne, in the end, feel cheated of a few more years?

Driving our dread of death is not only fear but greed. We want more days, more years, and when, against all odds, we receive those, we want more still. Why? wondered Montaigne. If you have lived one day, you have lived them all. "There is no other light, no other night. This sun, this moon, these stars, the way they are arranged, all of these are the very same your ancestors enjoyed and will entertain your grandchildren." When my time comes, I hope I can hold on to Montaigne's words.

No, chides Michel. *Not my words. Yours.* There is no such thing as an impersonal insight. Borrowed truths fit about as well as borrowed underwear, and are just as icky. You either know something in your heart or you don't know it at all. Live your life not as a standardized exam but, like Gandhi, as one grand experiment. In this sort of personal, lived philosophy, the goal is not abstract knowledge but personal truths: not to *know that* but simply to know. There's an enormous difference. I *know that* love is an important human emotion and has many health benefits. I *know* I love my daughter.

Montaigne's philosophy boils down to this: Trust yourself. Trust your experiences. Trust your doubts, too. Let them guide you through life, and to the threshold of death. Cultivate the capacity to be surprised, by others and by yourself. Tickle yourself. Remain open to the possibility of possibility. And, for God's sake, says Montaigne, joining hands with his compatriot Simone Weil, pay attention.

When I return to the hotel after a visit to Montaigne's tower, I grab a notebook and pen and assay to describe what I have seen. I draw a blank. Nothing. I wasn't paying attention. "Damn it," I say aloud.

"Give me a piece of paper," a voice replies.

Who said that? The voice is coming from the far side of the room. It sounds familiar.

"Sonya?"

"Give me a piece of paper, Dad."

She has roused from hibernation. I hand her a piece of paper and a pencil. She begins to write, to draw. After five minutes, she hands me the paper.

I'm floored. She has drawn a remarkably accurate rendering of Montaigne's tower, in great detail and complete with labels such as "Window

Number Two" and "Old Horse Saddle Number Three." I had assumed the tour of Montaigne's tower bored her and that she had mentally checked out. Not for the first, or last, time I remind myself to always question assumptions.

A few days later, Sonya hands me another piece of paper: translations of the sayings carved into the rafters of Montaigne's tower. Glancing at the paper, one short quotation stands out. From the Greek philosopher Sextus Empiricus: "It is possible and it is not possible."

I stare at the quote for a long time. It's one of those philosophical riddles that are either extremely wise or extremely absurd. Possibly both. I decide to try it out, assay it, Montaigne-style. Old Man pen in hand, I write in my Old Man notebook:

It is not possible for a 16th-century flatulent Frenchman with itchy ears to teach us anything. It is possible.

It is not possible to travel to France with a moody thirteen-year-old and maintain your sanity—even learn a thing or two about life, and death. It is possible.

It is not possible to face death—and, yes, life—fearlessly and intimately. It is possible.

At least I think it is. What do I know?

EPILOGUE

Arrival

5:42 p.m. On board Metrorail's Red Line, en route from Washington, D.C.'s Union Station to Silver Spring, Maryland. Heading home.

Familiarity doesn't breed contempt. It breeds numbness. We fail to see the beauty of the proximate, or hear the music of home.

It's tempting to blame our surroundings. I do. Metrorail isn't Swiss nice. No views of the Alps, or much else, either. Only the sweaty back of the commuter standing too close. I'm surrounded by Schopenhauer's porcupines, needles extended, approaching and retreating, approaching and retreating.

Yet, if my journey has taught me anything, it is that perception is a choice. The world is my idea. Why not make it a good idea?

I exit the train and walk a few blocks. I do not stroll like Rousseau or saunter like Thoreau. Mine is the hurried gait of the commuter.

I'm standing on a street corner, waiting for the Walk sign. I can't endure twenty seconds without external stimuli, so I reach for my smartphone. I fumble (I wasn't paying attention) and it slips from my hands, landing on the pavement hard, screen first. This can't be good.

Sure enough, the screen has shattered. A spiderweb of fissures radiates from ground zero in the upper left corner. Shards of glass protrude. I attempt to text my wife but quit after a few letters, bleeding profusely.

There are people who handle life's minor setbacks with aplomb. As you've probably surmised by now, I am not one of these people. The shattered screen is a sign, I conclude, and not a propitious one. There was, I calculate, only a one-in-two chance of my phone landing screen-down, and yet it did. Case closed. The universe is out to get me. Like a locomotive, the shattered phone pulls along boxcars of melancholia and angst. The broken phone signifies a broken life. It is Schopenhauer's Will at work, devouring everything in its path, including me. Where is my "portion of the infinite," as Thoreau called it?

I spend the next several minutes pouting and cursing and googling "shattered screen" on my shattered phone. I must have lost a pint of blood.

Then I surprise myself. I pause. Not a Socratic Mighty Pause—more of a mini-pause—but a start. The pause invites questions, and wonder. I wonder why, having spent the past few years imbibing the life-enhancing poetry of fourteen of history's greatest thinkers, it hasn't occurred to me to consult them. If philosophy can't help me navigate this mini-crisis, what good is it?

I hear voices. Comforting voices. Chiding voices. Wise voices. Socrates urges me to stop and question my assumptions. I assume my smartphone is necessary for my happiness, my *eudaimonia,* but is it? Like so many, I strive to achieve ever-greater connectivity at ever greater speeds, but rarely stop to question the assumption that connectivity and speed are inherently good. I don't know this to be true, Socrates reminds me. Is the demise of my smartphone catastrophic? Maybe, maybe not.

Epicurus spits at my so-called crisis. My phone was neither a natural nor necessary pleasure. Good riddance. Sei Shōnagon reminds me that the phone, like the cherry blossom, is impermanent. Accept that fact. *Celebrate* it. The Stoics, naturally, dispense no pity. Had I practiced premeditated adversity, I would have seen this coming. I can't control the events that led to my broken phone, but I can control my reaction. I can assent to my "pre-emotion" or not. I can sulk or not. It is my choice. *Man up!*

So many voices. They threaten to overwhelm my own. I retreat to a coffee shop: nothing special, but good enough. Squirrelling a few of Thoreau's "fugitive moments," as he called these stray bits of time, I let my eyes linger on the shattered screen. I don't look more closely, not exactly. I look differently. First from this angle, then that. I am not so much looking at my broken phone as conversing with it. Seeing is a dialogue—usually a humdrum one, but occasionally the discourse takes on a poetic quality. For someone like Thoreau, fluent in the language of the eye, life was one continuous poem.

After a few minutes, I see—and I know this sounds weird—art. Not MOMA art, but art nonetheless. The way the shards form shapes and patterns: triangles and rectangles and rhomboids, too. The way, seen as a whole, the screen resembles a stained-glass window I once saw in a Florentine church. Collateral beauty, right before my eyes.

I tuck my phone—my beautiful, broken phone—into my pocket and walk home, grateful for the visual verse I had just experienced. Mine is not a full poem. A stanza, perhaps, but I'll take it. My portion of the infinite, at last.

What had changed? Not my phone. It is still shattered. Not the laws of nature. They are immutable. My conversation with myself had changed. I thought otherwise, so I saw otherwise. It was the slightest shift in perspective; tiny, really, but as Sei Shōnagon reminds me, there is great power, and beauty, in the small.

As I walk, one last voice rises above the rest. It is not speaking to me. It is shouting! Nietzsche. He reminds me I will walk this selfsame street again and again. I will fumble my phone and it will fall—facedown every time. Forever. I will bleed and I will fret, again, and for all eternity. *Can you live with that?* he asks. *Can you* love *that?*

As I walk, my answer materializes. Two short words: foreign yet familiar, absurd yet plausible, more real than real. *Da capo.*

Again, again.

Notes

In the interest of keeping the endnotes relatively brief, I've cited only secondary sources here, as well as clarified points of controversy. Primary sources—the words of the philosophers themselves—can be found in the bibliography.

INTRODUCTION: DEPARTURE

xiii *"Knowledge is knowing that a tomato":* Cited in Gyles Brandreth, ed., *Oxford Dictionary of Humorous Quotations* (Oxford, UK: Oxford University Press, 2013), 84.

xiv *"misliving":* William Irvine, *A Guide to the Good Life: The Ancient Art of Stoic Joy* (New York: Oxford University Press, 2009), 13.

xvi *"radical reflection":* Maurice Merleau-Ponty, *The Phenomenology of Perception*, trans. Donald Landes (New York: Routledge, 2012), xxxv.

xvii *"life-enhancing poetry":* Daniel Klein, Foreword to *Epicurus: The Art of Happiness* (New York: Penguin, 2012), viii–ix.

xix *"Sooner or later":* Quoted in Robert Solomon, *The Joy of Philosophy: Thinking Thin versus the Passionate Life* (New York: Oxford University Press, 1999), 10.

1: HOW TO GET OUT OF BED LIKE MARCUS AURELIUS

5 *We have a common enemy:* Marcus and I both follow the path of Portuguese poet Fernando Pessoa. "The essence of my desire is simply this: to sleep away life," he said. *The Book of Disquiet*, trans. Richard Zenith (New York: Penguin, 2002), 428.

6 *Suicide, said the French:* Albert Camus, *The Myth of Sisyphus and Other Essays*, trans. Justin O'Brien (New York: Vintage, 1983), 3.

6 *The Scottish philosopher:* David Hume, *A Treatise of Human Nature* (New York: Penguin, 1985), Book III, Part I.

8 *Later, enamored of the Greek:* Frank McLynn, *Marcus Aurelius: A Life* (Cambridge, MA: Da Capo Press, 2009), 21.

9 *"his constant strivings":* Ibid. 251.

9 *possibly laced with opium:* A good deal of controversy surrounds the question of whether Marcus was ingesting, and possibly addicted to, opium. See Thomas Africa, "The Opium Addiction of Marcus Aurelius," *Journal of the History of Ideas* 22, no. 1 (1961): 97–102.

9 *Marcus had no intention:* "To Myself" is a more faithful translation of the title than *Meditations.*

10 *"a self-help book":* Gregory Hays, Introduction to Marcus Aurelius, *Meditations* (New York: Penguin, 2002), xxxvii.

10 *"someone in the process":* Pierre Hadot, *Philosophy as a Way of Life* (Oxford, UK: Blackwell), 251.

2: HOW TO WONDER LIKE SOCRATES

15 *Train of thought*: I had assumed that, like "off the rails," the expression "train of thought(s)" was born of the railroad age. It was not. The phrase was coined by the English philosopher Thomas Hobbes in 1651—more than a century before the first railroad.

16 *"Our culture has generally tended to solve":* Jacob Needleman, *The Heart of Philosophy* (San Francisco: Harper & Row, 1982), 7.

17 *"He seems to have entered":* Peter Kreeft, *Philosophy 101 by Socrates* (San Francisco: Ignatius Press, 2002), 25.

18 *Socrates was a practitioner of:* Drukpa Kunley, a fifteenth-century Buddhist monk, was perhaps the most famous practitioner of Crazy Wisdom. He called his penis "The Thunderbolt of Flaming Wisdom" and is credited with initiating the practice in Bhutan (still in vogue today) of painting phalluses on buildings to ward off evil spirits.

18 *"with a big, round":* Needleman, *The Heart of Philosophy*, 153.

18 *"great, smooth forehead":* Ibid, 153.

19 *"marvelous new naiveté":* Karl Jaspers, *The Great Philosophers* (New York: Harcourt, Brace, 1957), 31.

20 *"Every question is a cry":* Carl Sagan, *The Demon-Haunted World: Science as a Cradle in the Dark* (New York: Ballantine, 1996), 323.

20 *"Socrates was the first":* Quoted in Paul Johnson, *Socrates: A Man for Our Times* (New York: Penguin, 2002), 81–82.

21 *"Enlightened kibitzing":* Solomon, *The Joy of Philosophy*, 14.

23 *"All philosophy begins with":* Centuries later, Ralph Waldo Emerson added, correctly, that "[w]onder is the seed of science."

24 *"One time at dawn he":* Quoted in James Miller, *Examined Lives: From Socrates to Nietzsche* (New York: Farrar, Straus & Giroux, 2011), 42.

30 *"If you do not annoy":* Kreeft, *Philosophy 101 by Socrates*, 63.

30 *"planting a puzzle":* Ibid., 37.

30 *"Men pummeled [Socrates]":* Diogenes Laertius, *Lives of the Eminent Philosophers*, trans. Pamela Mensch (New York: Oxford University Press, 2018), 71.

33 *"The moment of insight":* Karen Armstrong, *The Great Transformation: The Beginning of Our Religious Traditions* (New York: Random House, 2006), 307.

34 *"like the sensation":* Leo Tolstoy, *The Death of Ivan Ilyich*, trans. Louise and Aylmer Maude (Bulgaria: Demetra, 1886), 88.

34 *I am embarking on a:* Michel de Certeau, *The Practice of Everyday Life* (Berkeley: University of California Press, 1984), 115.

35 *"Generosity just flows":* Solomon, *The Joy of Philosophy*, 76.

36 *"Ask yourself if you are happy":* John Stuart Mill, *Autobiography* (CreateSpace, 2018), 49.

3: HOW TO WALK LIKE ROUSSEAU

39 *"The flowers by the side":* Quoted in Wolfgang Schivelbusch, *The Railway Journey: The Industrialization of Time and Space in the 19th Century* (Oakland: University of California Press, 2014), 55.

40 *"All traveling becomes dull":* Quoted in Schivelbusch, *The Railway Journey*, 58.

40 *"follow this way or that":* Robert Louis Stevenson, *Robert Louis Stevenson's Thoughts on Walking* (London: Read Books, 2013), 5.

41 *"A difficult friend":* Leo Damrosch, *Jean-Jacques Rousseau: Restless Genius* (New York: Houghton Mifflin, 2005), 4.

42 *The Pentagon recently developed:* Joseph Amato, *On Foot: A History of Walking* (New York: New York University Press, 2004), 257.

46 *"I could not imagine the malice":* Maurice Merleau-Ponty, *The World of Perception*, trans. Oliver Davis (New York: Routledge, 2004), 63.

47 *"a book that is and is not":* Rebecca Solnit, *Wanderlust: A History of Walking* (New York: Penguin, 2000), 20.

48 *"to roll about, toss":* John Ayto, *Word Origins: The Secret History of English Words from A to Z* (London: A. & C. Black, 1990), 539.

48 *About six million years ago:* This is an estimate. Anthropologists are uncertain exactly when, or why, primates first took to two feet. For an overview of the re-

search, see Erin Wayman, "On Becoming Human: The Evolution of Walking Upright," *Smithsonian,* August 6, 2012. https://www.smithsonianmag.com/science-nature/becoming-human-the-evolution-of-walking-upright-13837658/.

49 *"It requires spending three-fourths":* Amato, *On Foot,* 3.

51 *"essentially unimproved":* Solnit, *Wanderlust,* 18.

52 *"a nobleman's carriage":* Damrosch, *Jean-Jacques Rousseau,* 485.

52 *"imagination is more important":* Albert Einstein, in an interview with the *Saturday Evening Post,* October 26, 1929.

53 *"sanctuary in time":* Abraham Heschel, *The Sabbath* (New York: Farrar, Straus & Giroux, 1951), 17.

4: HOW TO SEE LIKE THOREAU

56 *stumbled upon:* Kathryn Schulz, "Pond Scum," *New Yorker,* October 12, 2015.

56 *as the commuter train:* I am riding the Fitchburg Line. It reached Concord in June 1844, just thirteen months before Thoreau moved to his cabin on Walden Pond.

57 *"The biggest little place":* Henry James, *Collected Travel Writings: Great Britain and America* (New York: Library of America, 1993), 565.

57 *the shot heard round the world:* Most historians agree the phrase refers to the skirmish at Concord's North Bridge on April 19, 1775. That's where the first British soldiers fell in the battles of Lexington and Concord. However, shots were fired earlier that day in Lexington, and the two towns continue to dispute exactly where the Revolutionary War began.

59 *"a certain iron-pokerishness":* Quoted in Sandra Petrulionis, ed., *Thoreau in His Own Time: A Biographical Chronicle of His Life, Drawn from Recollections, Interviews, and Memoirs by Family, Friends, and Associates* (Iowa City: University of Iowa Press, 2012), xxiv.

62 *The scientist's detached:* The phrase "the view from nowhere" was coined by the contemporary philosopher Thomas Nagel and is the title of his 1986 book. Thoreau, though, was certainly aware of the concept of detached scientific observation, as well as the critiques of it.

62 *"A world that makes room":* Roger Scruton, *Beauty: A Very Short Introduction* (New York: Oxford University Press, 2011), 55.

63 *"fearless self-inspection":* H. H. Salt, animal rights advocate and an early biographer of Thoreau, quoted in Arthur Versluis, *American Transcendentalism and Asian Religions* (New York: Oxford University Press, 1993), 135.

63 *"sit motionless":* Concord native Joseph Hammer, quoted in Versluis, *American Transcendentalism and Asian Religions,* 102.

65 *"He walked as if a great deal":* Quoted in Petrulionis, *Thoreau in His Own Time,* 57.

66 *"innocence of the eye":* The phrase is John Ruskin's. Thoreau read Ruskin and was greatly affected by his thoughts on seeing. See John Ruskin, *The Elements of Drawing* (Mineola, NY: Dover, 1971), 27.

66 *thoroughly conscious ignorance:* The phrase comes from the nineteenth-century Scottish physicist James Maxwell. "Thoroughly conscious ignorance is a prelude to every real advance in knowledge." Quoted in Stuart Friedman, "What Science Wants to Know," *Scientific American*, April 1, 2012.

67 *"I stopped and looked":* Quoted in Walter Harding, "The Adventures of a Literary Detective in Search of Thoreau," *Virginia Quarterly Review*, Spring, 1992.

69 *There's a physiological basis:* This is due to the fact that the light hits the more sensitive periphery of the rods.

70 *a fun-pack of optical tricks:* Thoreau, the great seer, didn't care to see everything. When a farmer invited him to see a two-headed calf, Thoreau demurred. "We do not live for amusement," he said.

72 *thin, but very wide:* As Wittgenstein said: "The depths are *on the surface*."

72 *The glance is helpful:* Not all philosophers were fond of the glance. Kant dismissed it as *herumtappen*, "random groping."

74 *spiritual seeker named:* Not to be confused with the English poet William Blake.

5: HOW TO LISTEN LIKE SCHOPENHAUER

81 *"We cannot leave":* Nigel Warburton, *Philosophy: The Basics* (London: Routledge, 1992), 100.

84 *"It is as if time had stopped":* Bryan Magee, *The Philosophy of Schopenhauer* (New York: Oxford University Press, 1983), 164.

85 *Only in the last few years:* Toward the end of Schopenhauer's life, a British newspaper ran a favorable review of his collection of essays, and soon it became an ornamental must-have for every middle-class coffee table in Europe. His fame, though, came too late, and like a meal that's taken too long to arrive, he couldn't fully enjoy it.

85 *"playing with my new doll":* Quoted in Julian Young, *Schopenhauer* (New York: Routledge, 2005), 1.

85 *"Your mother expects":* Quoted in David Cartwright, *Schopenhauer: A Biography* (New York: Cambridge University Press, 2010), 43–44.

85 *"I wish you learned to make yourself":* Quoted in Rüdiger Safranski, *Schopenhauer and the Wild Years of Philosophy* (Cambridge, MA: Harvard University Press, 1989), 53.

88 *"The sound, which like all music":* William Styron, *Darkness Visible: A Memoir of Madness* (New York: Random House, 1990), 66.

88 *cognitive recovery after a stroke:* Kil-Byung Lim et al., "The Therapeutic Effect of Neurologic Music Therapy and Speech Language Therapy in Post-Stroke Aphasic Patients," *Annals of Rehabilitation Medicine* 74, no. 4 (2016): 556–62.

88 *Patients in minimally conscious:* Helen Thomson, "Familiar Music Could Help People with Brain Damage," *New Scientist,* August 29, 2012, https://www.newscientist.com/article/dn22221-familiar-music-could-help-people-with-brain-damage/.

93 *a joy to read:* Philosophical writing, Schopenhauer said, should "resemble not a turbid, impetuous torrent, but rather a Swiss lake which by its calm combines great depth with great clearness, the depth revealing itself precisely through the clearness."

93 *is "more with you":* Magee, *The Philosophy of Schopenhauer*, 7.

94 *"a nasty piece of work":* Paul Strathern, *Schopenhauer in 90 Minutes* (Lanham, MD: Ivan R. Dee, 1999), 11.

95 *At night, he jumped:* Schopenhauer, the big-eared philosopher, would lose much of his hearing late in life. First one ear, then the other. The noise he so hated disappeared, but this provided little consolation, for so, too, did the music.

95 *According to one study:* Lisa Goines and Louis Hagler, "Noise Pollution: A Modern Plague," *Southern Medical Journal* 100, no. 3 (2007): 287–94.

95 *Another study found that the roar:* Stephen Stansfeld and Mark Matheson, "Noise Pollution: Non-Auditory Effects on Health," *British Journal of Medicine* 8, no. 1 (2003): 244.

6: HOW TO ENJOY LIKE EPICURUS

102 *A* New York Times *correspondent:* Quoted in Jeri Quinzio, *Food on the Rails: The Golden Era of Railroad Dining* (London: Rowan & Littlefield, 2014), 30.

102 *It is edible, yes:* Amtrak recently announced it will be curtailing its dining car service. Luz Lazo, "The End of an American Tradition: The Amtrak Dining Car," *Washington Post,* September 21, 2019.

103 *"air and genius of gardens":* Quoted in David Cooper, *A Philosophy of Gardens* (New York: Oxford University Press, 2008), 6.

105 *"for many years he was unable":* Quoted in Klein, *The Art of Happiness,* 82. Diogenes dismissed these rumors, though. "The critics are all crazy," he wrote.

106 *the "Four-Part Cure":* The Epicurean Philodemus summarizes the Four-Part Cure this way: "Nothing to fear from god, nothing to worry about in death. Good is easy to obtain, and evil easy to endure." Tim O'Keefe, *Epicureanism* (New York: Routledge, 2010), 6.

107 *was a "tranquillist":* O'Keefe, *Epicureanism,* 120.

107 *"Happiness is definitely":* Ad Bergsma et al., "Happiness in the Garden of Epicurus," *Journal of Happiness Studies* 9, no. 3 (2008): 397–423.

107 *"pure pleasure of existing":* Hadot, *What Is Ancient Philosophy*, 115.

111 *"I too am an Epicurean":* Quoted in James Warren, ed., *The Cambridge Companion to Epicureanism* (Cambridge, UK: Cambridge University Press, 2009), 1.

112 *Two of Epicurus's early influences:* Klein, *The Art of Happiness*, ix.

7: HOW TO PAY ATTENTION LIKE SIMONE WEIL

120 *If I had more time, I'd read:* Before the advent of rail travel, hardly anyone read while traveling overland. The novelty of reading while moving quickly captured the imagination of a restless, literate public, and by the 1840s English booksellers established stalls at rail stations. One touted its "Literature for the Rail—works for sound information and innocent amusement."

121 *"in her presence all 'lies'":* The poet Jean Tortel quoted in Francine du Plessix Gray, *Simone Weil* (New York: Viking Penguin, 2001), 168.

122 *"For the moment, what we attend":* William James, *The Principles of Psychology* (Cambridge, MA: Harvard University Press, 1983), 428.

122 *As many studies reveal, we do not:* The most famous of these is the so-called invisible-gorilla study. Psychologists Daniel Simons and Christopher Chabris asked participants to watch a video of people passing a basketball and count the number of passes. Halfway through the video, a woman dressed in a gorilla suit enters the scene, thumps her chest, then walks away. Afterward, fully half of the participants didn't recall anything unusual during the video. Psychologists call this phenomenon "inattentional blindness." We only see what we expect to see. See Christopher Chabris and Daniel Simons, *The Invisible Gorilla: How Our Intuitions Deceive Us* (New York: Crown, 2009).

122 *"a condition so rewarding":* Mihaly Csikszentmihalyi et al., *The Art of Seeing: An Interpretation of the Aesthetic Encounter* (Los Angeles: J. Paul Getty Museum, 1990), 19.

122 *"One forgets oneself":* Quoted in Mihaly Csikszentmihalyi et al., eds., *Optimal Experience: Psychological Studies of Flow in Consciousness* (New York: Cambridge University Press, 1998), 220.

123 *"There is no primary act":* Francis Bradley, "Is There a Special Activity of Attention?" *Mind* 11, no. 43 (1886): 305–23.

123 *"Everyone knows what attention":* James, *The Principles of Psychology*, 170.

124 *we routinely overestimate our ability:* As one example, see David Sanbonmatsu et al., "Who Multi-Tasks and Why? Multi-Tasking Ability, Perceived Multi-Tasking Ability, Impulsivity, and Sensation Seeking," *PLOS One*, January 23, 2013.

124 *"No such upper bound":* Alan Allport, "Attention and Integration," in *Attention: Philosophical and Psychological Essays*, ed. Christopher Mole et al. (New York: Oxford University Press, 2011), 29.

125 *"I envied her for having a heart":* Simone de Beauvoir, *Memoirs of a Dutiful Daughter* (New York: HarperCollins, 1958), 239.

126 "Mi-usine, mi-palais": Alfred Meyer, quoted in Schivelbusch, *The Railway Journey*, 189.

128 *"the only great spirit":* Quoted in John Hellman, *Simone Weil: An Introduction to Her Thought* (Eugene, OR: Wipf & Stock, 1982), 1.

129 *"sloppy, almost careless":* Simone Pétrement, *Simone Weil: A Life* (New York: Pantheon, 1976), 39.

130 *Patient people are happier:* Sarah Schnitker, "An Examination of Patience and Well-Being," *Journal of Positive Psychology* 7, no. 4 (2012): 263–80.

132 *"In a moment everything is altered":* Iris Murdoch, *The Sovereignty of Good* (New York: Routledge & Kegan Paul, 1970), 82.

134 *"philosopher of margins":* A. Rebecca Rozelle-Stone and Benjamin David, "Simone Weil," *Stanford Encyclopedia of Philosophy*, March 10, 2018.

135 *"She was boiling with ideas":* Pétrement, *Simone Weil*, 492.

135 "But she is mad!"*:* Quoted in ibid., 514.

135 *"The steadiness of her writing":* Ibid., 521.

139 *"freewheeling, tequila-soaked":* Mary Karr, Twitter: @marykarrlit, July 8, 2019.

141 *fell into a funk:* Despondent, Hemingway wrote to his friend Ezra Pound: "All that remains of my complete works are three pencil drafts of a bum poem . . . some correspondence . . . and some journalistic carbons."

8: HOW TO FIGHT LIKE GANDHI

144 *invented the concept of zero:* Some scholars believe other cultures, including the Sumerians and Babylonians, may have invented the concept of zero earlier. For a summation of the various arguments, see: Jessica Szalay, "Who Invented Zero," *Live Science*, September 28, 2017, https://www.livescience.com/27853-who-invented-zero.html.

152 *surprised to find a fit:* Louis Fischer, *Gandhi: His Life and Message for the World* (New York: New American Library, 1954), 149.

152 *Gandhi considered it "unmanly":* Even Gandhi's adversaries admired his courage. "A Lesson in True Manliness," read the headline of one South African newspaper, after Gandhi forced the Transvaal government to back off from one of its demands.

153 *"Have you no shame?":* Quoted in Fischer, *Gandhi*, 28.

155 *"You have the right to work": The Bhagavad Gita,* trans. Eknath Easwaran (Tomales, CA: Nilgiri Press, 1985), 53.

157 *"emerged from Gandhi's hands":* Rajmohan Gandhi, *Why Gandhi Still Matters: An Appraisal of the Mahatma's Legacy* (New Delhi: Aleph, 2017), 133.

157 *Gandhi eventually settled:* Gandhi had some help devising a new name for his form of nonviolent resistance. While in South Africa, he held a contest in the newspaper *Indian Opinion*. Gandhi tweaked the winning entry to come up with *satyagraha*.

158 *"The officers ordered them":* Quoted in Homer Jack, ed., *The Gandhi Reader: A Sourcebook of His Life and Writings* (New York: Grove Press, 1956), 250–51.

160 *In a comprehensive study:* Erica Chenoweth and Maria Stephan, *Why Civil Resistance Works: The Strategic Logic of Nonviolent Resistance* (New York: Columbia University Press, 2011), 9.

161 *movement to Euclid's Line:* This is what Gandhi had to say about the connection between his ideas and Euclid's geometry: "Euclid's line is one without breadth, but no one has so far been able to draw it and never will . . . if Euclid's point, thought incapable of being drawn by human agency, has an imperishable value, my picture has its own for mankind to live."

163 *"What appears to be the end":* Mark Juergensmeyer, *Gandhi's Way: A Handbook of Conflict Resolution* (Los Angeles: University of California Press, 1984), 4.

166 *uttering the words* Hey Ram: Lately, some have cast doubt on whether these were, in fact, Gandhi's last words. His personal assistant, Venkita Kalyanam, claimed a decade ago Gandhi never uttered the words. More recently, he told the Press Trust of India: "I never said Gandhiji did not say 'Hey Ram' at all. What I had said was I did not hear him saying 'Hey Ram.'" "Never said 'Hey Ram' Weren't Bapu's Last Words: Gandhi's PA," *Times of India*, January 30, 2018.

166 *"To live with Gandhi":* A man identified as Chandwani, quoted in Manuben Gandhi, *Last Glimpses of Bapu*, trans. Moli Jain (Agra: Shiva Lal Agarwala, 1962), 253.

9: HOW TO BE KIND LIKE CONFUCIUS

170 *He didn't write it:* Some uncertainty surrounds the question of what Confucius did and did not write. Most scholars believe *The Analects* was compiled by Confucius's disciples well after his death.

171 *"Swords and shields":* Michael Schuman, *Confucius: And the World He Created* (New York: Basic Books, 2015), 27.

172 *"an uptight fuddy-duddy":* Ibid., 18.

173 *"and you can turn the whole world":* Quoted in Philip Ivanhoe and Bryan Van Norden, eds., *Readings in Classical Chinese Philosophy* (Indianapolis: Hackett, 2003), 121.

173 *"Do not roll the rice":* Quoted in Daniel Gardner, *Confucianism: A Very Short Introduction* (New York: Oxford University Press, 2014), 27.

175 *"an island of kindness":* Adam Phillips and Barbara Taylor, *On Kindness* (New York: Farrar, Straus & Giroux, 2009), 105.

177 *"All people have a heart":* Quoted in Paul Goldin, *Confucianism* (New York: Routledge, 2014), 46.

177 *"Given the right nourishment":* Quoted in Armstrong, *The Great Transformation*, 304.

178 *"Every spectacular incident":* Stephen Jay Gould, "A Time of Gifts," *New York Times*, September 26, 2001.

178 *Observing acts of kindness:* Lara Aknin, Elizabeth Dunn, and Michael Norton, "Happiness Runs in Circular Motion: Evidence for a Positive Feedback Loop Between Prosocial Spending and Happiness," *Journal of Happiness Studies* 13, no. 2 (2012): 347–55.

10: HOW TO APPRECIATE THE SMALL THINGS LIKE SEI SHŌNAGON

184 *he created layers:* One of Aristotle's most famous works is called "Categories," part of a larger collection known as the Organon.

184 *"I perceive value":* Susan Sontag, *As Consciousness Is Harnessed to Flesh: Journals and Notebooks, 1964–1980*, ed. David Rieff (New York: Farrar, Straus & Giroux, 2012), 217.

184 *"The list is the origin":* Umberto Eco, in an interview with *Der Spiegel*, November 11, 2009, https://www.spiegel.de/international/zeitgeist/spiegel-interview-with-umberto-eco-we-like-lists-because-we-don-t-want-to-die-a-659577.html.

187 *"a crazy quilt":* Meredith McKinney, Introduction to *The Pillow Book* (New York: Penguin, 1997), ix.

188 okashii, *or delightful:* Today the Japanese word means "amusing" or "strange," but in Shōnagon's time it meant "delightful."

190 *"The most precious thing in life":* Yoshida Kenkō, *Essays in Idleness*, trans. Donald Keene (New York: Columbia University Press, 1998), 3.

190 *"Beauty lies in its own":* Donald Richie, *A Tractate on Japanese Aesthetics* (Berkeley, CA: Stone Bridge Press, 2007), 4.

190 *"He is paying attention to things":* Russell Goodman, "Thoreau and the Body," in *Thoreau's Importance for Philosophy*, ed. Rick Furtak et al. (New York: Fordham University Press, 2012), 33.

192 *"the cult of beauty":* Ivan Morris, *The World of the Shining Prince: Court Life in Ancient Japan* (New York: Vintage, 1964), 170.

193 *"proper thickness, size, design":* Ibid., 187.

193 *"smart, good-looking":* Ibid., 188.

194 *"to demonstrate that things can be":* Ullrich Haase, *Starting with Nietzsche* (New York: Continuum, 2008), 25.

194 *"The man who for the first time":* Hermann Hesse, *My Belief: Essays on Life and Art* (New York: Farrar, Straus & Giroux, 1974).

11: HOW TO HAVE NO REGRETS LIKE NIETZSCHE

206 *"had none of the searching":* Quoted in Curtis Cate, *Friedrich Nietzsche* (New York: Overlook Press, 2005), 328.

210 *"a piece of pseudo-aesthetic":* Friedrich Ritschl, quoted in Miller, *Examined Lives*, 326.

210 *"Perhaps no one":* Stefan Zweig, *Nietzsche*, trans. William Stone (London: Hesperus), 54.

212 *"where doubts and rebellion grow":* Robert Solomon and Kathleen Higgins, eds., *Reading Nietzsche* (New York: Oxford University Press, 1988), 4.

214 *there are many more combinations:* Sometimes a higher number, 255,168, is cited, but that refers to the number of possible sequences, not games per se. See Steve Schaefer, "MathRec Solution (Tic-Tac-Toe): Mathematical Recreations (2002)," http://www.mathrec.org/old/2002jan/solutions.html.

214 *In chess, considerably more games:* For an explanation of how this number is arrived at, see David Shenk's *The Immortal Game: A History of Chess* (New York: Anchor, 2007), 69–70.

216 *what one scholar calls:* Maudemarie Clark, *Nietzsche on Truth and Philosophy* (New York: Cambridge University Press, 1990), 270.

217 *a hearty* Da capo!: An Italian musical term, *Da capo* means "from the beginning" (literally, "from the head").

218 *like Sisyphus happy:* "We must imagine Sisyphus happy," Albert Camus said in his essay "The Myth of Sisyphus."

218 *possibly due to syphilis:* For a long time, the consensus among scholars was that Nietzsche died from neurosyphilis, but lately that conclusion has been called into question. Some researchers believe he suffered from a hereditary stroke disorder called CADASIL while others say it was meningioma, a slow-growing tumor that forms in the membranes surrounding the brain and spinal cord. Two British researchers, relying, in part, on Nietzsche's own medical notes, conclude he died from frontotemporal dementia. We'll probably never know for sure. Nietzsche, a champion of perspectivism, would no doubt smile at our uncertainty.

218 *"an experiment in reorienting":* R. J. Hollingdale, ed., *A Nietzsche Reader* (New York: Penguin, 1977), 11–12.

12: HOW TO COPE LIKE EPICTETUS

224 *including George Washington and John Adams:* Carl Richard, "The Classical Founding of American Roots," in Daniel Robinson and Richard Williams, eds., *The American Founding: Its Intellectual and Moral Framework* (New York: Continuum, 2012), 47.

225 *"I had a good voyage":* Laertius, *Lives of the Eminent Philosophers,* 314.

225 *"No tree becomes rooted and sturdy":* Quoted in Donald Robertson, *Stoicism and the Art of Happiness: Practical Wisdom for Everyday Life* (New York: McGraw-Hill, 2013), vii.

228 *James Stockdale, an American pilot:* See James Stockdale, *Thoughts of a Philosophical Fighter Pilot* (Stanford, CA: Hoover Institution Press, 1995).

230 *"We don't typically get angry":* A. A. Long, *From Epicurus to Epictetus* (New York: Oxford University Press, 2006), 379.

233 *Forgoing pleasure is one of life's:* As William Irvine says, "Leave it to the Stoics to realize the act of forgoing pleasure can itself be pleasant." Irvine, *A Guide to the Good Life,* 117.

234 *"rehearse them in your mind":* Seneca, quoted in Antonia Macaro, "What Can the Stoic Do for Us," in Patrick Ussher, ed., *Stoicism Today: Selected Writing I* (Stoicism Today, 2014), 54.

239 *"Let your tears flow, but let them also cease":* Quoted in Irvine, *A Guide to the Good Life,* 154.

241 *"Do you suppose that wisdom":* Quoted in William Stephens, "A Stoic Approach to Travel and Tourism," *Modern Stoicism,* November 24, 2018, https://modernstoicism.com/a-stoic-approach-to-travel-and-tourism-by-william-o-stephens/.

241 *I turn to Epictetus:* Epictetus died in AD 135. Mourners heralded him as a "friend of the immortals." He had inspired a Roman emperor. He would inspire Shakespeare and birth a form of psychotherapy, cognitive behavioral therapy, that is still practiced today. Not bad for a former slave.

13: HOW TO GROW OLD LIKE BEAUVOIR

247 *"Chronological age is not":* Jan Baars, *Aging and the Art of Living* (Baltimore: Johns Hopkins University Press, 2012), 52.

252 *"The utter daring!":* Quoted in Claude Francis and Fernande Gontier, *Simone de Beauvoir: A Life, a Love Story* (Paris: Librairie Académique Perrin, 1985), 359.

253 *The word "work":* Francis and Gontier, *Simone de Beauvoir,* 198.

253 *"Everyone hopes to reach":* Marcus Cicero, *How to Grow Old: Ancient Wisdom*

for the Second Half of Life, trans. Philip Freeman (Princeton, NJ: Princeton University Press, 2016), 11.

254 *"I don't recognize"*: Martha Nussbaum and Saul Levmore, *Aging Thoughtfully: Conversations About Retirement, Romance, Wrinkles & Regret* (New York: Oxford University Press), 19.

257 *"His movement is quick"*: Jean-Paul Sartre, *Being and Nothingness*, trans. Hazel Barnes (New York: Washington Square Press, 1992), 101.

261 *And it was Sylvie who rescued:* Friends, worried Beauvoir might commit suicide, wouldn't leave her alone. She fell physically ill, too. She spent a month in the hospital, suffering from pneumonia and cirrhosis of the liver, the result of a lifetime of heavy drinking. When Beauvoir was discharged, she agreed to a strict health regime, and eliminated all her vices, save Scotch and vodka. "I need those," she said. Sylvie secretly watered down her Scotch, just as Beauvoir had done for Sartre.

261 *"It was as if she had put it all behind her"*: Quoted in Deirdre Bair, *Simone de Beauvoir: A Biography* (New York: Touchstone, 1990), 588.

263 *"At my age"*: Quoted in Wayne Booth, ed., *The Art of Growing Older: Writers on Living and Aging* (Chicago: University of Chicago Press, 1992), 159.

265 *"the certainty of a crushing"*: Camus, *The Myth of Sisyphus and Other Essays*, 54.

266 *"wider and more impersonal"*: Bertrand Russell, "How to Grow Old," in *Portraits from Memory and Other Essays* (Nottingham: Spokesman Books, 1995), 52.

266 *The person who departs this world:* Many of the philosophers I've encountered are good role models in this regard, especially Thoreau. Says author William Cain: "He persisted with his journal until serious illness intervened, and on his deathbed he was still writing: adding to his calendar of flowers and shrubs, compiling lists of birds, making selections from his journals, and preparing articles from his journals." William Cain, ed., *A Historical Guide to Henry David Thoreau* (New York: Oxford University Press, 2000), 4.

14: HOW TO DIE LIKE MONTAIGNE

272 *at an alarming rate:* It was one such slaughter, in which ten thousand Protestants were killed, that gave the world a new word, *massacre*, from the Old French for butchery.

272 *Killed by a tennis ball!:* He was playing a game called *courte-paume*, or court tennis, a precursor to the modern game, which used a heavier ball. But, still: killed by a tennis ball!

273 Que sais-je*:* *Que sçay-je* in the Middle French that Montaigne spoke.

275 *"He is a thinker who attacks"*: Henry Miller, *The Wisdom of the Heart* (New York: New Directions, 1960), 77.

278 *not bad at all:* Israeli prime minister Yitzhak Rabin, mortally wounded by an assassin's bullet, said something similar. "Don't worry. It's not bad. No, not so bad," he said, just before dying. Patrick Cockburn, "Assassin 'Told Guards Bullets Were Fake,'" *The Independent*, November 8, 1995.

281 *"Persuade yourself that each new"*: Quoted in Pierre Hadot, *What Is Ancient Philosophy?* (Cambridge, MA: Harvard University Press, 2002), 196.

SELECTED BIBLIOGRAPHY AND FURTHER READING

GENERAL READING ON PHILOSOPHY

Craig, Edward. *Philosophy: A Brief Insight*. New York: Sterling, 2002.

Curnow, Trevor. *Ancient Philosophy and Everyday Life*. Newcastle, UK: Cambridge Scholars Press, 2006.

——. *Wisdom: A History*. London: Reaktion, 2015.

Durant, Will. *The Story of Philosophy: The Lives and the Opinions of the Great Philosophers of the Western World*. New York: Simon & Schuster, 1926.

Hadot, Pierre. *Philosophy as a Way of Life*. Translated by Michael Chase. Oxford, UK: Blackwell, 1995.

——. *What Is Ancient Philosophy?* Translated by Michael Chase. London: Belknap, 2002.

Jaspers, Karl. *The Great Philosophers: The Foundations.* Translated by Ralph Manheim. New York: Harcourt, Brace & World, 1962.

Lehrer, Keith, B. Jeannie Lum, Beverly A. Slichta, and Nicholas D. Smith, eds. *Knowledge, Teaching and Wisdom*. New York: Springer, 1996.

Macfie, Alexander, ed. *Eastern Influences on Western Philosophy: A Reader*. Edinburgh, Scotland: Edinburgh University Press, 2003.

Magee, Bryan. *Confessions of a Philosopher: A Journey Through Western Philosophy*. New York: Random House, 1997.

——. *The Great Philosophers*. New York: Oxford University Press, 1987.

——. *Ultimate Questions*. Princeton, NJ: Princeton University Press, 2016.

Miller, James. *Examined Lives: From Socrates to Nietzsche*. New York: Farrar, Straus and Giroux, 2011.

Monk, Ray, and Frederic Raphael, eds. *The Great Philosophers: From Socrates to Turing*. London: Orion, 2001.

Needleman, Jacob. *The Heart of Philosophy*. New York: Harper & Row, 1982.

Nozick, Robert. *The Examined Life: Philosophical Meditations.* New York: Simon & Schuster, 1989.

Rodgers, Nigel, and Mel Thompson. *Philosophers Behaving Badly.* London: Peter Owen, 2005.

Solomon, Robert. *The Joy of Philosophy: Thinking Thin versus the Passionate Life.* New York: Oxford University Press, 1999.

Solomon, Robert, and Kathleen Higgins. *A Short History of Philosophy.* New York: Oxford University Press, 1996.

Sternberg, Robert, and Jennifer Jordan, eds. *A Handbook of Wisdom: Psychological Perspectives.* New York: Cambridge University Press, 2005.

Van Norden, Bryan, and Jay Garfield. *Taking Back Philosophy: A Multicultural Manifesto.* New York: Columbia University Press, 2017.

Walker, Michelle. *Slow Philosophy: Reading Against the Institution.* New York: Bloomsbury, 2017.

Warburton, Nigel. *Philosophy: The Basics.* London: Routledge, 1992.

GENERAL READING ON TRAIN TRAVEL

Nye, David. *American Technological Sublime.* Cambridge, MA: MIT Press, 1994.

Quinzio, Jeri. *Food on the Rails: The Golden Era of Railroad Dining.* New York: Rowan & Littlefield, 2014.

Revill, George. *Railway.* London: Reaktion, 2012.

Schivelbusch, Wolfgang. *The Railway Journey: The Industrialization of Time and Space in the Nineteenth Century.* Oakland: University of California Press, 1977.

Wolmar, Christian. *The Great Railroad Revolution: The History of Trains in America.* New York: Public Affairs, 2012.

Zoellner, Tom. *Train: Riding the Rails That Created the Modern World—from the Trans-Siberian to the Southwest Chief.* New York: Penguin, 2014.

1: HOW TO GET OUT OF BED LIKE MARCUS AURELIUS

Aurelius, Marcus. *Meditations.* Translated by Gregory Hays. New York: Modern Library, 2002.

Briley, Anthony. *Marcus Aurelius: A Biography.* New York: Barnes & Noble, 1966.

Camus, Albert. *The Myth of Sisyphus and Other Essays.* Translated by Justin O'Brien. New York: Vintage International, 1991.

Hadot, Pierre. *The Inner Citadel: The Meditations of Marcus Aurelius.* Translated by Michael Chase. Cambridge, MA: Harvard University Press, 1998.

Kellogg, Michael. *The Roman Search for Wisdom.* Amherst, NY: Prometheus, 2014.

McLynn, Frank. *Marcus Aurelius: A Life.* New York: Da Capo, 2008.

Needleman, Jacob, ed. *The Essential Marcus Aurelius.* Translated by John Piazza. New York: Penguin, 2008.

2: HOW TO WONDER LIKE SOCRATES

Gower, Barry, and Michael Stokes, eds. *Socratic Questions: New Essays on the Philosophy of Socrates and Its Significance.* New York: Routledge, 1992.

Johnson, Paul. *Socrates: A Man for Our Times.* New York: Penguin, 2011.

Kreeft, Peter. *Philosophy 101 by Socrates: An Introduction to Philosophy via Plato's* Apology. San Francisco: Ignatius, 2002.

May, Hope. *On Socrates.* Belmont, CA: Wadsworth, 2000.

Morrison, Donald, ed. *The Cambridge Companion to Socrates.* New York: Cambridge University Press, 2011.

Plato. *Plato: Complete Works.* Indianapolis: Hackett, 1997.

Taylor, C. C. *Socrates: A Very Short Introduction.* New York: Oxford University Press, 1998.

3: HOW TO WALK LIKE ROUSSEAU

Amato, Joseph. *On Foot: A History of Walking.* New York: New York University Press, 2004.

Damrosch, Leo. *Jean-Jacques Rousseau: Restless Genius.* New York: Houghton Mifflin, 2005.

Delaney, James. *Starting with Rousseau.* New York: Continuum, 2009.

Gros, Frederic. *A Philosophy of Walking.* Translated by John Howe. New York: Verso, 2015.

Rousseau, Jean-Jacques. *The Confessions.* Ware, Hertfordshire, UK: Wordsworth, 1996.

——. *Emile: or On Education.* New York: Basic Books, 1979.

——. *Reveries of the Solitary Walker.* Translated by Peter France. New York: Penguin, 1979.

——. *The Social Contract* and *Discourses.* London: Everyman's Library, 1973.

Solnit, Rebecca. *Wanderlust: A History of Walking.* New York: Penguin, 2000.

Wokler, Robert. *Rousseau: A Very Short Introduction.* New York: Oxford, 1995.

4: HOW TO SEE LIKE THOREAU

Cameron, Sharon. *Writing Nature: Henry Thoreau's Journal.* New York: Oxford University Press, 1985.

Casey, Edward. *The World at a Glance.* Bloomington: Indiana University Press, 2007.

Cramer, Jeffrey S., ed. *The Quotable Thoreau*. Princeton, NJ: Princeton University Press, 2011.

Goto, Shoji. *The Philosophy of Emerson and Thoreau: Orientals Meet Occidentals*. Lewiston, NY: Edwin Mellen, 2007.

Harding, Walter. *The Days of Henry Thoreau: A Biography*. New York: Knopf, 1965.

Leddy, Thomas. *The Extraordinary in the Ordinary: The Aesthetics of Everyday Life*. Calgary, Alberta, Canada: Broadview Press, 2012.

Petrulionis, Sandra. *Thoreau in His Own Time*: A *Biographical Chronicle of His Life, Drawn from Recollections, Interviews, and Memoirs by Family, Friends, and Associates*. Iowa City: University of Iowa Press, 2012.

Richardson, Robert. *Henry Thoreau: A Life of the Mind*. Berkeley: University of California Press, 1986.

Sullivan, Robert. *The Thoreau You Don't Know*. New York: Harper Perennial, 2009.

Tauber, Alfred. *Henry David Thoreau and the Moral Agency of Knowing*. Berkeley: University of California Press, 2001.

Thoreau, Henry David. *A Year in Thoreau's Journal: 1851*. New York: Penguin, 1993.

———. *Letters to a Spiritual Seeker*. Edited by Bradley Dean. New York: W. W. Norton, 2004.

———. *The Major Essays of Henry David Thoreau*. Ipswich, MA: Whitston, 2000.

———. *Selected Journals of Henry David Thoreau*. New York: Signet, 1967.

———. *Walden* and *Civil Disobedience*. New York: Barnes & Noble, 2012.

———. *Walking*. Boston: Beacon Press, 1991.

———. *A Week on the Concord and Merrimack Rivers*. Mineola, NY: Dover, 2001.

Versluis, Arthur. *American Transcendentalism and Asian Religions*. New York: Oxford University Press, 1993.

Young. J. Z. *Philosophy and the Brain*. New York: Oxford University Press, 1987.

5: HOW TO LISTEN LIKE SCHOPENHAUER

Cartwright, David. *Schopenhauer: A Biography*. New York: Cambridge University Press, 2010.

Janaway, Christopher, ed. *The Cambridge Companion to Schopenhauer*. New York: Cambridge University Press, 1999.

Lewis, Peter. *Arthur Schopenhauer*. London: Reaktion, 2012.

Magee, Bryan. *The Philosophy of Schopenhauer*. New York: Oxford University Press, 1983.

Odell, S. *On Schopenhauer*. Boston: Cengage Learning, 2001.

Safranski, Rudiger. *Schopenhauer and the Wild Years of Philosophy*. Translated by Ewald Osers. Cambridge, MA: Harvard University Press, 1991.

Schirmacher, Wolfgang. *The Essential Schopenhauer: Key Selections from* The World as Will and Representation *and Other Writings*. New York: HarperCollins, 2010.

Schopenhauer, Arthur. *Essays and Aphorisms*. Translated by R. J. Hollingdale. New York: Penguin, 1970.

——. *The World as Will and Representation*. Vol. 1. Translated by Judith Norman. New York: Cambridge University Press, 2010.

Sim, Stuart. *A Philosophy of Pessimism*. London: Reaktion, 2015.

Yalom, Irvin. *The Schopenhauer Cure: A Novel*. New York: HarperCollins, 2005.

Young, Julian. *Schopenhauer*. New York: Routledge, 2005.

6: HOW TO ENJOY LIKE EPICURUS

Cooper, David. *A Philosophy of Gardens*. New York: Oxford University Press, 2006.

Crespo, Hiram. *Tending the Epicurean Garden*. Washington, D.C.: Humanist Press, 2014.

Epicurus. *The Art of Happiness*. Translated by George Strodach. New York: Penguin, 2012.

——. *The Epicurus Reader: Selected Writings and Testimonia*. Translated by Brad Inwood and L. P. Gerson. Indianapolis: Hackett, 1994.

——. *The Essential Epicurus: Letters, Principal Doctrines, Vatican Sayings, and Fragments*. Translated by Eugene O'Connor. Buffalo, NY: Prometheus, 1993.

Klein, Daniel. *Travels with Epicurus: A Journey to a Greek Island in Search of a Fulfilled Life*. New York: Penguin, 2012.

Long, A. A. *From Epicurus to Epictetus: Studies in Hellenistic and Roman Philosophy*. New York: Oxford University Press, 2006.

Lucretius. *The Way Things Are*. Translated by Rolfe Humphries. Bloomington: Indiana University Press, 1969.

Nussbaum, Martha. *The Therapy of Desire: Theory and Practice in Hellenistic Ethics*. Princeton, NJ: Princeton University Press, 1994.

O'Keefe, Tim. *Epicureanism*. Berkeley: University of California Press, 2009.

Seneca. *Letters from a Stoic*. Translated by Robin Campbell. New York: Penguin, 1969.

Slattery, Luke. *Reclaiming Epicurus: Ancient Wisdom that Could Save the World*. New York: Penguin eBooks, 2012.

Warren, James. *The Companion to Epicureanism*. Cambridge, UK: Cambridge University Press, 2009.

7: HOW TO PAY ATTENTION LIKE SIMONE WEIL

Gray, Francine. *Simone Weil*. New York: Viking Penguin, 2001.

Hellman, John. *Simone Weil: An Introduction to Her Thought*. Eugene, OR: Wipf and Stock, 1982.

Mole, Christopher, Declan Smithies, and Wayne Wu, eds. *Attention: Philosophical and Psychological Essays*. New York: Oxford University Press, 2011.

Murdoch, Iris. *The Sovereignty of Good*. New York: Routledge, 2001.

Pétrement, Simone. *Simone Weil: A Life*. Translated by Raymond Rosenthal. New York: Pantheon, 1976.

Seneca. *On the Shortness of Life*. Translated by C. Costa. New York: Penguin, 2004.

von der Ruhr, Mario. *Simone Weil: An Apprenticeship in Attention*. New York: Continuum, 2006.

Weil, Simone. *An Anthology*. New York: Grove, 1986.

——. *Formative Writings, 1929–1941*. Translated and edited by Dorothy McFarland and Wilhelmina Van Ness. New York: Routledge, 2010.

——. *Gravity and Grace*. Translated by Arthur Wills. London: Octagon Books, 1979.

——. *Late Philosophical Writings*. Translated by Eric Springsted and Lawrence Schmidt. Notre Dame, IN: Notre Dame University Press, 2015.

——. *Waiting for God*. Translated by Emma Craufurd. New York: HarperCollins, 2009.

8: HOW TO FIGHT LIKE GANDHI

Dalton, Dennis. *Mahatma Gandhi: Nonviolent Power in Action*. New York: Columbia University Press, 1993.

Easwaran, Eknath, trans. *The Bhagavad Gita*. Tomales, CA: Nilgiri Press, 1985.

Fischer, Louis. *Gandhi: His Life and Message for the World*. New York: Penguin, 1954.

Gandhi, Manuben. *Last Glimpses of Bapu*. Translated by Moli Jain. Agra, India: Shiva Lal Agarwala, 1962.

Gandhi, Mohandas. *The Bhagavad Gita According to Gandhi*. Translated by Mahadev Desai. Floyd, VA: Sublime, 2014.

——. *Mahatma Gandhi & The Railways*. Ahmedabad, India: Navajivan, 2002.

——. *The Penguin Gandhi Reader*. New York: Penguin, 1996.

——. *The Story of My Experiments with Truth*. New York: Dover, 1983.

Gandhi, Rajmohan. *Why Gandhi Still Matters: An Appraisal of the Mahatma's Legacy*. New Delhi: Aleph, 2017.

Guha, Ramachandra. *Gandhi Before India*. New York: Knopf, 2014.

Homer, Jack, ed. *The Gandhi Reader: A Sourcebook of His Life and Writings*. New York: Grove, 1994.

Juergensmeyer, Mark. *Gandhi's Way: A Handbook of Conflict Resolution*. Los Angeles: University of California Press, 1984.

9: HOW TO BE KIND LIKE CONFUCIUS

Armstrong, Karen. *The Great Transformation: The Beginning of Our Religious Traditions*. New York: Anchor, 2007.

Confucius. *The Analects*. Translated by D. C. Lau. New York: Penguin, 1979.

Dan, Yu. *Confucius from the Heart: Ancient Wisdom for Today's World*. Translated by Esther Tyldesley. New York: Atria, 2006.

Gardner, Daniel. *Confucianism: A Very Short Introduction*. New York: Oxford University Press, 2014.

Goldin, Paul. *Confucianism*. Berkeley: University of California Press, 2011.

Ivanhoe, Philip, and Bryan Van Norden, eds. *Readings in Classical Chinese Philosophy*. Indianapolis: Hackett, 2005.

Mencius. *Mencius*. Translated by D. C. Lau. New York: Penguin, 1970.

Ni, Peimin. *On Confucius*. Belmont, CA: Wadsworth, 2002.

Phillips, Adam, and Barbara Taylor. *On Kindness*. New York: Farrar, Straus and Giroux, 2009.

Puett, Michael, and Christine Gross-Loh. *The Path: What Chinese Philosophers Can Teach Us About the Good Life*. New York: Simon & Schuster, 2016.

Schuman, Michael. *Confucius and the World He Created*. New York: Basic Books, 2015.

Tuan, Yi-fu. *Human Goodness*. Madison: University of Wisconsin Press, 2008.

Van Norden, Bryan. *Introduction to Classical Chinese Philosophy*. Indianapolis: Hackett, 2011.

10: HOW TO APPRECIATE THE SMALL THINGS LIKE SEI SHŌNAGON

Hume, Nancy, ed. *Japanese Aesthetics and Culture: A Reader*. Albany: State University of New York, 1995.

Morris, Ivan. *The World of the Shining Prince: Court Life in Ancient Japan*. New York: Vintage, 2003.

Richie, Donald. *A Tractate on Japanese Aesthetics*. Berkeley: Stone Bridge Press, 2007.

Saito, Yuriko. *Everyday Aesthetics*. New York: Oxford University Press, 2007.

Shōnagon, Sei. *The Pillow Book*. Translated by Meredith McKinney. New York: Penguin, 2006.

Tanizaki, Junichiro. *In Praise of Shadows*. Translated by Thomas Harper. New York: Vintage, 2001.

Tuan, Yi-fu. *Passing Strange and Wonderful: Aesthetics, Nature, and Culture*. Washington, D.C.: Island, 1993.

11: HOW TO HAVE NO REGRETS LIKE NIETZSCHE

Cate, Curtis. *Friedrich Nietzsche*. New York: Overlook, 2005.

Danto, Arthur. *Nietzsche as Philosopher*. New York: Columbia University Press, 2005.

Haase, Ullrich. *Starting with Nietzsche*. New York: Continuum, 2008.

Magnus, Bernd. *Nietzsche's Existential Imperative*. Bloomington: Indiana University Press, 1978.

Nietzsche, Friedrich. *Basic Writings of Nietzsche*. Translated by Walter Kaufmann. New York: Random House, 2000.

——. *Ecce Homo: How One Becomes What One Is*. Translated by R. J. Hollingdale. New York: Penguin, 1979.

——. *The Gay Science*. trans. Thomas Common. New York: Barnes & Noble, 2008.

——. *Human, All Too Human*. Translated by R. J. Hollingdale. New York: Cambridge University Press, 1986.

——. *A Nietzsche Reader*. trans. R.J. Hollingdale. New York: Penguin, 1977.

——. *Thus Spoke Zarathustra: A Book for Everyone and No One*. Translated by R. J. Hollingdale. New York: Penguin, 1961.

Reginster, Bernard. *The Affirmation of Life: Nietzsche on Overcoming Nihilism*. Cambridge, MA: Harvard University Press, 2006.

Safranski, Rudiger. *Nietzsche: A Philosophical Biography*. Translated by Shelley Frisch. New York: Norton, 2003.

Solomon, Robert. *Living with Nietzsche: What the Great "Immoralist" Has to Teach Us*. New York: Oxford University Press, 2003.

Solomon, Robert, and Kathleen Higgins. *What Nietzsche* Really *Said*. New York: Schocken, 2000.

Steinhart, Eric. *On Nietzsche*. Belmont, CA: Wadsworth, 2000.

Zweig, Stefan. *Nietzsche*. Translated by Will Stone. London: Hesperus, 2013.

12: HOW TO COPE LIKE EPICTETUS

Graver, Margaret. *Stoicism and Emotion*. Chicago: University of Chicago Press, 2007.

Long, A. A. *Epictetus: A Stoic and Socratic Guide to Life*. New York: Oxford University Press, 2002.

——. *Hellenistic Philosophy: Stoics, Epicureans, Sceptics*. Berkeley: University of California Press, 1974.

Epictetus. *The Discourses*. London: Orion, 1995.

——. *The Handbook*. Translated by Nicholas White. Indianapolis: Hackett, 1983.

Irvine, William. *A Guide to the Good Life: The Ancient Art of Stoic Joy*. New York: Oxford University Press, 2009.

Robertson, Donald. *Stoicism and the Art of Happiness*. London: Hachette, 2013.

13: HOW TO GROW OLD LIKE BEAUVOIR

Baars, Jan. *Aging and the Art of Living*. Baltimore: Johns Hopkins University Press, 2012.

Bair, Deirdre. *Simone de Beauvoir: A Biography*. New York: Simon & Schuster, 1990.

Beauvoir, Simone de. *All Said and Done*. Translated by Patrick O'Brian. New York: Putnam, 1974.

———. *The Coming of Age*. Translated by Patrick O'Brian. New York: Norton, 1996.

———. *The Ethics of Ambiguity*. Translated by Bernard Frechtman. New York: Open Road, 1948.

———. *Force of Circumstance*. Translated by Richard Howard. New York: Harper & Row, 1977.

———. *Memoirs of a Dutiful Daughter*. Translated by James Kirkup. New York: Harper Perennial, 2005.

———. *A Very Easy Death*. Translated by Patrick O'Brian. New York: Pantheon, 1965.

Booth, Wayne, ed. *The Art of Growing Older: Writers on Living and Aging*. Chicago: University of Chicago Press, 1992.

Cicero, Marcus. *How to Grow Old: Wisdom for the Second Half of Life*. Translated by Philip Freeman. Princeton, NJ: Princeton University Press, 2016.

Cox, Gary. *How to Be an Existentialist: or How to Get Real, Get a Grip and Stop Making Excuses*. New York: Bloomsbury, 2009.

Nussbaum, Martha, and Saul Levmore. *Aging Thoughtfully: Conversations About Retirement, Romance, Wrinkles, and Regret*. New York: Oxford University Press, 2017.

Sartre, Jean-Paul. *Existentialism Is a Humanism*. Translated by Carol Macomber. New Haven: Yale University Press, 2007.

Stoller, Silvia, ed. *Simone de Beauvoir's Philosophy of Age: Gender, Ethics, and Time*. Boston: De Gruyter, 2014.

Tidd, Ursula. *Simone de Beauvoir*. London: Reaktion, 2009.

Wartenberg, Thomas. *Existentialism: A Beginner's Guide*. Oxford, UK: Oneworld, 2008.

14: HOW TO DIE LIKE MONTAIGNE

Bakewell, Sarah. *How to Live: Or A Life of Montaigne in One Question and Twenty Attempts at an Answer*. New York: Other Press, 2010.

Beauvoir, Simone de. *All Men Are Mortal*. Translated by Leonard Friedman. New York: Norton, 1992.

Frame, Donald. *Montaigne: A Biography*. New York: North Point Press, 1984.

Frampton, Saul. *When I Am Playing with My Cat, How Do I Know She Is Not Playing with Me? Montaigne and Being in Touch with Life*. New York: Vintage, 2012.

Friedrich, Hugo. *Montaigne*. Translated by Dawn Eng. Berkeley: University of California Press, 1991.

Malpas, Jeff, and Robert Solomon, eds. *Death and Philosophy*. New York: Routledge, 1999.

Montaigne, Michel. *The Complete Essays of Montaigne*. Translated by Donald Frame. Stanford: Stanford University Press, 1958.

Zweig, Stefan. *Montaigne*. Translated by Will Stone. London: Pushkin, 2015.

Acknowledgments

Socrates believed philosophy is a group activity. So, too, is writing a book about philosophy, as I discovered. Throughout my journeys, from New Delhi to New York, friends and strangers alike provided insight and inspiration, support and succor. I am deeply grateful to each of them.

In the early stages of my research, Stanford University professors Ken Taylor and Rob Reich graciously offered their time and wisdom. Later, Tim LeBon channeled the ancient Stoics over lunch in New York, and Rob Colter kindly agreed to enroll me in Stoic Camp in the wilds of Wyoming. In Concord, Massachusetts, Richard Smith, Michael Frederick, and Tom Blanding generously shared their insights into all things Thoreau. New York University professor Moss Roberts enlightened me about Confucius.

Farther afield, in Paris, Gunter Gorhan and Catherine Monnet shared their philosophical insights with me over café au lait and croissants. In Athens, I was fortunate enough to break bread with the savant Brady Kiesling, as well as a pair of top-notch Epicureans: Christos Yapijakis and Elli Pensa. In Switzerland, Roland Kaehr helped me follow in Rousseau's footsteps, and Peter Villwock in Nietzsche's. In Tokyo, the great Junko Takahashi provided guidance, translations, and good company.

Authors, like philosophers, need a place to think, and write. I am grateful to the Virginia Center for the Creative Arts for providing just such a place. In New York, David and Abby Snoddy graciously supplied me with a room of my own, as well as sake and camaraderie.

My research assistants, Alyson Wright and Alec Siegel, dug tirelessly, finding the right person in the right place, and unearthing hidden philosophical gems, too. John Lister and Josh Horwitz read early drafts of this book and offered valuable suggestions.

No less important was the moral support proffered by friends and strangers. My informal clutch of writer-friends, the Writers Who Lunch, supplied a steady diet of encouragement and curry. Friends Stefan Gunther, Lisa Goldberg, Laura Blumenfeld, and Jacki Lyden steadied me whenever the winds of self-doubt reached gale force. A special shout-out to my Bulgarian publisher, and friend, Neyko Genchev, for painstakingly translating my words and attracting so many readers in his corner of the globe.

My agent, Sloan Harris, believed in the project from the outset, and never wavered in his support. I am grateful for that, as well as his wise counsel. I owe a particular debt to Ben Loehnen, my editor at Simon & Schuster's Avid Reader Press, for his faith in me and my book, and for wielding his razor-sharp editorial knife with skill and kindness. Avid Reader's Carolyn Kelly expertly shepherded my manuscript through the editorial gauntlet. Thank you to Simon & Schuster's president and publisher, Jonathan Karp, for being Jonathan Karp.

A big thank-you to my daughter, Sonya. She tolerated my absences from home, as well as my many annoying philosophical questions. On the road, she was a good sport, even when the sport was not of her choosing. She is my foil and my muse. This book is for her, too.

Most philosophers were unlucky in love. I could not be luckier. My wife, Sharon, stood by me during thick and thicker. She read rough first pages and, with her love and encouragement, gave me my second, third, and fourth winds. I could not have written this book without her.

Index

Page numbers beginning with 289 refer to endnotes.

INDEX

INDEX

About the Author

ERIC WEINER is an award-winning journalist, bestselling author, and speaker. A philosophical traveler, he writes about the intersection of place and idea. His books include the bestselling *The Geography of Bliss* and *The Geography of Genius*, as well as the spiritual memoir *Man Seeks God*. They've been translated into more than twenty languages. A former foreign correspondent for NPR, he is a regular contributor to the *Washington Post* and *AFAR*, among other publications. He lives in the Washington, D.C., area, with his wife, daughter, and a menagerie of rambunctious cats and dogs.